Bringing Children to Literacy:
Classrooms at Work

Bringing Children to Literacy:
Classrooms at Work

Edited by
Bill Harp
Northern Arizona University

Christopher-Gordon Publishers, Inc.
Norwood, Massachusetts

The contributors would like to thank their students who allowed them to reproduce portions of their work.

Christopher-Gordon Publishers, Inc.
480 Washington Street
Norwood, MA 02062

Printed in the United States of America

10 9 8 7 6 4   98 97

ISBN: 0-926842-29-3

Brief Contents

Long Contents

Chapter Three

Bringing Children to Literacy Through Shared Reading   45

Debbie Manning, Fresno, California
Jean Fennacy, Fresno, California

Chapter Four

Bringing Children to Literacy Through Guided Reading   65

Mary Giard, Bangor, Maine

Chapter Five

Bringing Children to Literacy Through the Writing Process   85

Mary Kitagawa, Amherst, Massachusetts

Chapter Six
Bringing Children to Literacy Through Theme Cycles   105

Donna Byrum, Sherman, Texas
Virginia Lazenby Pierce, Sherman, Texas

Chapter Seven
Bringing Children to Literacy Through Reading and Writing Demonstrations by the Teacher   123

Kittye Copeland, Columbia, Missouri

Chapter Eight
Bringing Children to Literacy Through Drama   141

Sheryl McGruder, Hallsville, Missouri

Chapter Nine

Bringing Children to Literacy Through Technology   161

Denise DeFranco, Reston, Virginia

Chapter Ten

Bringing Children to Literacy Through Integrated Basic Skills Instruction   177

Bill Harp, Flagstaff, Arizona

Epilogue   199

Bill Harp, Flagstaff, Arizona

Contributors   203

Index   207

Preface

Bringing Children to Literacy: Classrooms at Work invites the reader to walk through a variety of classrooms in which instruction is designed from a whole language perspective. Whole language is not an approach or method. It is a mind set about how children and teachers should work together to maximize learning. Whole language classrooms are child centered. The focus is first and foremost on children rather than texts, tests, or materials.

In whole language classrooms children are invited to behave as real readers, real writers, and real learners. Real readers read texts, often of their own choosing, which confirm what the reader knows about how language works. Real readers read texts that inform, persuade, or entertain. And so in whole language classrooms children are engaged with texts that make sense, tell stories, inform, and persuade. They use reading in the same ways that real, mature readers use it. Real writers write from their knowledge base for a variety of real, authentic purposes. In whole language classrooms children are invited to use writing to communicate their ideas and needs in the same ways that real, mature writers use writing. Finally, real learners determine their own next learning steps. They take responsibility for their learning. They set their own learning purposes. And so it is in whole language classrooms. Children are empowered to be responsible learners, setting their own learning agendas within parameters carefully defined by the teacher.

Whole language is not something a teacher or children do. Whole language is an educational philosophy that guides teachers in creating a learning environment that encourages children to come to literacy in the same natural, normal, developmental ways they became fluent language users. Whole language teachers create classroom environments in which children are immersed in texts of all kinds with an expectation that they will come to literacy successfully. Within this text-rich environment children see a myriad of demonstrations by the teacher and others of reading and writing processes, and have multiple opportunities to use (practice) reading and writing for authentic communicative purposes. While the teacher is ultimately responsible for that environment, he or she creates situations in which children take responsibility for their own learning—often making important decisions about how they will be engaged in learning.

This book invites readers into nine classrooms in which the kind of instruction described above is the norm. From a whole language perspective teachers plan instruction. Strategies of instruction and resources selected are born of this educational philosophy. Instruction is driven by the philosophy, not the strategies or materials. However, there are instructional strategies evolving within whole language instruction that are proving powerful in bringing children to literacy. Within each chapter of this book a practicing whole language teacher will describe how she is making successful use of an instructional strategy for bringing children to literacy. For example, Shelor carefully describes, in Chapter One, the way in which she uses literature in the primary grades. In Chapter Two, Porterfield describes the ways in which literature studies are carried out in her fourth/fifth grade classroom. Later, Copeland vividly discusses writing demonstrations by the teacher, while DeFranco shows how technology adds a new dimension to her classroom. So it is throughout the book—thoughtful teachers focus on remarkable literacy events for the reader and share their insights and methods for planning for such moments.

I have a concern about structuring a book on whole language this way. We do not mean to communicate that whole language is simply a set of strategies or approaches. I am afraid that by focusing on thematic teaching in one chapter, literature studies in another, and guided reading in another that the reader may conclude that whole language instruction is a set of discrete parts. It would be erroneous to conclude that by simply learning each of the parts and putting them together one would be a whole language teacher. Yet, it makes sense to highlight certain strategies that are, *taken as a whole, employed by a teacher coming from a firm whole language knowledge base,* proving successful in bringing children to literacy.

In putting this book together we set a challenge for ourselves. We challenged ourselves to constantly be aware of the knowledge base and the philosophical understandings from which we operate as whole language teachers. So, in each chapter the teacher shares some of the knowledge base and philosophy that under gird the classroom practices he or she employs. We hope that in doing this, the reader will see how the strategy is consistent with the philosophy.

Sit back, relax and enjoy this national tour of whole language classrooms at work.

B.H.
February, 1993

Foreword

This volume was written in response to professionals who, from their own needs and in their own voices said, as one teacher did recently, "I accept the theories that support whole language, but it's all so out of focus. *I need to see.*" This collection of experiences is for those who *would see.*

For both the experienced as well as the starting-off teacher, the stories presented here bring into focus classrooms at work. Seasoned teachers will find fresh ideas, searching teachers will gain new insights, and all of us will rekindle our quest to understand real learning and reflective teaching. This down-to-earth, yet scholarly, book is highly useful, largely because every experience described here embodies a feature that is essential to practicality—theory. Theory and practice come together in a harmonious whole in these working classrooms. Within the complete contexts of their creative curricula the authors invite us to see. Once we accept the invitation and adjust our spectacles we are enabled to view beyond the pages of this book, to the potential contextualization of our own classrooms.

The locale of these classrooms ranges from Maine to California and reflect creation and learning in primary through intermediate grades, including cross-age groupings. Although the topics are familiar to whole language teachers, much is said on these pages that has not been said before—about thematic cycles, literature study, shared reading, portfolios, literacy displays, teacher demonstrations, invitations, creative expression, journaling, and all the other experiences we might expect to find in classrooms where children are invited to read and write naturally. But there is more than the *stuff* of whole language to be found here. These learning fields are alive with the *essence* of whole language and they are filled with important and growing things like kids, stories, songs, plants, play, and language, language, language.

As I read these chapters I was struck by the timeliness of the messages and of teachers' receptiveness to the sharing of credible classroom experiences. Although the forum is a book, it was as if I were at a teacher support meeting. In such meetings, the conversation might begin with a question from a distraught teacher about organizing the classroom in order to facilitate authentic learning, or with a comment from an enthusiastic teacher about successful partnership with parents. The curriculum shared through the stories here, as in support groups, are the *very best* experiences not second best, nor are they experiences unconnected to strong beliefs. The stories from these working classrooms catch us up in conversations with the authors who, because they are eager to support us as their colleagues, have become our teachers. We are the beneficiaries of the rich and varied experiences of professionals who care not only about their students, but about other teachers as well.

It becomes evident with each chapter that these teachers' artistry springs from constant reflection on their own practices and from their persistent inquiry into the theory that supports their practices. Each author deals with some important and specific curricular issue, and in doing so, illuminates the broader nature of whole language. Standing next to masterful teachers, we share their vantage point, from which, with their pointing, we can see the contour of the whole.

This volume dispels some false assumptions about learning and teaching. I'll mention two. *Whole language classrooms are unorganized* and *curriculum is 'off the top of the teacher's head.'* To bring children to literacy, teachers work hard at understanding students, literature, learning, teaching, and themselves. Teachers, along with their students, are at the heart of learning and it is from this solid base that curriculum is weighed, measured, negotiated, and finally set into motion. In the chapters here, we see that there are intellectually important things going on in these working classrooms. Students are putting their heads to tasks that are important, and they are doing it in classrooms that are appropriately organized. The routines designed by the learners (students and teachers) are not ruts, and the schedules are not straight-jackets. The authors of these pieces show us that the organizing structure is part of the process, to be used and enjoyed rather than to be overtly or covertly resisted. In these chapters we are invited to see how organization facilitates an ebb and flow within classrooms in which learning and teaching are natural and are the rule rather than the exception.

This leads us to another myth. *Once you become a whole language teacher, it all (curriculum, evaluation, organization, etc. etc.,) falls neatly into place. It's just a matter of introducing the strategies.* The writers in this volume let us in on their struggles. Now we can breathe a sigh of relief when we listen to or watch teachers who make it all look so simple and easy. When we stumble in our efforts we can be comforted by the fact that such classrooms are never simple and seldom easy. These masterful teachers worked long and hard, at both their theory and their practice, to create purposeful and sensitive classrooms. When things went wrong they learned from their experiences and they were brave enough to try again and again. Their courage was bolstered by their theory and, as importantly, by their students. These teachers needed that courage because they did something very risky—they redefined curriculum.

Who is this book for? It is for educators who are eager to continue the conversations started here, who are inspired to redesign for their own classrooms the ideas and experiences shared, and to create stories with their own students. Of course, the volume is for those who *need to see,* but more importantly it is for those who *would see.*

Dorothy J. Watson
University of Missouri—Columbia
Columbia, Missouri

1

Bringing Children to Literacy Through Literature in Primary Grades

DEBBIE SHELOR

We begin our tour of exemplary literacy classrooms in Shelor's primary class. Note how carefully she creates a classroom environment that fosters the productive use of literature. She recognizes fully the importance of context for literature study, and encourages a wide range of responses to literature from learners. I am impressed by the way children became sensitive to other's needs through the buddy reading system. Shelor underscores the importance of reading by persons of all ages and walks of life by having her children read to adults all over the school. This helps them realize that reading can offer a vast array of ideas and connections in their world. This classroom is notable for the atmosphere Shelor creates that is sensitive to children, to individual needs, to individual decision-making, and to choice in learning.

For six of the past seven years I have taught first grade in a school of about 600 students in a diverse community that includes the wealthy and the poor, the educated and the uneducated, native Virginians and immigrants from more than 25 foreign countries. As the 1990–91 school year drew to a close, my principal, my students, their parents, and I decided to keep my class intact and move on to second grade together. During the course of the 1991–92 school year, several children came and went, but for most of the year 16 of my original first graders remained as second graders. My classroom is currently comprised of 21 students from backgrounds as varied as our larger community, including eight children for whom English is a second or other language. Several people have helped me support my students, including a teaching assistant, (four hours per day in first grade, but only 30 minutes per day in second grade as mandated by our school budget), an ESOL (English as a Second or Other Language) specialist, occasional parent volunteers, two tutors from the nearby middle school who help out for 30 minutes per day, high school students who assist with special projects, and one or two university students per semester who average one to two hours of volunteer work in our classroom per week.

The practices about which I am writing are drawn from my experiences with first graders as well as what I have learned from moving on to second grade and spending a second year with the same group of children. Finding it difficult to separate my educational philosophy from my teaching practices, I have blended the two throughout this chapter, trying to highlight for the reader the beliefs and values to which I adhere.

Bringing children to literacy through literature in the primary grades . . . what a journey!! In trying to write this chapter, I found it impossible to address the issue of using literature with young children without describing the whole setting, thus establishing the context that supports this multifaceted goal.

The Setting

The best place to start is to paint a picture of the classroom in which my children and I live, learn, work, and play each day. Because our classroom is a home away from home for all who live and learn there, I work hard to create an environment that is comfortable, safe and secure, aesthetically pleasing, and child-centered. Because the room belongs to all of us, I involve the children in arranging and organizing the classroom and learning materials. We typically set up the room to include eleven areas: the check-

Figure 1-1   Classroom Set-Up

Area	Description
Check-in center	Where children are responsible for taking attendance and signing up for lunch each morning and where news and announcements for the day are posted for all to see.
Large-group meeting area	Furnished with a rug, a rocking chair, a small stool (which enables me to sit a little higher than the children but still remain close to their level), a tape recorder/ player and cassette collection of stories and songs, and a display shelf filled with the books we are currently sharing as a group.
Listening center	Complete with a small sofa, a cassette tape player and an ever-changing collection of books and matching audio cassettes stored in Zip Lock baggies and hung on a dowel.
Conference corner	Located in a relatively secluded area of the room that includes a table, some shelves, and a chalkboard for working with individuals or small groups of children.
Computer area	Houses our Macintosh computer and printer as well as educational software (e.g., *Kid Pix, The Writing Center, Where in the U.S.A. Is Carmen Sandiego?*).
Science center	Includes our class guinea pigs and gold fish, a shelf for storing equipment (microscopes, magnifying glasses, kaleidoscopes, prisms, containers of all shapes and sizes), supplies (pet food, food coloring, magnets), and two small tables for displaying items of interest or experiments in progress (bones, rocks, insects, or seedlings).
Sand/water table Building area	Serves as an extra display table when not in use. Includes a 4′ × 4′ section of floor space and a shelf for storing blocks, Legos, Lincoln Logs, and any other building supplies that may be available.
Art area	Where the easel, paints, water colors, Craypas, markers, chalk, colored pencils, clay, yarn, and containers of recyclable materials (e.g., popsicle sticks, pieces of foam, fabric scraps, buttons, juice can lids) are stored.
Map center	Complete with a globe, a United States map, a world map, and a large atlas.
The loft	Built by parents so the children would have a place on the "top floor" for quiet activities and space on the "bottom floor" for dramatic play.

in center, the large-group meeting area, the listening center, the conference corner, the computer area, the science center, the sand/water table, the building area, the art area, the map center, and the loft (See Figure 1-1).

Various shelves housing materials used by the children on a regular basis are also located around the room. The math shelf contains commercially purchased manipulatives (pattern blocks, unifix cubes, tangrams, cuisenaire rods) and teacher/student made materials. The puzzles/games shelf houses jigsaw puzzles, brain teasers, checkers, board games, decks of cards, tic-tac-toe, and dominoes. The writing supplies shelf includes pencils and pens, erasers, staplers, hole punches, tape, glue, date stamps and ink pads, envelopes, and paper of all shapes, sizes, colors, and textures.

During the first few weeks of first grade, I spend a lot of time orienting the children to the classroom and the materials, modeling appropriate ways of using and caring for the areas and the supplies available to them. EVERYTHING is labeled with print and pictures to assist the children in locating and storing materials, and perhaps most importantly, in beginning to understand the practical functions of the printed word. Because our school population includes many students for whom English is a second or other language, I often include the native language of my particular students on these labels as well, thus helping those children connect their own language to the English word while also exposing the American children to different languages from other cultures.

The children each have a coat hook and shelf (located just outside our classroom) for backpacks and lunch boxes and an individual cubby (in the classroom) in which their journals, notebooks, spelling file boxes, supplies, and other personal belongings are stored. Scattered around the room are five tables (some rectangular and some round) which serve as work spaces for the children throughout the day. Each table is identified by a sign suspended from the ceiling. Each sign has a different color, symbol, or name related to the table's placement in the room (e.g., the science table is next to the science center). Having tables instead of individual desks adds to the community atmosphere of our room and encourages the children to interact with each other as they learn. During the early months of first grade, I assign the children specific seats to enhance their feelings of ownership and belonging within the larger classroom community. Assigned seats soon become unnecessary as the children grow secure and comfortable in the environment they help to create. With my second graders, we keep a "table sign-up sheet" on which the children select and sign up for a seat at a specific table for a period of two or three weeks at a time. They base their choices on the particular location of the tables, proximity to certain areas of the room, number of people at a given table, and the seating choices of their friends. While this seems to be a simple matter of classroom organization and management, I see it as a valuable way to give children control and decision-making power within their own learning environment. It is not uncommon for me to hear comments like the following on a Monday morning when children are signing up for new tables. "Kelly, wanna sit at the conference table this week so we can have some privacy?" asks Emily. Or "Hasan and me are sitting at the science table so we can keep an eye on the guinea pigs," informs Adrian. Or "Hey, Jim, let's sign up together so we can work on our book this week," urges Chris. At times, their choices work out beautifully and at other times it becomes necessary for me to intervene and suggest an alternative. The underlying principle is that the children have control and responsibility for their own choices and behaviors and if they are to learn to make wise, responsible decisions, they must have opportunities to exercise that control as often as possible.

In our classroom, the children and I negotiate the rules by which we are all expected to live as a community of learners. While I encourage input and allow much discussion among the children during the first few days of school, I usually condense their suggestions into three basic rules:

1. Be safe.
2. Be considerate.
3. Be a thinker.

Everything we say and do in our work and play together can be defined by these simple but powerful guidelines. When there are problems that involve a number of the children or decisions to be made that affect us all, we have a class meeting to work things out together.

Access to Good Literature

You may have noticed that the classroom description does not include a library or book corner. Because I want children to understand how literature can be connected to all aspects of their lives, there are tubs, baskets, and shelves filled with books of all kinds in every part of the room. Stories about famous artists as well as books containing suggestions for projects are on the art shelf. Books about counting, telling time, the days of the week, patterns, and using money are shelved near the math area. Next to the building area, children can find books about building houses and other structures. Nonfiction books and magazines fill one of the science shelves, and the map center has a basket of related nonfiction books as well as some easy reference books about different countries and cultures. In the large group meeting area, a suspended dowel supports our big books and magazines hung by skirt hangers. Spaced throughout are shelves that contain as many as eighteen different tubs of books organized according to theme, author, genre, and/or approximate reading level (See Figure 1-2).

A large bookshelf in the conference corner houses books not currently being used by the children. These books are shelved in alphabetical order for easy adult access. The rotation of books from the storage shelf to the classroom is an ongoing process negotiated by the children and me throughout the

Figure 1-2   Examples of Book Baskets

Organizer	Book Basket
Social Studies Theme	Family & Friends
Social Studies Theme	Life Long Ago
Science Theme	Light, Color, & Shadows
Author/Illustrator	Books by Tomie de Paola
Author/Illustrator	Books by Rosemary Wells
Author/Illustrator	Books by Barbara Cooney
Genre	Biographies
Genre	Fairy Tales
Genre	Predictable Pattern Books
Reading Level	"Step Into Reading" Books
Reading Level	"I Can Read" Books
Reading Level/Genre	Short Novels

year. I keep a computerized record of all the books in our classroom library, which now exceeds 1700 titles. Each entry includes the book title, author, illustrator, series (if applicable), topic or related theme, and any extra information such as Caldecott status, video versions, or audio-cassette tape accompaniment.

This data base allows me to produce a list of books sorted by a particular author or related to a specific theme and make them available to the children (See Figure 1-3).

For instance, noticing a keen interest in humor among many of the children, I decided to add a new book basket to our current selections. Labeled "Books to Tickle Your Funny Bone," the basket included joke

Figure 1-3   Sample Entry from Book Data Base

Title:	*The Patchwork Quilt* (1985).
Author:	Valerie Flournoy
Illustrator:	Jerry Pinkney
Series:	n/a
Genre:	Fiction; Picture Book
Season:	n/a
Theme:	Quilts; Family; Tradition
Other Info:	Coretta Scott King Award; Reading Rainbow featured book

books, riddles, limericks, and other humorous stories. During group time, I pulled out a copy of *Supposes* (1989) by Dick Gackenbach and asked, "What do you think this book will be about?" Children began to speak in unison, but I heard Karen explain: "It must be a funny book because you put it in the 'Books to Tickle Your Funnybone' tub. And besides, it has a silly illustration on the cover!"

Intrigued by the title, the children begged me to read the book to them. "Suppose a cat ate lemons . . . she would turn into a sourpuss!! Suppose a polar bear had money . . . he'd put it in a snow bank!!" As a light bulb flashed in Emily's mind, she exclaimed, "Hey, that's MY kind of book!! It's just like *The King Who Rained* (1987) and *Chocolate Moose for Dinner* (1976) by Fred Gwynne." She was exactly right because all of these books use word play to capitalize on common, and often humorous, misunderstandings of children and adults. Only an environment overflowing with exposure to books and easy access to many different kinds of literature will lead young children to identify with real authors and make such rich connections on their own without prompting.

Working around the parts of our day over which we have no control (like lunch, P.E., library, and music), I arrange the day's schedule to include large blocks of time to accommodate a balance of teacher-planned experiences and child-initiated activities (See Figure 1-4 a & b). We often adjust if we need to spend more time on a certain activity on any given day. Each day, I post the schedule on the wall or the chalkboard in our large-group area using magnetized cards. As the children become accustomed to this routine and are able to read the cards independently, they eventually assume the responsibility for posting the schedule. Again, this is a practical demonstration of one function of print and a way to provide stability and predictability for the children in my classroom.

Cooperative Thematic Planning

Based on my belief that children learn best when their activities are self-chosen and meaningful to them, I involve my students in the planning of our themes and units of study. Sometimes I suggest the topic (based on my observations about the children's interests or the grade level curriculum guide) and let the children determine the direction the unit will take. Occasionally, I simply ask the children what topic they would like to explore. To foster the notion that reading, writing, and math are valuable tools which can help us all to understand the world around us, I try to integrate all areas of the curriculum by planning themes into which literature, math, science, and social studies can all be interwoven.

As part of my belief that children learn to read by reading, I provide a large amount of time each day for meaningful engagement with print. In our classroom, the children are learning to make sense of print throughout the day as they read the menu before signing up for lunch, check the board

Figure 1-4a   1st Grade Schedule

8:00–9:00	Business Centers
9:00–9:30	Large-group Time
9:30–11:00	Language Arts Block
11:00–11:25	Recess
11:30–12:00	Lunch
12:00–1:05	Integrated Curriculum (Math/Sci./S.S.)
1:10–1:40	P.E.
1:45–2:15	Follow-up Activities
2:30——	Dismissal

Figure 1-4b   2nd Grade Schedule

8:00–8:45	Morning Business, Centers or Math Stations
8:45–9:15	Large-group Time
9:15–10:30	Readers' Workshop (M,W) Writers' Workshop (T,TH) R.W./W.W.(F)
10:30–10:50	Snack/Recess
10:50–11:20	Spelling
11:25–11:55	P.E.
12:00–12:30	Journals (M,W) Sharing Time (T,TH) Music (F)
12:35–1:05	Lunch
1:10–2:15	Integrated Curriculum (Math/Sci./S.S.) or Buddy Reading
2:30——	Dismissal

for announcements about the day's schedule, and read signs and labels in order to sign up for activities of their choice during centers time. But, the most formal and concentrated reading instruction takes place during what we call Readers' Workshop.

We typically start by gathering together in our large-group meeting area. Early in the school year our focus is on getting acquainted with the books in our classroom, how they are organized, how to choose a book, and how to derive meaning from that book. As the year progresses, a typical day starts with some singing and chatting about the previous day's events and going over our schedule for the day. Then we usually share a book or two together that are related to our current theme of study ("Family and Friends," "Life Long Ago," "Light and Color") or books that are part of a genre study (mysteries, fairy tales, adventure stories, biographies) or new books that are being added to our classroom library.

During our "Life Long Ago" unit, we began by generating lists of things that we already knew about life in the past and things that we wanted to learn. The children's curiosity was wide-ranging as they wondered about the pyramids of ancient Egypt, the activities colonial children did for entertainment, the houses of families in Brazil, and ways of getting food before there were grocery stores. Through the course of the unit, I read ten to fifteen books aloud to help the children learn and understand what life was like in various historical periods around the world, paying particular attention to the questions the children had raised. One large-group session was devoted to comparing two such books: *When I Was Young in the Mountains* (1982) by Cynthia Rylant and *I Go With My Family to Grandma's* (1986) by Riki Levinson, both of which were illustrated by Diane Goode. After many comments about the overall beauty of this artist's work, the children noticed that each book contained a family portrait. Intrigued by the similarities in the faces of the characters, the children were content to study and comment on Diane Goode's illustrations for half of that day's thirty minute session. As is often the case, I was pleasantly surprised by their keen observations and sophisticated comments.

I was equally surprised about four months later when Carol, an ESOL child from Taiwan, bounded into the classroom bursting with excitement. "Miss Shelor!! Look!!" she said. "Look what I checked out from the library yesterday!" She thrust a copy of *Cinderella* (1988) into my hands. We were currently involved in our fairy tale unit, so I assumed that was the impetus for her enthusiasm and said as much. My response did not satisfy her, so she pressed on. "Look, Miss Shelor, this book is illustrated by Diane Goode." I still did not get her point and with a sigh of frustration at my lame reaction, Carol stalked over to one of the storage shelves. She returned momentarily with two books in hand—*When I Was Young in the Mountains* and I *Go With My Family to Grandma's*. It was only after Carol blatantly displayed all three books in front of me that *I* made the connection which *she* had easily made for herself. Obviously, Diane Goode's work had made a lasting impression on Carol and I appreciated her patience and perseverance as she so ably taught me.

During our large-group sessions, we occasionally listen to author tapes to help us get acquainted with a particular author in hopes of coming to understand her books even better. During this same unit, we read several books by Barbara Cooney, including *Miss Rumphius* (1982), *Island Boy* (1988), and *Hattie and the Wild Waves* (1990). The children enjoyed her stories and were enthralled with her simple yet detailed illustrations. At the peak of their interest in her books, I introduced a commercially produced recording of an interview with the author/illustrator. As they listened, each child cued into something different that she had to say. "Hey, she liked to write plays when she was a little girl just like us," quipped Amanda and Laura. Cindy chimed in, "She lives in Maine. Have you ever seen her when you go there for the summer, Miss Shelor?" "Did you hear that? Her favorite thing at school was math! I love math too," noticed Karen. In reference to her illustrations, Billy tuned in to her explanation, "She *does* draw faces that look like her own. I wonder if she looks in the mirror when she paints." Several weeks later, when Rico wondered out loud about another author, Jeremy suggested, "You could ask Miss Shelor if she has a tape about that author. Then you could find out."

Developing the Use of Reading Strategies

During some large-group sessions, we spend time talking about specific reading strategies that children are using to help them figure out new words or tackle harder books. Hasan and Adrian are experts at drawing information about the text from the pictures in their books. Emily likes to skip over troublesome words and use the context to "figure them out." Rico writes the hard words down on his bookmark so he can refer to them if he encounters them again later. We often list such strategies on a chart or role play to give the children an opportunity to practice in a supportive situation.

One day Rhiannon was particularly eager to share a recent success with her classmates. Grinning from ear to ear, she held up a copy of *Papa, Please Get the Moon for Me* (1986), by Eric Carle. She proudly announced:

"I just wanted to tell everybody that I finished reading *Papa Please Get the Moon for Me*. And you know what? It was an easy book for me to read 'cuz I *interviewed* it first!"

I smiled and listened as Rhiannon excitedly told the group about her book.

Rhiannon meant that she had "previewed" her book before she read it, a technique I encourage the children to use whenever they are choosing a new book or beginning to read a selection for the first time. In previewing a book, we simply study the cover and think about the title in order to get an idea of what the book will be about. We then go through the book page by page looking at the illustrations and making predictions about the content. If an adult or a more experienced reader is present, she may point out vocabulary words which may be new or difficult for the child who is attempting to read the book for the first time.

The purpose of this process is to prepare the reader *before* the actual reading in hopes of ensuring success with the book. It is possible during the previewing that the reader may decide to abandon this book (if it's too easy or too hard or if the content is not appealing) and choose another book. In the case of Rhiannon, her apparent *faux pas* was in reality an accurate description of the way she had interacted with Eric Carle's text. She had indeed "carried on a conversation" with the author and the book as she previewed it by searching the illustrations to find the meaning. As she was able to point out herself, this process helped to ensure her success in reading the book.

At the end of large-group (which may last anywhere from fifteen to forty minutes), the children disperse to any area of the room to begin their own private reading. The term "private reading" has evolved over the years in my classroom as I have studied what it is that children actually do during this part of the workshop. At one time we called it "silent" reading, but I soon realized that for most young children who are just learning to read, this activity is far from silent! In examining the children's behaviors *and* my goals for this segment of the Readers' Workshop, I decided that "private" reading was the most appropriate term. I want the children to spend time on their own interacting with self-chosen books in ways that have been modelled for them during our large group sessions and during interactions with more experienced readers. As the school year progresses, the amount of time the children need for private reading increases from five minutes to thirty minutes. I use quiet music to signal the beginning of this time and to set a calm, relaxed tone in the room.

While recognizing that readers need time to interact privately with their own books each day, I also realize that reading is a social activity. Readers of any age need to *talk* about what they read in order to fully understand and construct their own meaning from another person's words. After the music stops (signaling the end of private reading time), the children have several choices for the remaining thirty to forty minutes of Readers' Workshop. They may continue to read on their own, share their books with friends, listen to stories at the listening center, or respond to their books by writing in their response journals, painting pictures, or acting out the stories. Again, these activities are modeled for the children in the beginning of the year and a list is posted to serve as a reminder.

The children have opportunities apart from Readers' Workshop throughout the week to share their reading with others. At least twice a week, we have a thirty to forty minute "Sharing Time" in which the children may sign up to read a piece that they have written or share a book they have read with the class. When sharing a book, they may pick a passage to read orally, give a book talk, or share their response to the book with us. When feasible, we do this in conjunction with children from other classes by sending and inviting visiting authors and readers from all over the school to share their learning.

Our Buddy Reading System

Our school also has a "Buddy Reading System" in which children from different grade levels are paired to read with each other for twenty to thirty minutes each week. My second graders have had reading buddies in fourth grade to whom they could look for help and advice about challenging books of interest to them. They've also had kindergarten buddies for whom they've taken their roles as mentors and teachers quite seriously. Through wide exposure to all types of literature, young children can become competent critics. One day while my students were preparing to read to their kindergarten buddies, I overheard several of them talking about their book selections. Jeremy said: "My buddy likes books with lots of adventure and good pictures, so I'm gonna read him *The Berenstain Bears Go to Camp* (1982)."

"Well, my buddy just loves *Mortimer* (1985), so I think I'll try reading *Thomas's Snowsuit* (1985) to him. It's by Robert Munsch too," decided Cindy. Jennifer seemed to be having difficulty picking out a book for her buddy. I offered my assistance and she explained: "My buddy really likes to read to me, so I'm trying to find something that won't be too hard for her. Maybe I'll wait 'til she gets to our room and then we can pick out something together."

Not needed at all during our buddy reading times, I have the privilege of sitting back and watching peer relationships develop as children discuss their books and their reactions to what they read.

To boost the children's confidence, increase their exposure to readers of all ages and walks of life, and help them realize that reading can offer a vast array of ideas and connections in their world, I make arrangements for students to read to adults all over the school. They read to the principal, the secretaries, the bookkeeper, the custodian, the librarian, the music teacher, and anyone else who will listen! We set aside special times to invite parents and other community members to come in and share their favorite books with our class.

Because I want each child to take responsibility for his or her own learning, it is important to teach the children to be responsible in caring for and keeping track of the books they read. To that end, each child has a book tub (an $8'' \times 12'' \times 4''$ plastic container) in which to store the books that he or she is currently reading. At the beginning of the year, depending on the personalities and habits of the children in any given class as well as the availability of books, we negotiate the number of books that can be kept in a tub at any given time. Initially, I usually suggest that each child choose three to four books to keep in the tub. Sometimes I qualify this by asking each child to find one book that he or she can read all by herself (often a book that I have read to the class in a large-group setting), one or two books that he or she wants to learn to read, and one book to look at or have another person read to him or her. As the year progresses and the demand for books increases, we meet to renegotiate. By January of 1991, for example, my first graders generally kept nine books in their book tub at a time—three they could read independently, three they were trying to learn, and three they enjoyed looking at or having someone else read to them.

During a spring discussion about book selection, I asked the children to describe for me how they go about choosing a new book to read. Amanda spoke first, saying, "Well, I pick books that my friends have read and told

Figure 1-5   Monthly Chart

September Reading

| 1. | | 3. | |
| 2. | | 4. | |

| 5. | | 7. | |
| 6. | | 8. | |

| 9. | | 10. | |
| 11. | | 12. | |

me about." Karen added, "I know I like mysteries and biographies, so I always look in those baskets when I need a new book." Billy chimed in, "You have to make sure the book you pick isn't too easy or too hard. It should be just right for you." Jim said, "I like to read all the books in a series like the Pee Wee Scouts or the Kids at the Polk Street School." Jessica summed it up by saying, "You have to find a book that *fits* you. You know, it's got something in common with you and it's not too easy and not too hard. Then you know it will be just right for you!"

In addition to helping the children select, locate, and store their own reading materials, I teach them to keep track of the books they read during Readers' Workshop. Over time, most children become more interested and able to keep records of their own reading by recording titles on a monthly chart (See Figure 1-5). Some entries are recorded by the adult and some are recorded by the children. Another option is a "Reading Log" on which the children independently record the date, the title and author, and a brief comment about each book they read privately, with a friend, or in a conference with an adult (See Figure 1-6).

Reading Response Journals

The final vehicle I have used is having the children keep a "Reading Response Journal" in which they regularly record the date, the book's title and author, and a written and/or pictorial response to the book. Modelled after our group discussions about books we read together, the children's responses often summarize the story, give their opinion of the book and its

Figure 1-6   Reading Log

Books I've Read	Date	My Comments

illustrations, tell what the book reminded them of, or explain how it made them feel.

For example, after reading *Sonny's Secret* (1991), a Pee Wee Scout book by Judy Delton, Amanda wrote: "It was about a secret. Sonny's mom is getting married. I liked the book because it was about a secret and I like secrets."

Chris' response to a nonfiction book about Michael Jordan written by Richard Brenner, was "It made me feel that you can do it if you try! And the pictures were cool! I think other people should read it." Rico enjoyed reading *The Secrets of the Super Athletes* (1982) by David Fremon and responded by writing:

> It made me feel like I was playing basketball and it made me feel like I made a slam dunk. I like tackling other guys and I like the color of the basketball. Basketball is fun. It makes you smart and it makes you strong.

After reading E.B. White's *The Trumpet of the Swan* (1970), Karen wrote, "This book is of the realistic fiction genre and it makes me think of how I am saving up for college." Kelly's response to a book called *The Gymnasts* (1991) by Elizabeth Levy, was: "Well, what happens is, well first, I'm a gymnast too, so when I'm reading this book I sort of go into a daze and I feel like I'm in the gym."

Readers' Workshop

During Readers' Workshop, I circulate through the room, assisting with book selection and having individual or small group conferences with children. Early in the year with my first graders, we set up a weekly conference schedule and post it in the conference corner. Each child's conference is

Figure 1-7   Reading Conference Form

_____'s *Reading Conferences*

Date	Books	Strategies	Working on next . . .

scheduled on the same day each week along with conferences for three or four other readers, providing a predictable routine for the children and ensuring a weekly meeting with each child.

Each day, the children whose conferences were scheduled for that day meet in the conference corner at the beginning of private reading time. I make my way around the table, spending ten to fifteen minutes working with each child. Though the goal and function of the actual conference varies somewhat from reader to reader and from book to book, I use a conference form as a guide and record-keeping tool (See Figure 1-7).

In their book tubs, the children have folders in which they store copies of poems and songs learned in class, their monthly charts, reading logs or response journals, and their conference forms. When I sit down to read with a child, I have ready access to past notes as we begin the new conference. I usually start by asking about the book(s) we recorded under 'Working on next . . .' during the previous conference. If appropriate, I ask the child to read aloud from one of those books for me. If not, the child reads another self-chosen selection. As the child reads, I make note of his or her choice and its appropriateness (in terms of topic and level), the behaviors and strategies I observe as he or she reads (body posture and comfort level, attendance to picture cues, phonetic decoding strategies, use of context clues, and comprehension of the text), and specific comments he or she makes during the reading. Sometimes my role is that of a quiet observer, listening and recording; sometimes I become an involved participant, interacting with the child and the text by making comments and asking questions. The last step of the conference is to help the child choose a book to work on next. Again, sometimes I simply allow the child to make the choice and I record it on the conference form. In other situations, the child might ask me to help him or her find a book about a particular topic or discover a topic he or she might like to explore. In yet another situation, I might deem it necessary to intervene and make suggestions or limit the choices of a child who is choosing inappropriately or floundering in a sea of "too many books to choose from." During a September reading conference with Chris (a second grader), I asked what book he had chosen to read. He pulled *Little House On the Prairie* (1935) by Laura Ingalls Wilder out of his tub. "I'm getting ready to start reading this," he said very seriously, but with a hint of hesitation in his voice. "That's an interesting choice, Chris. Can you tell me why you want to read this book?" was my reply. In the same serious tone, Chris answered: "Yeah, my mom really likes this series, and I've seen Karen and Jim reading them, so I thought I'd try one and see if I like it." Making note of his reasoning, I asked if I could listen in as he started to read. "Sure," he replied and began to read. It only took a minute and the first three sentences for Chris to realize that he was in over his head. Resisting the urge to intervene and suggest an alternate book, I recorded his attempts and waited to see what he would do. As he thumbed through the pages, my attention turned to a different area of the room. I excused myself from Chris' conference, promising to return shortly. When I returned momentarily, I found Chris struggling to read the first page of *These Happy Golden Years* (1943), another book from the same series. Chris explained why he had changed books, "The other book had 335 pages and this one only has 289 pages, so I thought this might be a better one to start with." Again, I sat quietly and observed as he attempted to read the first page of his newly chosen book. Once more, I was called away to tend to a situation in another part of the room. Upon returning for the second time, I found that Chris had traded the second book in for one with still fewer pages in hopes that he would be able to successfully read it. As I struggled to decide whether or not it was time for me to intervene, Chris closed the book and said, "I don't think I'm ready to read these books yet. I think I'll pick something else." Thankful that I had let him come to this conclusion on his own, I acknowledged his decision and asked if he'd like some help making another choice. Together, we settled on a Pee Wee Scout book called *Cookies and Crutches* (1988), one that would challenge but not frustrate Chris. Six months later, Chris successfully read *Little House On the Prairie* for the first time!!

When there are other adults in the room during Readers' Workshop, they also circulate and read with children or carry out specific tasks which I have planned for readers who need assistance in a particular area. The conference form also gives all the adults who work with a child access to necessary information about that child's reading selections and development.

From time to time throughout the school year, I restructure the reading conference schedule to accommodate some small group shared reading. Sometimes I set up the day's group to include children who have similar reading interests or abilities so that we can use the conference time during Readers' Workshop to read and discuss a common book as a group. Sometimes I ask the children to form their own groups and conduct peer conferences. In the spring, my second graders decided they wanted to have "Book Clubs" in which four readers would meet together, decide on a common book, series, or author, and spend two to three weeks reading and discussing their choice. When they finished their reading, they worked on a project for sharing their book with the rest of the class. Ideas included written responses, puppet shows, and art projects. Each club recorded the names of its members, their reading plans, and their intended response on a contract form and proceeded with little intervention or supervision from me. This proved to be a successful way for the children to share common books and have fun presenting their books to their classmates.

Observing and making note of the way children interact with me, with their peers, and with books during large-group sessions enhances my understanding of their knowledge about and appreciation for literature. Having regular individual reading conferences helps me to assess each child's growth and development as a reader. Periodically checking their Reading Logs or reading their Response Journals gives me added insight into the independent reading my children are doing in the classroom. This continuous contact with my children in large-group sessions and as individual readers ultimately guides the planning of my reading instruction.

One priority I must not neglect to mention is building a strong connection between home and school for my children. I meet with parents early in the school year to provide information about our curriculum and establish some vehicles for our regular communication throughout the school year (e.g., the use of home journals, telephoning procedures, parent/teacher conferences). For ESOL children or those with other special needs, I use this initial contact to gain as much information as possible from parents and to set goals and plan instruction accordingly. For ESOL students, it is particularly helpful to know the parents' expectations for their child's educational experiences and their long-range plans for staying in the United States or returning to their native country. Some of my colleagues and I invite parents to come in for occasional evening workshops during which we focus on one area of the curriculum at a time and explain more thoroughly the kind of instruction their children are receiving. When necessary, I send home written correspondence about specific classroom activities (e.g., Readers' Workshop, Book Tubs, Reading Buddies), and in weekly newsletters, I inform parents about our current unit of study and the upcoming special activities for that week. I also elicit their help and expertise in the classroom. For example, during our "Life Long Ago" unit we dipped candles and made our own quilt with the help of some parents. During our fairy tale unit, many parents sent in books and one sent in a puppet theatre and a set of marionettes for the children to use. We also had German, Arabic, and Taiwanese parents who were willing to share their native folklore with our class.

To keep parents abreast of their children's ongoing reading in the classroom, the children take home a Zip Lock baggie one or two nights each week containing some of the books they are learning to read. This gives the children a chance to practice at home and let their parents see what they are working on at school. I also include a small index card for the parents with notes about their child's current repertoire of reading strategies and suggestions on how to help and encourage their child's reading development. The

ESOL children often borrow books and matching cassette tapes from our listening center as another way for their families to hear the English language. During our periodic parent/teacher conferences, I share the children's book tubs, conference forms, Reading Logs, and Response Journals with their parents.

Bringing children to literacy through literature in the primary grades . . . what a journey!! I hope the picture I have painted for you offers some ideas and springboards which will challenge your thinking about your own philosophy and teaching practices. Writing this chapter has certainly done that for me. I have come to believe that all of learning is really like a journey, part of which has important anticipated landmarks along the way, and part of which is uncharted and developed as we go. There is no clear final destination which is the same for all of us. There are only stopping off points, at some of which we choose to linger longer than at others. From all of them, we can discover more about who we are as learners, where we want to go next, and how and with whom we want to travel.

Bibliography

The following bibliography includes some of the professional literature which has challenged my thinking and shaped my teaching practices during the past seven years:

Atwell, N. (1989). *Workshop 1 by and for teachers: Writing and literature.* Portsmouth, N.H.: Heinemann.

Atwell, N. (1990). *Workshop 2 by and for teachers: Beyond the basal.* Portsmouth, N.H.: Heinemann.

Baskwill, J. & Whitman, P. (1988). *Evaluation: Whole language, whole child.* New York: Scholastic.

Butler, A. & Turbill, J. (1987). *Towards a reading-writing classroom.* Portsmouth, N.H.: Heinemann.

Clay, M. M. (1985). *The early detection of reading difficulties.* Portsmouth, N.H.: Heinemann.

Graves, D. H. (1991). *The reading/writing teacher's companion: Build a literate classroom.* Portsmouth, N.H.: Heinemann.

Griffiths, R. & Clyne, M. (1988). *Books you can count on: Linking mathematics and literature.* Portsmouth, N.H.: Heinemann.

Hansen, J. (1987). *When writers read.* Portsmouth, N.H.: Heinemann.

Hansen, J., Newkirk, T. & Graves, D. (1985). *Breaking ground: Teachers relate reading and writing in the elementary school.* Portsmouth, N.H.: Heinemann.

Routman, R. (1988). *Transitions: From literature to literacy.* Portsmouth, N.H.: Heinemann.

Routman, R. (1991). *Invitations: Changing as teachers and learners K–12.* Portsmouth, N.H.: Heinemann.

Children's Books Cited in the Chapter

Berenstein, S. & Berenstein, J. (1982). *The Berenstain bears go to camp.* New York: Random House.

Carle, E. (1986). *Papa, please get the moon for me.* New York: Scholastic.

Cooney, B. (1990). *Hattie and the wild waves.* New York: Viking.

Cooney, B. (1988). *Island boy.* New York: Viking.

Cooney, B. (1982). *Miss Rumphius.* New York: Viking.

Delton, J. (1988). *The pee wee scouts: Cookies and crutches.* New York: Dell Publishing.

Delton, J. (1991). *The pee wee scouts: Sonny's secret.* New York: Dell Publishing.

Flournoy, V. (1985). *The patchwork quilt.* New York: Dial Books for Young Readers.

Fremon, D. (1982). *The secrets of the super athletes.* New York: Dell Publishing.

Gackenbach, D. (1989). *Supposes.* San Diego, CA: Gulliver Books

Gwynne, F. (1976). *A chocolate moose for dinner.* New York: The Trumpet Club.

Gwynne, F. (1987). *The king who rained.* New York: Prentice Hall.

Levinson, R. (1986). *I go with my family to grandma's.* New York: The Trumpet Club.

Levy, E. (1991). *The gymnasts.* New York: Scholastic Inc.

Munsch, R. (1985). *Mortimer.* Toronto: Annick Press.

Munsch, R. (1985). *Thomas' snowsuit.* Toronto: Annick Press.

Perrault, C. (1988). *Cinderella.* New York: Alfred A. Knopf.

Rylant, C. (1982). *When I was young in the mountains.* New York: E.P. Dutton.

White, E.B. (1970). *The trumpet of the swan.* New York: Harper & Row.

Wilder, L.I. (1935). *Little house on the prairie.* New York: Scholastic Inc.

Wilder, L.I. (1943). *These happy golden years.* New York: Harper & Row.

2

Bringing Children to Literacy Through Literature Studies

KATHY PORTERFIELD

Porterfield extends the concepts of using literature to teach reading to the intermediate grade levels. Her philosophy statement is particularly interesting because it reveals Kathy as a learner herself—a "teacher on the grow." She clearly articulates how she creates an environment in which children become self-directed explorers and learners while she serves as a "guide on the side." Porterfield shares with the reader a variety of activities for engaging children with text that lead to intrinsic motivation to read—a goal all of us want to achieve. The teacher new to literature studies will find her sequence of activities for initial literature studies and tips for beginners especially helpful.

In this chapter I will share the way I teach literature studies in my fifth/sixth multi-grade classroom. This will not be a formula for literature study but rather a snapshot representing what works for me with my students at this time. Several years from now, our literature studies may look quite different.

My journey toward the use of literature study began with discussions with my language arts colleagues when I was a special education teacher in a middle school. We were all experimenting with various methods of exploring literature with children. When I moved to an elementary school, I continued to experiment with literature studies with my younger special education students. I also worked with general education teachers to further refine my understanding of literature studies. When I moved from special education to a multi-grade intermediate general education classroom my literature study process continued to grow and flourish undaunted. The process I am sharing with you will undergo transformation as my community of learners extends our understandings of literature.

> Treat people as if they were what they should be and you will help them become what they are capable of becoming.
>
> *Johann Wolfgang von Goethe*

Philosophy

I believe that my philosophy of how children learn is the anchor for all decision making in my classroom. If I want to build a literate community in my classroom, I must have a defined philosophy or the classroom would become nothing more than a collection of activities. Children learn best when they are invited to participate in activities that are whole, real, relevant, and functional. Children must have opportunities to deal with the whole before they look at the individual pieces of a concept, process, or literacy event. Reading is a dynamic and constructive process and literacy events must be authentic, with children reading real texts or writing for a real purpose. The focus of learning must be on the *process* of learning, not just the product.

It is my responsibility to guide students, and then step back and see what happens when children work together and produce results. Lev Vygotsky, a Russian psychologist, developed the theory of the "zone of proximal development."

Vygotsky defined the zone of proximal development as the distance between a child's 'actual developmental level as determined by independent problem solving' and the higher level of 'potential development as determined through problem solving under adult guidance or in collaboration with more capable peers.'

Wertsch, 1985, p. 67–68

The implications of Vygotsky on my educational philosophy are powerful. It means that in the classroom community the goal is for students to discuss a variety of experiences and ideas with one another. By working together and constructing new meanings, we all extend our zones of proximal development. In fact, what each member of the classroom does alone is less than the sum of the parts as we work together.

My philosophy has also been shaped by the work of Louise Rosenblatt. Rosenblatt (1976, p. 94) believes that students bring to their reading personal experiences, the values and backgrounds of their communities, and their personal moral stances. In fact, the sum of who they are is brought to the reading setting. She also states (1976, p. 107) that since most students bring narrow beliefs, attitudes, and backgrounds to the reading experience, they will be helped to enlarge their perspective through the reading experience. She believes that unless readers become aware of the interaction between the text and their belief systems, it is unlikely that a new foundation of knowledge will be built. She states that, "Only when this happens has there been a full interplay between book and reader, and hence a complete and rewarding literary experience." I believe reading is a dynamic process and through cooperative experiences optimal learning takes place.

As students bring their newly constructed knowledge to a literature discussion group and discuss the book they increase their depth of meaning from their common literature experiences and personal world view. It is hoped that each child will leave a literature discussion with new and enlarged perceptions of the meaning of the work.

Laying the Foundation

There are thirty students in my multi-age, suburban school classroom. Our school staff is developing and implementing a whole language philosophy with the support and encouragement of our building administrator. Students are rarely pulled out for special services but consultative assistance is available when needed.

My first priority is building a literate community in my classroom. I strive to create an environment that embraces Frank Smith's concept of the "Literacy Club." He states that the "Literacy Club is, of course, a club of people who use written language. Children join the literacy club . . . with the implicit act of mutual acceptance: 'You're one of us, "I want to be just like you.'"

I believe, as a community, we all have a share in constructing a learning environment in which learning will occur. The students take responsibility to arrange the room physically. They also accept responsibility to create and organize ways in which classroom routines and procedures will be carried out. These activities are built on a foundation of interpersonal and social skills which are essential for successful literature studies.

In order for literature studies to be successful, it is important that extensive groundwork be laid before the students and I ever meet in a literature discussion group. The activities which follow are not necessarily done sequentially. They are interrelated and are introduced during the first quarter of the school year. These activities will change as we all grow and learn.

At the beginning of the year I have lunch with each student during which I conduct a personal interview. I try to learn as much as possible about their families, personal interests, their perception of individual strengths and weaknesses, as well as what they enjoy (and don't enjoy) about school. Student complete a personal interest inventory as well as more detailed descriptions of the literary genres they like, their experiences, and interests. You can develop your own questionnaire asking questions such as the following:

What are your favorite kinds of stories?

Do you have any favorite books?

What do you like about these books?

Do you have any favorite authors?

What do you like about these authors?

What are three favorite things you like to do outside of school?

How did you get interested in these things?

The interest survey forms the basis for conversations in which we discuss the selection of books for personal reading.

The class also takes part in "Critic's Corner." As students complete books, they sign up to share during Critics' Corner times. The purpose of this activity is for students to act as "literary critics," giving class members a "commercial" for their completed book, which also includes their opinions as to why other students should read the book.

As a part of the classroom community, I also share books that I have recently read as well as feature new additions to our classroom reading library. It is vital that students view me as a lover of books. I cannot communicate values I do not have and which children do not see. They are quick to identify adult lack of authenticity; students need to see that reading is a valued activity.

It is essential that I establish D.E.A.R. (drop everything and read) time the first day of school. D.E.A.R. time is when it is silent in the classroom because everyone is reading. I begin with just ten minutes or so a day and build to at least forty-five minutes each day. The purpose of D.E.A.R. is to encourage students to read as much as they can in as many genres as possible. For this to occur it is essential that I have a classroom library with a wide range of reading material at various interest and ability levels. The building of my classroom library is a never ending process with a continuous search for the largest possible range of materials. As the year progresses, the students often spend entire mornings reading.

At the beginning of the year, it is imperative that students view me as a part of our reading community. This is really a case of, "do as I do". I read during D.E.A.R. and talk with students about books I am reading. Eventually as the routine becomes established, I can begin conferencing and holding literature discussions with groups of students. These activities are ones that guarantee all students "their share" of the teacher's time. It should be noted, however, that on occasion throughout the year I elect to read with the class. This is a purposeful choice on my part as I want to model participation in our reading community.

Book Lover's Journals and Book Teas are two of the building blocks for our literate community. All of my students have their own "Book Lover's Journal" in which they write titles and comments about books they have read. This is *not* a book report as most of us would know it. The students discuss their books with one another, sharing information and opinions in the same way adults might talk together about what they have been reading as they sit around the dining room table (Atwell, 1987). When eight students have completed entries in their journals, we arrange a time for a Book Tea. Cookies and juice are served at the conversation table and students talk about their books with me and each other. This activity usually takes about a half hour. These teas take place about twice a month and participation is neither graded nor required.

Figure 2-1   Book Tea Form. *Created by Katherine Porterfield*

Book Tea Form

Title: _____

Author: _____

Date Read: _____

Comments: _____

             _____

             _____

             _____

All these activities contribute to students becoming intrinsically motivated to read for the sheer pleasure of it. Without the enthusiasm these kinds of activities generate, reading will not be the rich experience necessary for successful literature studies.

Formal Reading Instruction in my Classroom

After these activities or similar ones are installed in my classroom, more formal reading instruction can take place in a nonthreatening environment. It is imperative that I develop a clear sense of how each individual student deals with a variety of texts. This gives me the information I need to make critical instructional decisions as I begin to structure our literature studies. As a total classroom or as individuals, we review and discuss students' perceptions of the personal challenges books may present. In addition, we discuss what "supports" the books have for them. Challenges or supports may be level of interest in the book topic, background knowledge, personal experience with the topic, the genre itself, the relative difficulty of the vocabulary, the physical layout of the text, and so forth. These are some questions I have asked students regarding challenges and supports in books they are reading:

> What makes it easy for you to read this book?
>
> What helps you to do deal with vocabulary you do not already know?
>
> How does using the context make it easier for you when you come to ideas and words you may not know?
>
> What do you already know about the topic of this book that may help you as you read?
>
> Have you had any experiences related to the topic of your book?
>
> How do you use those experiences to make reading the book easier?
>
> How can you deal with changes in setting in the book and still understand what is happening?
>
> How do prologues and epilogues help you as you read? Do they help you predict or better understand the book you have read?
>
> How does the author's use of tension and conflict affect you as a reader, pulling you through the book?

This activity is patterned after the New Zealand model in which students deal with challenges and supports of the reading material they may encounter. The purpose of this activity is for students to become active evaluators of reading materials as opposed to passive recipients.

Individual reading conferences are extremely important in the development of my understanding of my students as readers. During these conferences challenges and supports are discussed. In addition, the conference itself becomes a stage for exploration of individual reading processes and the strategies children develop to become more efficient readers. Reading strategies that might be explored during reading conferences could include: what to do when a reader comes to an unknown word, skipping unfamiliar words, and self-correction as readers learn to process information in context. Initially I meet every student during D.E.A.R. time on a weekly basis. As I come to know my readers better, individual schedules for reading conferences will differ, based on the competence of the readers. These conferences usually take about five minutes, although they may last longer depending on the needs of each student. This kind of interaction lessens as typically proficient readers become more so. I continue to conference with my least proficient readers on a regular basis, and use other strategies for selected students with special needs. The reading conference form I use for this activity is shown below in Figure 2-2.

Each day I read aloud to my students. Reading aloud to them is an essential element in building a base for literature studies. It is during read-aloud time that we begin our discussions and investigations into meanings as a class through discussions emphasizing meaning-making. I carefully select a piece of fiction that will draw the students into the literature selection. I select Caldecott and Newbery selections, medal winners from other countries, notable books, and personal favorite. I also use reviews from professional magazines. Some of my personal favorites include *Hatchet* (1987) by Gary Paulsen, *Summer of the Monkeys* (1976) by Wilson Rawls, *Roll of Thunder, Hear My Cry* (1977) by Mildred D. Taylor, *Call It Courage* (1941) by Armstrong Speery, *A Wrinkle in Time* (1963) by Madeline L'Engle, and *Sounder* (1970) by William H. Armstrong, among others. The selections I read to students do not define the limits of their personal reading. Students may choose a wider variety of reading material including magazines, serial books, nonfiction, books embodying family values, and other works selected by students' families. Children will ultimately make their own choices as to what constitutes good literature to them, as well as make personal decisions to read varying kinds of material which may not fit my personal definition of good literature.

Selections for literature study and read-alouds must reflect the wide variety of essential literary elements found in good literature. These include: story structure, characterization, setting, plot, conflict, resolution, mood, point of view, similes, metaphors, symbolism, and others. A good reference in this areas is *A Critical Handbook of Childrens' Literature* (1990) by Rebecca J. Lukens. The read-aloud time serves as an opportunity for students to begin to discuss the more complex elements of making personal meaning from what they have heard. We identify and discuss a variety of literary elements that are a part of the read-aloud. Students have some small group discussions focusing on particular elements of literature as they arise during the read-aloud selection.

My students have spiral notebooks ("Literature Logs") in which they

Figure 2-2 Reading Conference Form. *Created by Cheryl Ames and Katherine Porterfield.*

Name _____

+ Strategy Used / Good
− Strategy Not Used / Poor
✓ Instruction Provided

Retelling

Date	Book	Predicting	Omit/Synonym/Blank	Back Track/Read On	Accurate Self Corrections	Rate/Fluency	Characters	Setting	Events	Problem	Resolution	Author's Lesson	Personal Reaction	Comments

Comments

write responses to the read-aloud story and literature study books. Initially I have the students focus on three open-ended questions, "What did you notice?" (I am looking for a cognitive response, usually focusing on an element of literature the student finds particularly outstanding). "What did you think?" (I am looking for affective responses in which children state their feelings and opinions as well as personal connections to the story. "What did you wonder?" (I ask students to write honest questions to which they do not have answers). Students' answers to these questions become the foundation for our literature discussions throughout the course of the year. Of course, there are no "right" answers, permitting all students the freedom to share openly and honestly with their classmates in a non-threatening atmosphere. It is amazing that I rarely find it necessary to ask leading questions because students' responses are often characterized by a depth beyond my own. I read certain responses aloud with the author's permission because they elevate the quality of others' written responses.

I have learned that written responses to literature can be overdone. When I began this process with students, I expected quality written responses weekly. I have learned that the overuse of this rich technique can become the "workbook" of literature studies. In this case, familiarity does tend to breed contempt. When used judiciously, the written responses of students are connectors between the students and me. They share parts of themselves which they bring to the reading process. This is reflected in the quality and depth of their written responses. The selections below illustrate the work of both a special and general education student. These are responses to *Hatchet,* a book read aloud in class. It was written by Gary Paulsen. Shawna, a general education student said:

> I wonder if Brian is scared and not always happy like the book says and always having good ideas. Deep down inside he is probably scared and lonely wishing he would just be found, saying "Enough of all this. Just give me my life back!." I would be praying if I were him. It would give him a better chance to get off the island. I can feel his anger inside of me, scared with him as if I've known him all of my life and I was part of him like part of his soul. I know that if I were him I would be frustrated and cry a lot . . . I thought he was going to die of thirst or cold or hunger but he didn't. That didn't surprise me though. There are a lot of wild animals out there and I am surprised that only a couple of them bothered him . . . I thought about how neat it is that from one story about twenty-five people in our classroom have different pictures in their heads and not one of them is alike.

After reading *Hatchet* the class decided to watch the film. John is a special education student. His response is a comparison between the film and the book:

I liked both but the book was mostly my favorite. I like the book better because you don't know what will happen. The book was interesting, but when you've seen the movie it was different . . . where he made the raft it was only one log not a bunch like in the movie. In the movie the bear came up two times. That wasn't in the book. I wonder why in the book it said he shot the twenty-two but in the movie he didn't . . . the book didn't say anything about him feeding the cub and the book didn't say that he killed the bear and left the cub some food to eat. I wonder if the cub died and if the mother and father got back together. This is the best story I ever heard in my life.

Literature Study Begins

Depending on the group of students, we are usually ready to begin literature studies by the middle of the first quarter of the school year. An advantage of a multi-grade classroom is that it does not take as long to begin since there is a cadre of students who were with me the preceding year.

It is important that my role be established as a facilitator of literature study groups. It is my task to be an active participant, a listener, a critic, and one who can bring greater clarity to the group discussion. I also need to have a clear direction in my own mind of the knowledge I hope my students will possess after two years in my classroom. Literature study is not about testing comprehension or reducing the study to some rigid, formal process but about helping students come to deeper understandings of literature.

Students need to understand that there are many purposes for reading. Reading done for no other reason than for the pure pleasure of it is certainly one of the goals for students in my classroom. They need to understand, however, that there is a difference between a book read purely for pleasure and one that is read in a literature study. They are read differently and the students will learn to approach them differently. Eeds and Peterson (1990) characterized these two types of reading as "extensive" and "intensive" reading. During extensive reading I encourage my students to read as much and in as many genres as possible. I encourage students to have fun with their reading, skipping part of books that are not of interest to them, skimming and re-reading when those activities seem appropriate and so forth. During literature studies, students are introduced to the need for more intensive reading. During discussion it is important that students come to realize the goal in literature studies is to develop a deep and thorough understanding of the text.

This is the process I use to set up literature studies:

- I use picture books as a vehicle to teach elements of literature.
- Discussions are held to help students with their choices of books.

- I share an overview of each book available for a particular literature study.
- Students select books of their choice.
- We practice how to discuss in groups e.g., listening skills, questioning, and so on.
- I share a variety of note taking methods.
- We review the basis of literature study evaluation.
- We set meeting times for group responses to literature.

Picture Books

I often begin with collections of picture books by particular authors. Some of my favorites are the books of Chris VanAllsburg, William Steig, Jan Brett, and Robert Munsch. These selections pose no threat to the students regardless of their reading abilities. During this beginning time, I have my students gather in small groups and focus on major elements of literature. Each group reads a different title from the collection. By the end of this activity students will have read and discussed several titles by one author. I then have the groups compare literature elements such as mood, theme, characterization, and others. I encourage students to look for similarities and differences between books. Picture books have proved to be a very successful vehicle for teaching about literary elements regardless of student age or reading ability.

A student, Brandon, shared the following in his literature log after reading *The Amazing Bone* (1985) by William Steig:

> I thought that this was a great story. I like how William Steig puts animals in the place of people. That's what makes his stories funny. I think that just because they are picture books doesn't mean they are for little kids.

Book Choice

When gathering books for literature studies, it is essential that I have read each book myself. In addition, I often have students read possible titles before I purchase books. I want the students' opinions about whether or not the books are interesting to them, and their recommendations as to whether or not that particular title should be added to our classroom collection. I also select a balance of titles and buy books of varying difficulty, with both female and male protagonists and from various genres. Genres of particular interest to a wide range of students include: survival, mystery, historical fiction, animal stories, fantasy, and realistic fiction. I also offer collections by individual authors like Natalie Babbitt, Katherine Paterson, and Gary Paulsen. These collections of books give students a choice within a choice. The standards for read-aloud books and literature study books are the same. A good source for suggested literature study books is *Grand Conversa-*

tions: Literature Study Groups In Action (1990) by Ralph Peterson and Maryann Eeds.

Book Talks

When gathering titles together for a book talk, I select five different titles (to discuss in the classroom) based on their probable worth as pieces of literature. Often they will coincide with areas of study in my classroom. I give the students a brief background about the author, and do a "commercial" for the book. It is important that students have opportunities to review the various choices before making their own selections.

Selection and Assignment of Books

After my book commercials I have students prioritize the books I have reviewed in order of interest to them. I have found that four literature groups are the maximum I can comfortably manage. However, I still share a fifth title which gives me flexibility in organizing groups. I have found that groups of four to seven students work best. I then assign students to literature study groups keeping in mind the following:

1. Their top two choices of books.
2. A balance of reading levels.
3. Individual student attitudes and behaviors.

Modeling Groups in Discussion

I have videotaped groups of students engaged in literature discussions. We watch the tapes as a group and analyze the strengths and weaknesses of the discussions. Students are quick to pick up on the dynamics of the group: Are they listening to one another; are they using their notes; have they completed the reading?

Note Taking

When I read books, I take notes, modeling this behavior for my students. These notes are invaluable in actual literature discussions. I model what works best for me, emphasizing that they may elect not to take notes. Some students like to take notes while they read, while others choose to go back after reading to take their notes. I encourage students to take notes keeping in mind the open-ended questions they use in their written responses. These notes consist of things students notice, wonder, think while they are reading. They also include unfamiliar vocabulary or things in the text they find particularly challenging. It is important that they cite page numbers related to their comments to help them during discussion. Some students choose to use "sticky notes" on individual book pages while note taking while others write notes in their literature logs. CAUTION: It is important that students do not get bogged down in note taking since it can make reading unpleasant for some of them. I have found that one page of notes in a literature log is ample for this purpose although some students really enjoy keeping copious notes. I have found that some students become discouraged by note-taking and if they are able to participate actively in discussion, notes are not a requirement.

Literature Study Assessments

Assessment takes the form of student self-evaluation at the end of literature study. Students analyze their preparation and participation in discussion. I have found it helpful for students to know the evaluative criteria prior to group discussions. (please refer to Figure 2-5, page 41).

Meeting Times and Group Responses to Literature

I meet with literature groups two to four times for each book. The number of meetings depends on the needs of each group, school activities, disruptions, and the like. Each discussion lasts fifteen to twenty minutes. Often students continue their discussion without me. Many students will finish reading a book in less than a week's time, though it may take two weeks for me to meet with all the groups. I have found that two weeks is the *maximum* time I want to spend on a particular selection.

At the first meeting we fill out a calendar detailing the number of pages to be read each day (Figure 2-3). We also discuss the content of the book and build background knowledge if it is necessary for the students to have a fuller understanding of the book. We discuss the particular elements of style, such as flashbacks and setting changes peculiar to the book to help students meet possible challenges in the text. It is during this first meeting that we set goals and expectations for note-taking, and review strategies for dealing with particular challenges the text may hold. I encourage students to keep notes regarding challenges they cannot meet alone.

During discussions I stress that students examine their own processes of coming to grips with challenges they have met. It is in sharing individual strategies that group members learn from one another and increase their understandings of how other people think, and how they can incorporate other students' ways of knowing into their own repertoires. Vocabulary concerns are resolved as they arise. I encourage students to find meanings of unknown words through the use of context and discussions among group members. Through discussion students develop a sense of what is essential to know and what is not, which words need formal definition to maintain meaning as they read and which do not. If there are particular words or concepts children feel they must know, the group may decide to investigate them further. They may also note their understandings of new words in their literature logs.

Figure 2-3   Literature Study Calendar. *Source: Grand Conversations—Modified by Kathryn Porterfield.*

Name _____

Date _____

Title _____

_____

Literature Study Calendar

During the weeks of _____ I agree to read the book titled

_____.

This book has a total of _____ pages. I will pace myself according to the schedule below.

Date_____	Date_____	Date_____	Date_____	Date_____
Date_____	Date_____	Date_____	Date_____	Date_____

I agree to complete at least _____ entries in my Literature Log to be turned in by. _____.

Student Signature _____

Teacher Signature _____

At the second meeting we discuss general impressions of the book. I follow the lead of the students as they bring up points of interest and questions from their notes as well as any particular challenges they may have encountered. I try to be a "guide on the side." As Maryann Eeds states, my job is to shoot literary arrows as students bring up particular elements and points of interest during the literature discussion. We are building meaning *together*. During this second discussion, I like to stress connections from their past experiences and knowledge. As children share their own constructed meanings from the text, one can see Vygotsky's theory of zones of proximal development in action. All participants in the discussion, including me, come to deeper understandings of the piece of literature. Following are excerpts of discussions from two novels, *The Great Gilly Hopkins* (1979) by Katherine Paterson and *The Sign of the Beaver* (1984) by Elizabeth George Speare.

From *Gilly Hopkins* we hear:

Sarah:	"I think she's getting more nice," "I don't know, it just seems like she is" ... "Um, like how she's writing to her mom and stuff, I don't know."
Rosemary:	" I've got something ... she's being nice by being nicer to W.E. ... "
David :	"But wasn't she doing that so that she could get the money?"
Chris:	"Oh, yeah, she's using him."
Christina:	"I think she really likes him because in the end, so after that when she isn't living with Trotter anymore she is nice to him 'cause she writes to him and stuff."
Chris:	"I think she is nicer than she was in the beginning of the book. At the beginning she was a brat."
Mrs. P.:	"Why do you think she was that way?"
Sarah:	"Because she's really sad or something."
Rosemary:	"She was raised to be tough, she says, well you have to be tough."
Sarah:	"I think she's mad. If you're switched around everywhere . . . ."
Brandon:	"I'd feel that way if I got sent to foster home after foster home."

From *The Sign of the Beaver* we hear:

Nicole:	"I thought the relationship between Matt and Attean was really strong because they would do like everything together."
Rian:	"I thought it was kind of a strange relationship because they looked out for each other but they didn't show feelings toward each other."
Erik:	"And he brought him food and medicine and stuff like that. And then Matt brought the Bible and stuff like that."

Kyle: "Like when they were out in the woods Attean made Matt feel kind of ridiculous because he didn't really know anything and Attean but Matt made Attean feel kind of ridiculous cause when he was teaching him to read and stuff."

Leslie: 1 "I thought Attean always made Matt feel that way because Matt felt stupid because he wasn't teaching Attean the right way. Ok, on page 47 Matt fell in the lake and Attean gave him a horrible grin."

During discussions I participate as well as take notes. These notes serve as a vehicle for our negotiations as to their assignments for the next meeting.

The third meeting is usually at the end of the book. We begin our discussion by addressing the assigned topic of the previous meeting. One can observe during the second meeting that the students have moved beyond the superficial details of the book. The discussions are much deeper. At this time we may also choose to focus on an element of literature which is particularly strong in the book. After agreeing upon a topic of investigation, students will also record examples of that element in their logs as they reread parts of the text.

CAUTION: Through experience I have found that the group can become too fixated upon specific elements to the detriment of their personal connections with the book. Students may see the task of literature study as one of merely identifying literary elements and in so doing, we may lose the richness of the discussions.

The *experience* of reading is always in the forefront of my mind in group meetings. I use a very helpful evaluation form which was created by a colleague at the Middle School. It helps me to track the progress of students during literature discussions (Figure 2-4).

If we have time for a fourth meeting we discuss their topics of investigation and complete self-evaluations for this meeting series. We often discuss similarities and differences they see in this book compared to others they have read. I encourage students to become literary critics by discussing and rating the books with their ratings supported by evidence from their experiences. Students have also completed their written response to the book and these are evaluated at this time.

Sarah, in response to *Tuck Everlasting* (1975), written by Natalie Babbitt wrote,

Tuck Everlasting is the best book I have ever read. There's so much foreshadowing in the prologue that it just pulls you in. It's like a book with hands. It pulls on you and pulls on you until you can't get out of the book like when it says, 'but sometimes people find this out too late.' Also when it says, 'when people are led to do things they are sure to be sorry for after'.

You don't really catch the foreshadowing until you go back. She hides the foreshadowing so deep that your mind finds it but you don't really process the information until later.

I think the man in the yellow suit is SO weird! I wonder lots of things about him. I wonder if he has a family. I also wonder *who* he is. It never says his name or anything. He is so mysterious. She only tells you *just* so the reader knows what's going on in the story, but that's all.

Her writing makes you think about life. Well, I guess it makes you think about death too, like what happens when you die, and would it really be great to live forever. What would it be like to live forever? That's kind of hard to explain or understand, forever. Weird!

Sometimes these evaluations are only between the student and me and sometimes the groups engage in discussion together. One of the values of this process is that the students are able to put personal closure to this particular reading experience.

Following the discussions, students respond to the book in a variety of ways depending on how they have interacted with the book. They may elect to investigate further something from the content of the book or to write reflecting their own opinions. Responses may also take the forms of drama, writing to the author, producing timelines, writing sequels, or artistic responses. I leave the decisions as to the kinds of responses in the hands of the students.

Grading

I find grading for literature studies to be relatively simple. I have set high expectations for the quality of both written work and discussion. Through the use of the monitoring form and students' self-evaluations, it is not difficult to assign grades, a requirement in my school.

While this may change based upon the dynamics of my classroom, grading for literature studies consists of some or all of the following:

1. Participation in discussion.
2. Completion of discussion assignments.
3. The completion of some sort of notes.
4. A written response to the book.
5. Their personal choice of response to the book.
6. Self-evaluation.

Figure 2-4 Literature Studies Group Evaluation.

Book Title _____

Period _____

Excellent	=	+
OK	=	O
Not Prepared	=	–

Group Members:

Discussion
Reading Completed
Log Caught Up
On Task
Evaluation
Indiv. Grade
Group Grade
Assignment

Comments:

Meeting # _____
Date _____
1
2
3
4
5
6
7

Meeting # _____
Date _____
1
2
3
4
5
6
7

Meeting # _____ Date _____

1
2
3
4
5
6
7

Meeting # _____ Date _____

1
2
3
4
5
6
7

I strive to have students involved in each step of the grading process and we usually collaborate. They self-grade and I have found them to be incredibly accurate. Students are measured only against themselves and the growth they make over time as learners. A grade of "A" is based upon doing their very best work possible.

It should be clear that the elements of grading noted above must not be constraining to the individual readers. It is important that students' uniqueness is not lost in a grading formula or devotion to expectations which may be meaningless and unnecessary for some readers. One must remember that the goal of literature studies is to create fully literate students who love reading for its own sake as well as students who are able to investigate literature on more formal levels.

For Those Beginning Literature Studies

1. It is easier to begin with *one* literature group at a time. This group should be carefully selected to insure success with this new endeavor. A goal for a teacher beginning this process might be to have each student complete one literature study during the year.
2. The video camera has proved to be a very useful tool to help students develop better discussion skills.
3. I have found it difficult to handle more than four literature study groups at one time. One might wish to build up to four groups over time, perhaps in a year or so.
4. I find that student participation in five to six groups during the course of a year is ample (this number may change based upon the interests of my students). I have found it useful to intersperse literature studies with many other activities: partner reading, plays, poetry, private reading, and so forth.
5. Following are some suggestions for accommodating the needs of readers who may have difficulties with their literature choice:
    a) Make certain that they carefully review all book choices before making their selections,
    b) Audio tape the books for literature study,
    c) Enlist parent support by requesting that they read with their child at home should the need arise,
    d) Consider partner reading. It is popular with all of my students and I often arrange for those with reading difficulty to read with a more proficient reader.

    Here are some comments from students' logs where they shared their feelings about literature study:

"I love lit study because there is always a theme and I learn from it."

"I really enjoy lit study because it gives you a chance to read new books that you probably wouldn't have read before. It doesn't seem

Figure 2-5   Literature Study Evaluation

Name _____ Date _____

Here is a checklist to help you self-evaluate your part in your literature study group. Please circle the correct rating.

Title _____

Author _____

Question

1. When reading the story I made sure it made sense   1 2 3 4 5
2. I have prepared for the discussion by:
    a. reading the assigned pages   1 2 3 4 5
    b. writing in my log and noting important page numbers   1 2 3 4 5
    c. thinking about what I want to say in group   1 2 3 4 5
    d. creating "I wonder questions"   1 2 3 4 5
    e. listing unfamiliar vocabulary   1 2 3 4 5
    f. drawing in my log (optional)   1 2 3 4 5
    g. doing some research (optional)   1 2 3 4 5
3. I relate the story to things that have happened to me . . . personal connections   1 2 3 4 5
4. I relate the story to other stories or poems I have read in terms of the following elements: setting, mood, plot, theme, characters, illustrations, and record in my log.   1 2 3 4 5
5. I look for patterns in the story . . . example: foreshadowing, repeated language, pictures.   1 2 3 4 5
6. Participation: I keep the discussion going well by . . .
    a. staying on the subject   1 2 3 4 5
    b. contributing important information   1 2 3 4 5
    c. encouraging other to speak   1 2 3 4 5
    d. listening to other members of the group   1 2 3 4 5
    e. show my attention by looking at the speaker and responding   1 2 3 4 5
    f. listening to opposing opinions   1 2 3 4 5
    g. ask for clarification when I don't understand   1 2 3 4 5
    h. speaking clearly and loudly enough to be heard by all group members   1 2 3 4 5

My literature Study grade is an _____

because _____
_____

like an assignment because it's so fun. At the end I like doing the log entry. It helps you kind of understand the book better. I like discussions because you get to find out what other people like about the book. It's also fun to hear things that people noticed that you missed in the book."

"I think literature study is a good idea. It helps us express our opinions and also to hear other people's opinions. It also helps to get your questions answered."

"I think lit study is fun because it takes you to a different world. It's easy for me because I take a lot of notes and then I write a long log response. It's fun for me. I get more out of a book when I write about it. I would much rather do a lit study than a workbook."

If you wish to begin literature studies, you must give yourself the gift of time. In addition to implementing the entire process, it will take time to get a feel for the discussions and how they are conducted. Some discussions are dynamic and have their own life while others barely get off the ground. The more you, as a teacher, step back and allow the students to take the lead, the more you will see them leading. Remember you don't have to be a "sage on the stage" but instead, "a guide on the side." The process and the teacher are always "becoming."

In the years I have been a teacher, my goal has been to help children to become active participants in their own learning process. It matters little what a book or idea means to me if it does not have meaning for my students. None of us learns in a vacuum and we must always remember the importance of genuine interaction. I believe sharing must be demonstrated. It does not happen by accident. Literature studies help students develop the skills of introspection, but even more importantly, they provide a means of sharing ideas with one another in an atmosphere of genuine mutual respect for ideas and for each other.

My philosophy is in evolution and I, of course, am still becoming.

The real purpose of books is to trap the mind into doing its own thinking.
Christopher Morley

References

Atwell, N. (1987). *In the middle: Writing, reading, and learning with adolescents.* Portsmouth, NH: Heinemann.

Lukens, R. (1990). *A critical handbook of children's literature.* Glenview, IL: Scott, Foresman and Company.

Peterson, R. & Eeds, M. (1990). *Grand conversations.* New York: Scholastic.

Rosenblatt, L. (1976). *Literature as exploration.* New York: Modern Language Association.

Smith, F. (1986). *Insult to intelligence: The bureaucratic invasion of our classrooms.* Portsmouth, NH: Heinemann.

Smith, F. (1992). Learning to read-the never-ending debate. *The Kappan.* *(73)*6. 432–441.

Wertson, J. & Vygotsky, L. (1985), *Formation of mind.* Cambridge, MA: Harvard University Press.

Children's Books Cited in the Chapter

Armstrong, W. (1970). *Sounder.* New York: Harper & Row.

Babbitt, N. (1975). *Tuck everlasting.* New York: Sunburst Publications. Farrar, Straus, & Giroux.

L'Engle, M. (1963). *A wrinkle in time.* New York: Dell.

Paterson, K. (1979). *The great Gilly Hopkins.* New York: Crowell.

Paulsen, G. (1987). *Hatchet.* New York: Puffin.

Rawls, W. (1976). *Summer of the monkeys.* New York: Dell.

Speare, E. (1984). *The sign of the beaver.* New York: Houghton-Mifflin.

Speery, A. (1941). *Call it courage.* New York: MacMillan.

Steig, W. (1985). *The amazing bone.* New York: Farrar, Straus, & Giroux.

Taylor, M. (1977). *Roll of thunder, hear my cry.* New York: Bantam Books.

3

Bringing Children to Literacy Through Shared Reading

DEBORAH A. MANNING

JEAN W. FENNACY

Central to Manning and Fennacy's philosophy is the concept that we do not teach children to read, but we can make it possible for them to teach themselves through texts that engage them. Evidence of their strong belief in this position is found throughout the chapter. Here they expand the concept of shared reading well beyond the use of big books as they underscore the importance of written material all can see, a proficient reader to lead the way, and a nonthreatening atmosphere. They demonstrate a variety of ways that shared reading can be used throughout the day for a wide range of purposes. It is a joy to read this piece and think about how children's perceptions of themselves and their classmates as readers changed throughout the year.

To learn to read, children need the attention of one patient adult, or an older child, for long enough to read something that pleases them both. A book, a person, and shared enjoyment: These are the conditions of success. The process should begin at an early age and continue as a genuine collaborative activity until the child leaves school. (Meek, 1982, p. 9)

For those of us who are more knowledgeable and more mature—parents and teachers—the responsibility is clear: to interact with those in our care in such a way as to foster and enrich their meaning-making. (Wells, 1986, p. 222)

Just as the children learn to say the nursery rhymes by hearing them said aloud, so they can learn to read whole units of meaning once they have heard the sounds of the sentences "ringing in their ears." (Martin, 1966, p. 2)

It is 2:25 p.m. on a spring afternoon. Outside, children are milling about. Ten minutes earlier they had been dismissed from school for the day. Some of the students are heading toward the playground, others are meeting parents who have come to pick them up after school. Most are traipsing toward the gate on their way home.

But the door to Room 4 hasn't even opened yet. These second graders are still in class and appear oblivious to the time of day. All 30 of them are clustered together on the rug at the front of the classroom reading in unison. As they finish what they are reading, Matthew pleads, "Mrs. Manning, let's read Jason's next. I really think it's funny." Then, together with their teacher, they all read Jason's piece out loud from the latest edition of their classroom newspaper. Finally the teacher declares that it really is time for them to go, but she promises they will read more tomorrow.

Such enthusiasm for Shared Reading experiences is not atypical for this group of children. They often read aloud together and enjoy doing so. Sometimes they read with partners or with small groups of friends. Sometimes a parent volunteer sits with four or five children around a table using multiple copies of the same book and they read in unison. Occasionally the teacher reads one-on-one with an individual child. But most often it is the whole class along with their teacher who engage in shared reading.

Reading plays an important role in this classroom. The teacher reads to the children several times each day. The class also has time daily to read independently selected trade books and magazines from their large classroom library. And they also experience shared reading on a regular basis. Because their teacher agrees with Frank Smith (1985) that the only way to learn to read is by reading, she makes certain that all of her students find their way into reading in a joyous and nonthreatening manner. Shared reading, essentially reading (or chanting or singing) along together, provides the support many of her students need to become successful readers.

Not all of the students in this class entered second grade with positive feelings about themselves as readers. A small number are quite proficient. Most are not. A few spent first grade in a literature-based classroom. Most experienced a year of traditional basal-driven instruction. For several of the children, English is their second language, yet they have not had the benefit of school literacy instruction in their first language. The class reflects the growing diversity of students found in central California. They represent a wide range of economic levels and cultural backgrounds including Hispanic, Afro-American, Anglo-American, and Southeast Asian. Regardless of their background or degree of literacy proficiency, shared reading is one of the many ways their teacher brings them to literacy in this classroom.

The purpose of this chapter is to clarify what we mean by shared reading, explore the role shared reading plays in nurturing reading development, and examine a number of ways we have used shared reading experiences in the primary classroom.

Shared Reading

Shared reading is commonly used in whole language classrooms as one means by which teachers bring children to literacy. Cochrane, Cochrane, Scalena, and Buchanan (1984) describe supportive reading and read-along as strategies teachers use to nurture reading. Both of these seem connected to what we define as shared reading. In our view the term shared reading covers a range of activities which have the following basic aspects in common:

- Written material which all involved can see and which is of interest and delight to the readers
- A proficient reader who leads the way, supporting the readers as long as they need support
- A nonthreatening atmosphere of shared enjoyment.

Each of these elements seems to be encompassed in what Don Holdaway (1979) described as the shared book experience which was introduced in New Zealand as a means by which children could benefit from an activity in school that was similar to the bedtime story reading many children experience at home. In a nurturing environment they are enticed into the literacy club (Smith, 1985).

Written Material Which All Can See

We have found a variety of ways to make material available for shared reading. Big books are perhaps the most widely recognized materials used for shared reading. However, there are numerous other ways to make printed text available for everyone. Sometimes we write poems, stories, or songs on large charts for easy viewing. On other occasions we use overhead transparencies. Sometimes we duplicate multiple copies of poems or students' authored pieces so all members of the class may have their own copies in hand. And we use class sets (or small group sets) of trade books or children's magazines. Even the local newspaper and our class-produced newspaper has provided us with materials to read together.

Whichever way we choose, our intent is to enhance the opportunity for our students to engage with the given text. The important point is that all the children be able to clearly see the print. This means when we have a shared reading experience with the whole class the print must be enlarged to a greater degree than when we are reading with a very small group or individual. To a certain degree our decision to use either multiple copies of an individual text, an overhead transparency, a chart, or a big book rests on the age, experience, and sophistication of our readers. For example, we are most likely to choose big books and charts when we work with kindergartners, but there have been times when multiple copies of poems have been appropriate for that age group.

Of the utmost importance is that we select texts that will be enticing and interesting to our students. We are convinced that children only become readers if and when they see reading as something personally worthwhile. We agree with Meek (1982) that if we want our students to read well they must have "compelling reasons for doing so" (p. 18). We do not teach children to read, but we can make it possible for them to teach themselves. Materials that make them want to read are therefore essential. By making sure the printed text is accessible to them, either at the front of the room enlarged for all to see or right in their own hands, we enhance the possibility that the children will explore the print and learn from it what they are ready to learn at the moment. However, the most important aspect is that once the children have had a taste of the text they will want more. The text must draw the children's interest and fascination.

A Proficient Reader Leading the Way

Even though we believe we do not teach children to read, we certainly believe as teachers we play an extremely important role not only in helping students learn to read but making it possible for them to do so. As Wells (1986) suggests, our responsibility is to foster and enrich our students' meaning-making. During shared reading, our enthusiastic reading provides a demonstration of how a particular piece can be read. In leading the way, we make the text accessible to the children. Particularly for our students who are not yet independent readers, when we read the text out loud to them first and then encourage them to read along with us, we play a role similar to the parent helping a youngster learn to ride a bike. The parent runs along side and helps balance the youngster who is just beginning to ride. Just as the parent does, we keep them going until they are ready go without our help. By reading a well-loved poem or story together over and over, our help is needed less and less. Soon, the children are taking off on their own. It is within what Vygotsky (1978) called the "zone of proximal development" that shared reading provides support for novice readers. What they can do with help today they will be able to do on their own tomorrow.

We would not want to suggest that it is only teachers who can play this supportive role. Older children who are invited to be reading buddies with younger ones can help the novice reader over some of the hurdles along the path toward independent reading. When time is regularly scheduled for reading buddies to get together, shared reading happens almost naturally. As each pair of buddies develops mutual relationships there is the added benefit that the older children are able to select books that are of particular interest to their individual reading buddies. As a result, the likelihood of the younger children coming into contact with reading materials they find especially compelling is enhanced.

Shared reading even occurs among peers. For example, a first grader who is already an independent reader or who is particularly familiar with a given text can read along with a less-proficient classmate. In this situation one child becomes the support for the other. Once again it is a proficient reader supporting the novice as he becomes a member of the literacy club.

A Nonthreatening Atmosphere

Because no child is singled out in shared reading, no one is put on the spot. No one has to perform, no one has to feel fearful of making a mistake. Children can enter into the collaborative reading as they feel comfortable doing so. No one is coerced. No one must risk punishment, failure, or embarrassment in order to participate. The activity is not hazardous (Smith, 1988). Instead, shared reading provides an atmosphere of shared enjoyment. We all have a good time. We enjoy what we are reading, we enjoy our shared voices, and we enjoy being together as we experience the text. In so doing, we are demonstrating that reading is, indeed, a delightful activity worth doing.

Shared reading is especially beneficial for the less proficient readers and those students for whom English is a second language. In the collaborative and nonthreatening community they can join in as they feel ready to do so. They can participate in the phrases or parts of the text with which they are most comfortable. As a result we support children's self-confidence, never making them feel unaccepted or incompetent as readers. Instead, we invite them into the joyous act of reading. No matter what their degree of proficiency, they are readers in this supportive context.

Shared Reading and Learning to Read

It is our theory of learning that leads us to choose shared reading as a beneficial classroom experience for our developing readers. In other words, we do
not engage our students in shared reading just because it is enjoyable. Instead, we conscientiously choose shared reading because it reflects our understanding of what reading is as well as how people learn to read. Just as we
recognize children will not learn to ride a bicycle unless they learn to coordi-
nate steering, balancing, and pedaling simultaneously, we recognize children
cannot learn to read unless they engage in the whole of reading.

Fundamentally, reading is a search for meaning (Goodman, 1984). It is
an integrated and unified act in which the reader simultaneously coordinates
strategies (predicting, confirming or disconfirming, integrating) while sampling the cueing systems. The only way to learn to perform this complex
behavior is to be involved in reading. Shared reading is by no means the only
way to engage our students in reading. It alone will not create a class full of
independent readers. However, it is one teaching/learning strategy we find
very beneficial, for it admits all children immediately into the reading club no
matter how far along they are on their path toward becoming independent
readers.

A good deal of research over the past quarter century has dramatically
changed our understanding of how children become literate (Doake, 1988;
Y. Goodman, 1983; Harste, Woodward, & Burke, 1984; Temple, Nathan,
& Burris, 1982). While it was once thought that children first had to master
letters, sounds, and basic sight words before they would read and only after
that could they learn to write, we now realize children learn a good deal
about reading and writing long before they enter school.

Much has been discovered by studying children who have learned to
read "naturally" without benefit of intentional instruction. Young children
tune into print in their environment. Long before youngsters read conventionally they are assigning meaning to product labels and commercial signs.
Just as they work to make sense of other things in their world, they strive to
figure out how print works.

Novice readers engage in reading-like behavior. No two young readers
follow exactly the same path or sequence of specific behaviors toward
proficient reading, but there are general trends in reading development.
Early on, children who have had experience with books learn to turn the
pages at more or less the appropriate time while reciting a story they have
heard, perhaps several times. By relying on prior knowledge of a story as
well as illustrations, they are able to behave like readers before they know
how to match written to spoken words. At this point children make good
use of the situation context as well as a story's syntax and semantic cues to
support their reading. As they have more and more literacy experiences,
they begin to pay more attention to print. In time they are able to identify
particular words and phrases in specific contexts while relying on picture

cues for help. Gradually they are able to match oral production to individual words on a page. At this point children often become preoccupied with reading exactly what is on a page and their once fluent reading becomes halting for a time as they work to control the grapho-phonemic cueing system in addition to syntax and semantics. Finally, with still more experience, children come to control the whole of reading, the complex interplay of strategies and cueing systems. As Weaver (1988) suggests, it is clear that children progress as readers from whole to part not from part to whole.

We recognize that children's natural development as readers moves from a more global to a specific understanding of how printed language works. Because of this, we find shared reading particularly useful no matter where our developing readers are on their path toward proficient reading behavior. For a child who has had little experience with stories, our reading and rereading of familiar texts helps them develop an understanding of how stories work. For the child who is just beginning to match oral production with print, we encourage their developing awareness by pointing to features of the text as we read aloud or when we invite a child to lead our reading, tracking along the enlarged text with a pointer. For those children who have begun to puzzle out the relationship between sounds and letters, we can select texts that highlight those relationships. We can even point these out after we all become familiar with the story, poem, or song. Finally, for those children who have already achieved balanced coordination in reading, their path can be enriched by the variety of texts our shared reading provides.

In spite of our awareness that children may engage in the various demonstrations of how printed language works through Shared Reading, we keep in the forefront of our minds that reading is for making meaning. Therefore we select texts that are rich in language and meaning. We often use trade books and in Figure 3-1 we have listed several of our favorite books for shared reading.

Shared Reading Experiences in the Classroom

We have used shared reading a number of different ways and for a number of purposes. We also have used shared reading throughout the school day, not only during the time of day primarily set aside for language arts. In our classroom we have used shared reading to

- Enjoy the sounds of language
- Make texts available to all our readers
- Support and nurture our most fragile readers
- Prepare for an activity
- Review and share information
- Perform before an audience.

Figure 3-1   Examples of Books for Shared Reading

Allen, P. (1982). *Who sank the boat?* New York: Putnam & Grosset Group.
Bennett, J. (1985). *Teeny, tiny woman.* New York: G.P. Putnam's Sons.
Brown, R. (1981). *A dark, dark tale.* New York: Dial.
Charlip, R. (1974). *Fortunately, unfortunately.* New York: Four Winds Press.
Delaney, A. (1988). *The gunnywolf.* New York: HarperCollins.
Fox, M. (1983). *Hattie and the fox.* New York: Bradbury Press.
Galdone, P. (1975). *The gingerbread boy.* New York: Clarion.
Goss, J. & Harste, J. (1985). *It didn't frighten me.* Worthington, OH: Willowisp Press, Inc.
King, B. (1992). *Sitting on the farm.* New York: Orchard.
Lindbergh, R. (1990). *The day the goose got loose.* New York: Dial Books.
Longstaff, J. (1977). *A hunting we will go.* New York: Macmillan.
Rounds, G. (1990). *I know an old lady who swallowed a fly.* New York: Holiday House.
Shaw, C. (1947). *Spilt milk.* New York: Harper & Row.
Wood, A. (1984). *The napping house.* Orlando, FL: Harcourt Brace Jovanovich.

Above all else, shared reading gives us the opportunity to focus on meaning as we enjoy and learn through language.

Enjoy the Sounds of Language

Each day as our students enter the classroom, they sign in, put away their belongings, check the message board, collect materials they know they will need for their morning activities, converse informally with one another, and begin to cluster on the rug at the front of the room. As everyone settles down together, the student leader begins the day's routine by calling on classmates who have signed up to share. When sharing has been completed the children know their teacher will move to the front of the room and they will all enjoy songs, stories, and poems together.

Songs play an important role in this classroom both as a means of enjoyment and as texts to read together. Among the songs the children enjoy the most are the songs they have written together with the help of a parent volunteer. When their teacher told them about a song-writing contest for a teacher magazine the class enthusiastically decided they wanted to participate. The children brainstormed possibilities, selected a Halloween theme tied to their study of dinosaurs. The parent who discussed their ideas with them helped them create the song found in Figure 3-2. She wrote the song on big chart paper and every time the children sang the song one of them would lead the class by pointing to the words as they sang along. It wasn't long before the children wanted their own copies of the song so they

Figure 3-2   Song Written by Students for Contest.

Dinosaurs Can't Wear Costumes

It's time for Halloween.
Kids' favorite time of year.
But dinosaurs are sad and blue,
There's something that they cannot do.

Dinosaurs can't wear costumes.
Their folks say they'd scare all the kids.
With their spikes, horns, claws and their long sharp teeth
They dare not go out and trick or treat.

But this year things are different.
No hiding anymore.
Be careful when you open your door
'Cause it might be a dinosaur.

Stegosaurus is a pirate.
Triceratops is a queen.
Watch out for the witch who throws a hex
'Cause it might be a Tyrannosaurus Rex.

This year things are different.
No hiding anymore.
Be careful when you open your door
'Cause it might be a dinosaur.

could take it home. Their teacher made individual copies available. The children proudly took their copies home, knowing they could share the song with others for they had sung it in class so many times.

In addition to singing, the children and their teacher often read big books together at the beginning of the day. When their teacher introduced them to *Hattie and the Fox* (1988) by Mem Fox, she first read the story fluently and expressively as she showed the pictures. Then, after the students made comments as they customarily do after hearing a story, she invited them to read along with her. As she tracked the words of the text, they all read together. Recognizing the children enjoyed the story and the sounds of its language, she decided to share this book with the class many times over the next several weeks. Sometimes they all read together, sometimes the class was divided into groups, each representing a different animal·in the story. Before long, Lydia and Erin were volunteering at sharing

time to read the book to the class themselves. Eventually, a group of children decided to use this story as the basis for a shadow puppet play which
they performed for their parents. Not only did the story become one of the
most enjoyed by the class, it became one that all the children could read.

Often our morning shared reading time includes numerous poems that
are either enlarged on chart paper or placed in individual poetry collections. We select poetry that has rhythmic structure making it easy to chant
aloud. It is fascinating to see how popular poetry becomes with our students when we read it to them first and then invite them to join in.

Make Texts Available to All Our Readers

After we have shared a few songs, poems, and/or stories, we sometimes use
this morning time over a period of days to read a chapter book together. We
pass out individual copies so everyone has their own book. We talk about
what has happened so far in the story and then the teacher begins reading.
Some children join in out loud while others silently follow along. Some
children almost echo read, saying the words just after the teacher has vocal-
ized them. We discuss strategies of how to find your place if you lose it, for
example by noticing when the teacher turns a page or looking to see where
other students are reading.

It has been our personal experience that second graders particularly enjoy shared reading in this manner. Because some are just on the verge of
reading chapter books independently this group support helps all of them
have access to books they will later be able to read on their own. Books the
students have enjoyed in this manner have included *Skinnybones* (1982) by
Park, *Fantastic Mr. Fox* (1970) by Dahl, and *Stone Fox* (1980) by Gardiner.

Our own classroom newspaper is another text our students enjoy reading together. They are anxious to share their newspaper with their families,
and by reading each edition of the paper together, the children become
familiar with all the published pieces. Since our newspaper has evolved to
include school news and interview articles, poetry, stories, reports, book
reviews, classified ads, and captions for pictures, it provides a wide variety
of types of text to read. Unlike other shared reading, we usually do not read
the newspaper first to the students. Instead, we just begin reading all together as described in the opening of this chapter. Figure 3-3 shows several
pages of one of the newspapers the students enthusiastically read in unison.

Support and Nurture Our Most Fragile Readers

One of the most beneficial aspects of shared reading is that it supports our
least proficient readers. During whole class experiences with songs, big
books, poetry, chapter books, and the class newspaper, these students behave as readers and read along as best they can. Never are they singled out
for their lack of proficiency.

We also find specific ways with shared reading to help these students

Figure 3-3   Classroom Newspaper.

ROOM 4'S TEAMWORK

MAY 1991   Vol. 1 No. 2   ©1991

Dailey School's new secretary Mrs. Keoshian. Student photographers Raedina Windsor and James Musso.

OUR NEW SECRETARY
Interview by Amanda Rodriguez   Commentary by Amanda Rodruguez

Amanda: How do you like it here?
Ms. Keoshian: Great.
Amanda: What do you like about Dailey?
Ms. Keoshian: The kids are wonderful.
Amanda: Do you like kids? And is that why you took this job?
Ms. Keoshian: Yes, I love all the children at Dailey.
Amanda: What do you do as a secretary?
Ms. Keoshian: I type and answer the phone.
Amanda: What do you like about your job?
Ms. Keoshian: I like the people and the children.

Everyday when I go to the office to take my enhaler for my asthma, Ms. Keoshian is a good secretary. She is nice to me when I go to the office and she treats me with respect. I like knowing someone cares about me.

Figure 3-3   Continued.

CLASSROOM HELPERS
MY GRANDMOTHER
By Maia Spight-Therkildsen

My grandmother comes to the classroom two mornings a week. She helps people with reading and writing. Sometimes she reads to the whole class. My grandmother loves to come to our classroom and we love to have her come too.

MRS. ARAGON
By Jalia Stephens

Thank you Mrs. Aragon for being such a good helper in our room. Thank you for spending your time with us. You've helped us make a quilt. You've cooked with us and helped us with plays and have just been a good friend. Mrs. Manning and Room 4 really appreciate you doing this for us. We all love you because you have done so much for us.

MISS SMITH
By Maia Spight-Therkildsen

Miss Smith comes into the classroom and sometimes she works with kids on reading books. She also works on the bulletin board with a group of kids. Then she talks with the group of kids. Today she took The Three Bears group to work on the play for the dessert theater. We are glad that she is here. Thank you, Fresno High.

OUR CLASS' WOOD CENTER
By Gina Starbuck

Maia is a girl in our great classroom. Her dad, Mr. Thorkleson brought a million boxes of wood into our classroom. Our teacher brought nails, hammers, and saws. We make stuff out of the wood like airplanes, cages, miniature beds and tables. I'm glad we have Maia's dad. He is great. We're lucky to have Maia's dad. He's cool.

GARDEN UPDATE
By Jason McDowell

We have a garden with flowers, rose bushes, and trees. We have two cherry trees, a peach tree, and a plum tree too. Our cherry trees have leaves on them and cherries too. We also have tomato plants growing in the grow-lab in the room. Soon we will plant them in our garden. The tomatoes probably won't be ripe before school is out.

THANK YOU
MR. MASKALERIS
By Jose Benitez

Dear Mr. Maskalris,
Thank you for saving our tree by putting a stick in the ground to help it stand up. Thank you for bringing our class the moth and letting us keep it. We will take care of the moth. Thank you for saving our tree or we wouldn't have a tree. You are a good friend and we like you very much .

Love,
Jose and Room 4

ROOM 4'S DESSERT THEATER
By Raedina Windsor

Room 4 is having a dessert theater June 5, at 6:30 P.M.. There will be reading, singing, and four plays. The plays are called The Three Bears, The Breman Town Musicians, Tacky the Penguin, and Hattie and the Fox. There will be a good time for all. There will be lots of good food to eat. So, please come and join us.

TISSUES
By Jason McDowell

Friends and people! Everyone in our classroom has snotty noses. PLEASE, PLEASE, PLEASE send us boxes of tissues. Do you know how many boxes we go through in one week? Please help.

Figure 3-3 Continued.

BOOK REVIEWS CONTINUED

STONE SOUP By Tony Ross
©1987 ISBN 0-8037-08904
        Reviewed by Sohan Sandhu

Once upon a time there were a whole bunch of rabbits and cats. One of the cats found the big bad wolf and the wolf found the cat. The cat didn't know the wolf was following him and when he got home the wolf begged them for food. They gave him some food and the wolf liked it. Then they found out that the wolf wasn't in their club and they told the wolf to get out. But the wolf wouldn't leave. I liked the book because the animals fed the wolf. And I liked when the cat chased the wolf out. Third graders should read this book because it's challenging.

SEE YOU IN SECOND GRADE
        By Miriam Cohen
        Illustrated by Lillian Hoban
©1989 ISBN 0-688-07139-2
        Reviewed by Blake Davis

I like when the kid says the ocean smells like french fries. I think he smells the hot dog stand. That's where I hang around. If I were her, I would not have cried. I would swim in the shorts and keep the shirt on. If I had to eat the bread, I would not eat it. I would have thrown it in the water. The class got back to school, but one kid was still wearing his swim shorts. He went home in the car and had fun. But he had more fun at the beach.

WEIR SPIDER
By
Matthew Caiati

Watch out all you spider lovers
There is a weir spider on the loose
He will eat you in one GULP!
So you better watch out
Because
He looks like this.

POETRY CORNER

Darkness
By Jeremy Travis
Darkness is a light
That is dull in the night.
So, don't be afraid,
Just turn on the light.
So when you go to bed
Have a night light beside you
And scare away the dark
By turning on the light.

Kitty
By Nigel Robertson
Kitty, kitty all around
Kitty, kitty on the ground
Kitty, kitty bound to drown
Kitty, kitty, wet, wet, wet.
Kitty, kitty gets dry again.
Kitty, kitty grows and grows
Kitty, kitty on your nose
Kitty, kitty everywhere.

Lizards
By Josh Brewer
A sly lizard pauses on a rock.
I watch him stir
As if he were a statue.
I watch him run away
As fast as lightning.

The Moon
By James Musso
The moon shines on the lagoon
The florescent moon that shines
The moon shines on the lagoon all night long
It shines so bright
Mermaids at night are very moonish
But they don't care over there
Because the moon shines on the lagoon
It's morning now at the mermaid lagoon
The light of the moon shines no more

in small groups as well as with individual students. We use materials such as those described earlier, especially poetry and multiple copies of books. During our reading workshop we invite a group of children perhaps, four or five, to read a book together. Such a grouping is not at all permanent. It is a group that meets for a day or two with a particular book such as *Sylvester and the Magic Pebble* (1969) by Steig, *The Greedy Old Fat Man* (1983) by Galdone, *The Pain and the Great One* (1985) by Blume, or *Spider's Web* (1983) by Back. With the teacher, parent, or grandparent volunteer leading the way, the whole group reads the book together. We read the book in quiet voices so as not to disturb the rest of the class, but loud enough to enjoy our voices in unison. We read at a comfortable pace, fast enough to keep the flow of natural language, and slow enough to allow the children to follow along. We take time to talk about what we have read, as well as examine and comment on the illustrations. When appropriate the teacher points out aspects of the print that will make written language available to the children based on their emerging needs. For example, we may choose to point out rhyming words or interesting words, or phrases that are repeated.

Sometimes a book proves to be of particular interest to a group and we find a way to read and reread it, a useful strategy for encouraging fragile readers. When one group of second graders enthusiastically enjoyed *The Little Red Hen* (1973) by Galdone we suggested they might want to take parts and perform it for the rest of the class. They like the idea and practiced and practiced their parts until they were ready to share their play with their classmates. With another group of second graders we read *Tacky the Penguin* (1988) by Lester and figured out how we could turn it into a play, adapting the story into a script format including a part for a narrator. Again in this instance the children read and reread the text in preparation for a performance. As we discuss later in the chapter, encouraging authentic ways for students to perform becomes a powerful means by which students engage in meaningful reading practice that is needed to develop into proficient readers.

Prepare for an Activity

In addition to engaging our students in shared reading in a variety of ways during our reading/language arts block of time each day, there are also other times during the day when shared reading becomes a very natural way to engage students in reading for real purposes. For example, prior to cooking and science activities we have found it very helpful to present to students an overview of what they will be doing in small groups. In order to do this, we share the written directions for activities with the students by first passing out multiple copies of directions, reading the directions to the students, and then inviting them to read them all together. Again, as with other shared reading, our focus is on constructing meaning, not testing children's word recognition. We talk about what we will be doing, and we return to the text when we need to clarify information.

Classroom cooking activities provide natural opportunities to read and re-read recipes and cooking directions. First, we talk about the cooking we will be doing. Then, as a whole class, we read the recipe we will be using. Then, while most of the class is involved in another activity, a small group of students meets in a designated area of the classroom to begin cooking. As a small group they again read over the recipe together, deciding how they will organize themselves to carry out the cooking. Once they are finished, another group takes their place and the cycle begins again. When we prepare food for gifts (such as banana nut bread for Christmas presents) the children each take a copy of the recipe home along with their prepared food. This gives us a good opportunity to choral read the recipe once again prior to taking the gift home.

We also use shared reading in conjunction with science activities. When we are about to engage in a whole class project, such as making green house gardens from shoe boxes, we distribute directions to everyone, read them as a shared reading activity, discuss the ideas, then proceed with the project. Again, when the projects go home, we reread the directions all together and the students take the printed directions home along with their projects.

On occasion, the students create their own set of directions and we read them all together. For instance, when we showed the students a store-bought kit for growing a peanut plant, we all decided we could do it ourselves. We studied the materials, drew on prior knowledge about growing plants, and figured out as a class how we might proceed. The class dictated written directions which we read and reread and revised several times making sure they made sense. Then, we proceeded to follow these directions, each planting our own raw peanut in a paper cup filled with yarn. Figure 3-4 shows the directions the children developed.

In these cooking and science activities, we use shared reading to clarify what we were going to do. Our focus is on understanding and shared reading provides us with a legitimate way to make the texts accessible to all our class.

Review and Share Information

Our students have many opportunities to work in small groups on various projects. One project each child gets to work on involves designing and creating a bulletin board. Each month during the year one group is responsible for the class bulletin board. By the end of the year, every child has had the opportunity to help participate on a bulletin board committee. In addition to the art work involved, each group also collaborates to create a written text that in some way clarifies the theme of their bulletin board. For example, a group of second graders decided to make the December bulletin board depict helping the needy at Christmas time. Undoubtedly the fact

Figure 3-4   Directions for Peanut Plant

How to Grow a Peanut Plant

by Room 4 Dailey Elementary School

Materials and Equipment:

Styrofoam or paper cup

36 inches of yarn

One raw peanut

A pencil

Scissors

12 inch ruler

Water

Paper towel or plate

Directions:

First you take your styrofoam cup and your pencil and poke a hole in the center at the bottom of the cup. If desired, put your name on your cup and decorate. Then measure 36 inches of yarn and cut the yarn. Place the yarn in the bottom of the cup. Take the peanut and crack the shell open. Be careful not to take the brown skin off of the peanut. Take the peanuts and put them on the yarn. Take the cup to the sink and turn on the water. Put the cup under the water faucet until it is $\frac{1}{4}$ full of water. Then let the water drain out of the hole that's in the bottom of the cup. Don't forget to turn off the water! Take the cup and the paper towel or plate over to the window sill (or table near the window). Put the paper towel or plate down and put the cup on top. Make sure your plant has plenty of sun, air, and water. Check your peanut plant every day. If it's dry, water it. Once it starts to sprout, replant your peanut plant into another pot with soil. Then water your plant again. After your plant has grown to 5–6 inches, replant your plant outside in a garden.

---

that the class was involved in collecting food and clothing for a family through the Salvation Army stimulated their idea for the theme. Their bulletin board showed a scene of a city where people were coming to the aid of people in need. The story they created to go along with their bulletin board is found in Figure 3-5.

Once the children had written their story and it was typed for them, they read it together several times with the help of the instructional aide who had worked with them on the bulletin board. When they were ready, they stood before the class reading their story together in unison. Then the

Figure 3-5   Bulletin Board Story.

A Christmas Morning

Dedicated to
Tiffany and Jack:
We wish we could do this for you.
Written by
Robert Gonzales
Robyn Taylor
Danette Strasheim
Aiza Dyangko
Raedina Windsor
Jason McDowell

One morning it was cold. It was Christmas morning and it was snowing. Poor people were in the alley. It was getting colder. The snow was coming down hard. The homeless were cold. They had to find trash cans and burn garbage for heat. The homeless hoped that someone would help them.

Some kids were building a snowman in the park. The kids saw the homeless and cried because they felt bad. They decided to help them by giving them presents, blankets, and pillows to sleep with. Some kids brought the homeless into their homes. Others were left outside, but they kept warm anyway.

The kids and the homeless felt very good and became friends. They thought this was the best Christmas ever.

---

rest of the class received copies of their story and the whole class read the story together.

Similarly, science projects provide our students with opportunities to collaboratively create texts which they review and share with their peers. When a small group chose to study silk worms they learned a great deal about these interesting creatures. The instructional aide read books to the group. The children studied the pictures, talked about what they were learning, and began taking care of real silkworms in the classroom. Once they had discovered enough information, they were able to collaboratively create a report by dictating it to the aide. Much like the children in the bulletin board committee, these students then practiced reading their report until they were satisfied that they were ready to share it. Then, along with posters and charts they had prepared as part of their committee work, they made a presentation to the rest of the class. Their presentation included a choral reading of their report. Figure 3-6 shows the small group's silkworm report.

Figure 3-6   Small Group's Silkworm Report

Silkworm Discovery

by Blake Davies Josh Brewer Jalia Stephens Aiza Dyangko

Silkworms started in China 5000 years ago. The Chinese used to be the only people who made silk, but other people took some eggs from them and now make their own silk. This is how silk is made.

A male and female moth mate by joining their bodies. The female has a fatter body than the male. The eggs that the female lays are light yellow at first, and then they turn dark blue-gray. We put our eggs in a cardboard box. In seven days they will begin to hatch. When the eggs are ready to hatch they get darker around the edges and look like a comma when they first hatch.

The newly-hatched worm begin eating leaves by holding the leaf with its three pairs of front legs. The worm eats continually and grows very fast. It sheds its skin many times.

Our worms will eat mulberry leaves. Other kinds of worms eat other kinds of leaves. The silkworm needs fresh leaves every day. You need to clean the leaves by putting three tablespoons of bleach and one drop of dishwashing detergent in one gallon of water. Leave them for three minutes and then rinse them off in cold water before putting them in the box with the worms. The worms eat for twenty-five to thirty days.

When the worm stops feeding, it spins its silk cocoon by moving its head back and forth in a figure eight. The silk cocoon will cover his whole body. Inside the cocoon the silkworm sheds his skin for the last time.

When the moth first comes out of the cocoon, it is wet like a chick before its wings dry out. Its antennae look like a comb. Some are kind of ugly because they are darkish brown and darkish black. Some are pretty. They are blue and red and other colors.

Perform Before an Audience

Presentations or performances by students extend beyond their own classroom and provide further possibilities for shared reading experiences. One of the most successful ventures we have been involved with occurred the year our students planned, practiced, and performed for their parents at a Dessert Theater. With the help of their teacher the children prepared desserts ahead of time in class and decorated the school cafeteria with flowers from their garden. Their evening program consisted of plays, songs, choral reading, and individual readings. Many of these productions involved shared reading activities.

One group presented *Hattie and the Fox* as a shadow puppet play. The students involved in this group rehearsed and rehearsed their parts, reading in unison and separately as they worked to get the story just right. A large group of students chorally read *The Day the Goose Got Loose* (1990) by Lindbergh. They, too, read and reread the poem over and over until most of them knew it by heart. One student in the group was Jose, a child who had attended school for less than a year prior to being placed in second grade. He was two years older than the rest of the class yet had very little understanding of how reading and writing worked. By the time of the Dessert Theater, his voice was the loudest and surest in the group and he carried along the less secure readers.

The important role that shared reading played in the preparation for and performance of the Dessert Theater cannot be understated. By reading together with the support of their teacher, the children blossomed, each in their own way. As a community of readers they shared special pride in a collaborative experience. As they performed they showed how enjoyable stories, songs, plays, and poetry can be. They were proud of their efforts and so were their parents.

The children's perceptions of themselves and their classmates as readers changed throughout the year. The Dessert Theater was perhaps the most dramatic evidence of this. They saw themselves as successful members of the literacy club (for they wrote as well as read in this class.) and they were confident enough to share their abilities in a public forum. Harste (1989) suggests that education is about altered and altering social relationships. When parents see their children develop as readers (and writers) they too change their perceptions about their children and this, in turn, changes social relationships. When one student's mother came to the teacher after the Dessert Theater and said, "Thank you for what you have done for my son. He has become a reader," this was her acknowledgment that her perception of her child had changed. Instead of seeing him as a struggling student, she was seeing him as a successful reader.

We would not want to suggest that shared reading was the only strategy we used over the course of the year to bring our students to literacy. Many, many real world literacy events were part of our experiences together. However, shared reading certainly played an important role in our meaning-centered classroom.

References

Cochrane, O., Cochran, D., Scalena, S., & Buchanan, E. (1984). *Reading, writing, and caring*. Winnipeg: Whole Language Consultants Ltd.

Doake, D. (1988). *Reading begins at birth*. New York: Scholastic.

Harste, J.C. (1989). The future of whole language. *The Elementary School Journal*, 90(2), 243–249.

Harste, J. C., Woodward, V.A., & Burke, C.L. (1984). *Language stories and literacy lessons*. Portsmouth, NH: Heinemann.

Holdaway, D. (1979). *The foundation of literacy*. Sydney: Ashton Scholastic.

Goodman, K. (1984). Unity in reading. *Becoming readers in a complex Society*. Eighty-third Yearbook of the National Society for the Study of Education. Chicago, Illinois: The University of Chicago Press.

Goodman, Y. (1983). Beginning reading development: Strategies and principles. R. Parker & F. Davis (Eds.). *Developing literacy: Young children's use of language*, (p. 68–83). Newark, DE: International Reading Association.

Martin, B. (1966). *Sounds of the storyteller—teacher's edition*. New York: Holt, Rinehart, and Winston, Inc.

Meek, M. (1982). *Learning to read*. Portsmouth, NH: Heinemann.

Smith, F. (1083). *Essays into literacy*. Portsmouth, NH: Heinemann.

Smith, F. (1988). *Joining the literacy club*. Portsmouth, NH: Heinemann.

Temple, C., Nathan, R. & Burris, N. (1982). *The beginnings of writing*. Boston, MA: Allyn and Bacon, Inc.

Vygotsky, L.S. (1978). *Mind in society*. M. Cole, V. John-Steiner, S. Scribner, & E. Souberman (Eds.). Cambridge, MA: Harvard University Press.

Weaver, C. (1988). *Reading process and practice*. Portsmouth, NH: Heinemann.

Children's Books Cited in This Chapter

Back, C. (1984). *Spider's web*. Englewood Cliffs, NJ: Silver Burdett.

Blume, J. (1984). *The pain and the great one*. New York: Bradbury.

Dahl, R. (1970). *Fantastic Mr. Fox*. New York: Penguin Books.

Fox, M. (1988). *Hattie and the fox*. New York: Bradbury Press.

Galdone, P. (1983). *The greedy old fat man*. New York: Houghton Mifflin.

Galdone, P. (1973). *The little red hen*. New York: Houghton Mifflin.

Gardiner, J. (1980). *Stone fox*. New York: Harper & Row.

Lester, H. (1988). *Tacky the penguin*. Boston: Houghton Mifflin.

Lindbergh, R. (1990). *The day the goose got loose*. New York: Penguin Books.

Park, B. (1982). *Skinnybones*. New York: Alfred A. Knopf.

Steig, W. (1969). *Sylvester and the magic pebble*. New York: Simon and Schuster.

Schwartz, A. (1984). *In a dark, dark room*. New York: Harper & Row.

4

Bringing Children to Literacy Through Guided Reading

MARY GIARD

*S*pending time in Giard's classroom even through the medium of this book is a delight! You will especially enjoy seeing the ways in which Mary creates responsibility for their own learning in her students. Clearly, the children in her classroom are active, responsible learners. Giard explains the prerequisites to guided reading and then carefully takes the reader through guided reading protocols that help us understand the ways in which she focuses on children learning, as readers, to think for themselves—to ask their own questions and to seek their own answers. The most stunning part of this chapter, for me, is the way in which Mary's children come to use very professional language to discuss their handling of the reading process. Each time I read this I am reminded that we too often sell children short in terms of our expectations for what they can do.

No matter what we were studying, she opened up new worlds for me. Even the simplest thing evolved into deeper learning. Josh Gass, age 12, former student.

I love to learn and I have always hoped that our room would not only be an atmosphere of learning but a place of great joy. I have always wanted to create an environment in which we could all learn and prosper. I cannot say that I have always been successful. Many people have contributed to my learning, both adults and children. I have read many books, articles, and position papers. I have participated in many classes, conferences, and workshops. People, for me, have made the difference. My father, a teacher, had great impact on who I am today as a teacher. He modeled for me the importance of knowing all learners and respecting them for who they were. He was the first in a long line of people who showed me that I can never assume anything—that new understandings will come to me as I continue to grow. Children and parents have impacted me.

Following are statements by people who have been a part of my learning and teaching. I asked each of them to respond to the question: "When you come into our classroom, what do you think I believe about teaching and learning?" Each person responded in a lengthy manner so I have taken a section from each piece. Everyone recognized that in our room every person is a teacher and a learner. The children take responsibility for their learning and are actively involved in decisions that affect their education.

Marie Gass, a colleague and parent of a former student, said, ". . . the entire population of her room is recognized as both teacher and learner. Each one knows that he/she and he/she alone is ultimately responsible for his/her own learning. Child empowerment, adult language and freedom of choice are part of the comfortable atmosphere. . . ."

Another colleague, Mary Moreau, stated, ". . . It is a room filled with literature, with authentic reading and writing, with learners and teachers, for Mary reminds both children and any grown-up in the room that we are all teachers and learners."

Janet Allen spent two years in our room. She is a high school English teacher in a graduate program. She said, ". . . The first of many shocks came the day Mary said to her students, "Whose job is it for you to learn to read?" the children chorused, "All of ours." In my 17 years of teaching at the secondary level, I have never heard kids take that kind of responsibility for their own learning . . . She had high expectations for herself and her students and they had high expectations for themselves, each other, and their teacher. It was an atmosphere of mutual caring and respect; a respect born out of the knowledge that their own teacher had given them something wonderful—the knowledge and ability that they could not only be learners, but also teachers . . ."

Finally, Giles Hoover, a University of Maine college student, became very involved in the room. His observations included, "The whole day follows like this: the kids taking responsibility for themselves and learning. These first graders often seem to act more like adults than most adults. I cannot help but believe that the desire to be active and responsible learners was instilled by Mary. There is always an aura of calmness about her, and it includes the way she interacts with the kids. It rubs off on them . . ."

Our classroom community is comprised of twenty-two first grade students, ages six through eight. Many of the family members are involved either in the classroom or in a supportive role. Other school professionals are part of our classroom and we have many visitors and volunteers associated with the College of Education at the University of Maine. The children and I plan our days; we try to control our schedule as much as possible to maintain a routine.

Typically the children enter the room and prepare for the day. Children sign in for attendance and hot or cold lunch. They get their work materials out, check the messages on the message board, discuss their plans for the day and finally meet in our gathering area for our morning meeting.

We established our gathering area on the first day of school. This spot is sacred for lessons, storytime, and discussions/meetings that we have. It is a part of our community, not unlike the town square. Each morning as we gather we discuss the schedule for the day, issues that need to be addressed, and discuss everyone's topics or roadblocks in writing. We typically have a mini-lesson (writing or reading to . . .) to get all our thoughts focused on the day. Children often leave the morning meeting with a peer to help them conference on their work or collaborate to undertake a new endeavor. Our mornings are very flexible and fluid. I meet with children individually, meet with shared and guided reading groups and monitor the progress of the entire group. During this time many volunteers work in the room as well. They might help children publish work or take stories from dictation. They might read to the children or read with them. Some of the volunteers were very interested in how we monitor our progress.

As we worked through our schedule during the fall, we brainstormed a list of work we do. The children used the list as transition to our current flexible schedule. Typical morning work may include: writing in draft books, conferencing with a peer or an adult, publishing work, doing research on a self-selected or group topic, writing mini-lessons, shared reading groups, guided reading groups, partner, or buddy reading as we call it, reading to self, responding to texts, listening to a read aloud or a tape, or taking a running record. Much goes on in a two and half hour block!

In this chapter I hope our philosophy and organization shine through. Because the focus is on the reading and writing processes, the chapter will be devoted to our mornings and specific work we do during our daily morning routine. May our class help you come to new understandings about (guided) reading.

There has been a lot of controversy over the years about the best way to help children learn to read. For me, as I work with young children, I find that using a variety of reading approaches best meets the needs of the learners with whom I work. Our classroom has a variety of activities going on simultaneously. Activities that visitors often see while in our room fall into one of the following three categories: reading and writing to children, reading and writing with children, and reading and writing by children.

Reading and Writing to Children

Throughout the day children gather in large and small groups to hear stories written by well-known writers and by authors in our room. I read to the children several times a day. In addition, volunteers, older children, other members of the school staff, and classmates often read to the children. We read picture books, poetry and chapter books, making sure that we read from a balance of genres to expose everyone to the wide world of literature. In addition to lots of reading, I frequently demonstrate the value and joy of writing by writing in front of the children daily. Writing messages, working on the easel, sharing a particular form of writing such as letter writing, family letters, webbing, and outlining as well as demonstrating the process through which I work as a writer. Many other people who work in our room demonstrate similar modeling and provide many opportunities for the room's emerging writers to see writing being used for a variety of purposes.

Reading and Writing with Children

As well as reading and writing to children, we read and write with children. Shared reading and writing are important components of our classroom program. These shared reading and writing experiences can be seen on a daily basis in our room. Many of the children are emerging as readers and need plenty of supportive opportunities to have positive literacy experiences. Having my voice support or that of another adult, a classmate or a tape recorder provides a bridge to literary that the emergent reader cannot yet make on his or her own. Some of the young readers have had little exposure and opportunity to interact with print and books. It would make little sense to move these children into a guided reading setting when they do not yet have the background of experiences and expectations that more mature and experienced readers bring to the reading process. Giving them the support and time they need to understand story and book language is necessary for these young learners as they develop a mind set towards literacy. The child who has little exposure to books, reading, and writing needs plenty of time to try it all out. The child needs plenty of opportunities to hear good books, see readers and writers at work, and try on literacy learning for him or herself. Models and support are needed to help the learner make sense of reading and writing.

Many of the adults who interact with the children in our room also use the language experience approach to demonstrate the bridge from the spoken to the printed word. Many stories, charts, letters, and books are produced. Through such experiences literacy learning continues for the emergent reader and writer.

Shared reading and writing, language experience, and reading and writing to children are important components of my classroom's schedule and instruction. Guided reading as an approach and the changes it fosters in young readers is the focus of this chapter. My understandings come from fifteen years of change and evolution as a learner and a teacher.

I have learned a lot about guided reading from New Zealand authors and speakers. *Reading in Junior Classes* (1985), a publication written by New Zealand's Department of Education and distributed by Richard C. Owen Publishers, Inc. introduced me to some information about the philosophy of guided reading. In addition, hearing Jan Duncan, a native New Zealander, talk about guided reading brought me to clearer understanding about the purpose and power of guided reading. Although I had initiated some of the components of guided reading in my classroom, it was not until I had the opportunity to openly discuss and debate the approach that I truly gained insight into the idea. Margaret Mooney's book, *Reading to, with and by Children* (1990) helped me continue to refine my knowledge and understanding of guided reading as one viable approach for helping young readers take their next steps.

The children have learned a lot from and about guided reading through our lessons and discussions. They clearly understand the impact guided reading lessons have made in terms of their personal evolutions as young readers. I, too, have come to new understandings about guided reading. Professional reading, open dialogue, and practice have contributed to changes in my understanding and skill in facilitating guided reading lessons.

> "Guided reading gives me a sense of what the page is about, it gives me hints." (Hannah, age 7)
>
> "Guided reading helps me know more about the book than I would be able to get on my own." (Melissa, age 7)
>
> "It (guided reading) makes it simpler for me to read other materials." (Michael, age 7)

These seven-year-olds have found value and understanding in their guided reading lessons. They meet with me a few times as members of a group that reads materials which have appropriate supports and challenges. The children's comments seem to indicate that they find the sessions meaningful and worthwhile. They are able to transfer what they learn and know to other situations.

What exactly is guided reading? I grappled with that concept for a long time and still find myself working through issues as I think about readers and texts. Sometimes my own learning still invades my decision-making. As I think back to when I used basals, linguistic readers, and total individualized reading, I realized how much my values have changed. Through much thinking, talking, and trailing, I came to some understandings about guided reading.

What Guided Reading is Not

Guided reading is not a set of prescribed questions purchased to go along with every story used with children. Having relied upon prepared questions that accompanied texts earlier in my teaching, I found many questions to be trite and the questions made the children dependent on the text's questions (not to mention the teacher). Guided reading promotes independence not dependence.

> "I did a great job with *Greedy Cat* (1991) once you guided us into
> the pattern Mrs. G." (Dan, age 7)

Guided reading is not a linear continuum through which each child must follow the same path. All children do not need to read the same texts or be subjected to the same set of questions for the text at hand. Teachers and children make decisions and think for themselves.

> "I can read aloud and sound like the character in the book. Now I
> know how to use strategies to read to people myself." (Heather,
> age 7)

Guided reading is not based on the assumption that children need to follow a sequence of skills in order to be able to handle specific texts, materials, or concepts. The children's individual needs determine the materials to be used and the appropriate time to use them.

> "I like how we have different questions each time we read with
> you. That helps me look at different books in different ways."
> (Michael, age 7)

Guided reading instruction does not imply that members of a group are grouped by their abilities. The children do not necessarily remain together for an entire year. Groups are flexible and are built on similar strengths.

> "I like it when someone new joins our group. We get new ideas
> from new people." (Melissa, age 7)

Guided reading is not the only approach to reading. It is not meant to be the sole opportunity for children to interact with each other and print. It is not for all children all of the time. A young child who has not been read to needs lots of book experience before moving into guided reading.

I have shared what I know is not reflective of the guided reading approach. But what is guided reading? What do I consider as I think about using that approach with the children in my class? The next segment of this chapter will focus on the considerations I explore as I plan for meeting the needs of the children in my class.

What Guided Reading Is

Group(s)

How are groups selected for guided reading lessons? Children have different interests and experiences they bring to the group. However, the group is relatively homogeneous in terms of strengths and needs. Although groups do not necessarily remain intact for an entire school year, they do remain intact until children either make faster progress or are unable to handle the challenges in texts the group reads. Groups in my room range from one group that has four students to one that has eight. Group make-up varies based on the attitudes, understandings, and the beliefs about reading children have. The children who are more mature and experienced as readers naturally form a group different than the groups of emergent and early readers. Guided reading groups are secure, comfortable places to learn, solve problems, and share ideas.

Materials

How are the materials selected? Books, stories, magazines, and poems are selected based on the supports and challenges the texts have to offer. Texts that are predictable often offer some supports for the young reader but may also offer challenges in the vocabulary the book uses. Language, format, concepts, illustrations, diagrams, and genre all play a part in the selection of the appropriate material to meet the needs of the members of the group. The text must offer supports, yet there must be challenges to warrant a guided reading lesson rather than an independent reading. The piece cannot offer too many challenges; the children would then be too dependent on the teacher for assistance. Materials must be of quality and of a challenge that will encourage strategic thinking through the guidance of a teacher. Two examples of lists that one group of children generated when they finished reading the texts in Figure 4-1. They felt each text had supports and challenges that affected how independent they could be as readers.

The children came to these understandings because we had done a lot of talking about what makes books easy and/or hard to read. I had also spent time discussing the process I go through making decisions about

Figure 4-1   Supports and Challenges Identified by the Children

The Day Jimmy's Boa Ate the Wash

Guided Reading Group (Dan B., Patrick, Jolena, Aaron J., Kirstin)

Supports	*Challenges*
pictures	small print
Mrs. Giard's questions	some individual words
words that weren't long	fantasy genre
knowing about a farm	Mother didn't believe the children

Nana Upstairs, Nana Downstairs

Guided Reading Group (Michael, Melissa, Hannah, Sarah)

Supports	*Challenges*
we know strategies like picture clues	some pages had lots of words
some of the same characters throughout the book	introduction of new characters
familiar illustrator	

texts to guide them through. They used the same language I used with them to articulate what they found supportive and what they found challenging in the texts they had read.

Scheduling

How does a guided reading lesson fit into the daily schedule? How long is a typical guided reading lesson? What are the other children doing while I am working with a group? I typically work with two guided reading groups a day. At the beginning of the year, because I work with young children, the lessons usually last ten to fifteen minutes. The children who are young, new to our room, are reading generally less challenging material and are slowly becoming familiar with the kinds of questions I ask. As time goes on, the lessons may run fifteen to twenty minutes because the pieces are a bit longer and more challenging and the discussions become livelier. While I am working with a group, the other children know they need to work independently or seek assistance from a classmate or adult who may be in the room. Writing, independent reading, paired reading, illustrating, responding to a book, or listening to a tape are typically happening as I work with a guided reading group.

Location

I try to have our guided reading lessons on the floor in the same spot where we gather several times daily for meetings, lessons, and storytime. It is comfortable, roomy, and already has the gathering and learning atmosphere associated with it. The children have plenty of room to spread out comfortably with their individual books. The other members of the classroom community also know that the area is where they expect to see lessons going on so they automatically know they need to refrain from interrupting when students are gathered here.

Planning for guided reading includes grouping, selecting materials, scheduling, and selecting a location for conducting the guided reading lessons. In addition, it is important for me to understand my role and help children come to understandings about their roles in guided reading lessons.

My Role as the Teacher

Through guided reading lessons I have the opportunity to set the stage for children to discover the strengths and understandings they possess about the reading process. It requires a good understanding of the reading process and the learners with whom I am working as well as taking care to select just the right material to meet the needs of the children. They readily respond to the exposure and practice they participate in each day. By providing a model of questioning, I try to get the children to think about reading in a meaningful way. I hope to see them transfer their understanding and strategies to their personal reading. My questions and comments guide the readers, helping them discover the resources within themselves and the reading material so that they can transfer their knowing to similar situations in other texts.

Guided reading offers me the chance to be a good teacher, decision maker, guide, and facilitator. I need to be clear in my purpose and sharp in my questioning. Both the timing and the types of questions and comments I make are crucial. I need to get the readers to predict, sample the text, integrate all that they know in order to confirm or reject their predictions as they read. I want to read for sense—to read on, read back, and read into the text to get the meanings of the texts they have read. Guided reading lets me be a thinker and a doer. I make the difference; not the manual or the questions at the end of the selection in commercially purchased materials. I help to set the purposes for reading so that later the children can sample texts on their own and come to their own understandings. Guided reading is always tailored to meet the needs of the individuals within the group. Working with young readers gives me the responsibility to help them develop good habits for their lifetimes of reading. The strategies they internalize become supports for them as lifelong readers and learners. The kinds of questions and prompts I pose determine whether the children I work with will be dependent or independent learners.

The Role of the Reader

Children need to have had many experiences with print including stories, songs, and poems before they are introduced to guided reading. They need to take on a certain amount of responsibility to see themselves as being in charge of their own learning. My questions force the children to think and make decisions for themselves. They soon realize that a one word answer is not going to be acceptable. Our community wants to know the process through which each child went to arrive at an answer. We want a map of mental problem-solving the child went through to arrive at his or her understanding. The child who answers these questions becomes clearer and more definitive in his or her thinking and problem-solving. In addition, the processing gives the other children and me a window into the thinking process of the child. Children can carry on in-depth conversations and discussions once they move beyond approaching the process of reading from only one stance. The children not only become cognizant of their own learning style or approach to learning but also become observers of the styles and strengths of their peers. Because the group works together on a daily basis, the children come to know one another's approaches to learning. The group experiences translate to independent work. Children naturally begin to ask themselves more questions as they read on their own. Typical questions might be: Does this make sense? Does this sound right? Does this look right? Do the pictures help me? What do I think is happening or what do I expect based on what I already know? Did what I just read make sense given what I know? I don't know this word, what am I going to do to figure it out? Putting the child in the driver's seat encourages the reader to take charge of his or her own learning.

To demonstrate the points I have made about guided reading, I am including a transcript from a guided reading lesson. The group, made up of six children, met in November of the school year. We met in the usual gathering spot for our lesson. I feel the transcript demonstrates my role as well as the responsibility and ownership taken on by the readers.

Prior to reading *The Very Busy Spider* (1984), Hannah, Kirstin, Missy, Dan B., Aaron J., Patrick, and I looked at the cover of the book and the children discussed the similarity of the cover illustration to that of a book we had read a couple of weeks earlier.

Dan: "This looks like the cover of *The Very Hungry Caterpillar* (1990)."

Missy:	"Yes, the art style looks like it must have been illustrated by the same illustrator."
Hannah:	"It is by the same person. See here in the corner. It is Eric Carle's name."
Mrs. G.:	"You are all right. It is by Eric Carle. Read the title to yourself then give some thought to what you might expect the book to be about."
Patrick:	"I think it will be similar to *The Very Hungry Caterpillar*. What I mean by that is that I think the spider will have some kind of purpose or job to do like the caterpillar did."
Aaron:	"I think it will have some facts too, not just be a story."
Dan:	"Yeah, usually his (Eric Carle) stuff is partly fiction and partly non-fiction."
Missy:	"I like his books."
Kirstin:	"Me too. Can we get on with the reading?"
Mrs. G.:	"Let's turn to the title page and see if we get any more information to help us with the reading of the story."
Patrick:	"The picture reminds me of *The Very Hungry Caterpillar* too. It must mean that it is going to be another story where work gets done during the day."
Mrs. G.:	"That may be true. Why do you suppose Eric Carle has entitled his book *The Very Busy Spider*?"
Patrick:	"I think it will be about how busy spiders are."
Mrs. G.:	"What do you mean?"
Missy:	"Spiders work hard spinning webs. They have different kinds of thread. They catch food. Did you feel the book? The thread is raised like a real web. I'll bet this book is going to be about the spider being busy trying to spin her web."
Mrs. G.:	"Well, Missy, you are helping to lead me to a question to prompt your thinking on the first two pages of the story. Would you all read the first two pages for yourself and see whether or not your predictions about the focus of the book are right?" (After a short time, all the hands flew up.) "Yes, yes," everyone said.
Aaron:	"We know that at least part of the story is going to be about the spider spinning her web."
Mrs. G.:	"How do you know that?" (Again all the hands go up.)
Mrs. G.:	"Tell a friend and see whether or not you came to the same conclusion."

Missy:	Hannah and I agreed because it says right here that the spider is on the fence, near a farm—maybe like Charlotte and Wilbur, and started spinning her web. It says it's silky too—maybe that's why we can feel it on the page." (All the other children nodded their heads and murmured in agreement.)
Mrs. G.:	"So, you were right and you clearly supported your answer! Let's turn the page. What do you suppose is going on here?"
Patrick:	"Well, maybe the horse wants to talk to the spider like Wilbur did with Charlotte."
Missy:	"Yeah, see the quotation marks? Mrs. Giard has shown us those before. The horse is talking."
Dan:	"Well the part about the spider is nonfiction, but with a horse talking there is some fantasy here too. Horses don't talk!"
Kirstin:	"Yeah, but this isn't as hard to read as something like *Charlotte's Web* (1980). That would be too challenging for everyone except Sarah. I think she can read anything."
Mrs. G.:	"Okay everyone. You're making some interesting observations. Let's continue with the reading! Why don't you read these two pages and find out how the horse fits into the story?" (Once again, the group read the small amount of text on the two pages. Everyone wanted to respond. They all looked to me wanting the permission to discuss their findings with the other members of the group. I nod, indicating that they should carry on and the tape picked up these pieces of conversation.)

"Did you get those first two words that the horse said? I tried to use some strategies but even sounding out didn't work—'e' and 'i' together don't make sense to me."

"I think the horse wanted to play with the spider and the spider was rude not to respond."

"I don't think the spider was rude. She was busy doing her work and the horse interrupted her."

Mrs. G.:	"Well, it seems that a variety of understandings came from these two pages. Let's talk about the 'e' and 'i' together—that seems to have caught several of you. Look up here on the easel. What is this word (sleigh)?"
Missy:	"That is easy—sleigh."

Dan:	"Oh, I get it—the other word must be neigh!"
Mrs. G.:	"That's right—but, Dan, how did you figure that out?"
Dan:	"Well, neigh is spelled very much like sleigh and neigh rhymes with sleigh. I thought about the sounds that horses make and sometimes they do make the neigh sound. The 'ei' spelling threw me off because I didn't know that they could make the 'a' sound." (All the other children raised their hands in support and agreement.)
Mrs. G.:	"So, what strategy did you have to use to finally make meaning?"
Hannah:	"We had to focus on if the word looked right."
Patrick:	"Yeah, we tried to use sounding out but we also had to use the other stuff."
Missy:	"We really had to use everything to make sense. Neigh was the only word we didn't know so most of us skipped it and read on. Even if we thought it might be neigh, as we read on, we still got confused because of the spelling. It sounded right and made sense but the letter sounds really messed us up. A lot of us know that horses make the neigh sound so our background knowledge helped us out. I guess we really did use everything. And, another thing, I don't think the spider was rude to the horse!"

The conversation I just shared with you not only shows the understandings these first graders have come to within the first three months of school, but also the literacy experiences they had prior to coming to our room. They are reading material that is relatively typical for young children at the earlier part of first grade, yet they are carrying on a conversation as though they were my colleagues. They use the same language I use with other teachers and are able to effectively convey their thoughts and ideas. They have gained an understanding of the cueing systems and clearly articulate how they arrive at the problem-solving choices they make.

The children are using sophisticated language and clearly demonstrate their knowledge of semantics, syntax, and graphophonics. Lifelong readers need to be able to self-monitor while they read. Here is another short segment of transcript from that day's guided reading lesson. It demonstrates children's shifts from making predictions to confirming or rejecting their ideas based on what they learn from the text.

Mrs. G.:	"Let's move on. What do you think is going to happen on these two pages?"
Aaron:	"I think the cow is going to ask her to go for a ride too

> and I think she won't answer because she will be too busy spinning her web." (Everyone read the pages and some smiles appeared.)

Missy: "Aaron was partly right."

Mrs. G.: "Go on."

Missy: "Well, the spider did keep spinning but the cow didn't ask her to go for a ride."

Aaron, grinning: "The cow didn't say neigh either—she said moo and asked the spider to eat some grass."

We continued through the text and discovered that indeed there was a pattern and we came to expect various animals to make their own proper noises. The entire lesson lasted approximately twenty minutes and the lesson was rich with observations and understanding. Throughout the lesson, the children repeatedly demonstrated that they were internalizing the many questions I had been asking over the past months in order to gain their own independence in reading. They knew my expectations were not just for them to produce correct answers, but to verbalize the various routes each of them used to solve the unknown. The children began to use strategies that would most quickly get them to a sensible answer and then crosschecked themselves to satisfy their inner needs to make sense of the text.

I have shared two important approaches for helping young children gain fluency in their reading. But another important approach, Reading and Writing by Children, also needs to be addressed. As I mentioned earlier in the chapter, the ultimate goal for me is to help children be well armed as readers and writers to work and learn independently. This last section is devoted to demonstrations of children taking their next steps in learning.

Reading and Writing by Children

What kind of evidence do I see that shows children transferring the understandings they gain from guided reading and large group strategy lessons to their own reading? Sometimes I just ask them what kinds of things are going on with them in reading. By December when I asked them what strategy (ies) they often relied upon when they encountered unknown text or concepts, they were able to give the following responses:

"I rerun to get the meaning."

"I skip it first, I read back, and then I read on."

"I skip it first, read to the end, go back to the beginning, then if I have to look at the word more closely, I sometimes sound it out."

"I skip it, go back then figure it out with other strategies."

"I think about the word, when I think I have it right, I rerun all over again to be sure it makes sense."

"I think about whether I have heard of the word. If I have never heard of it, sounding it out won't do me any good and I still probably won't be able to get it because I won't be able to get the meaning and make sense."

Besides talking to children, I have gathered other evidence that has convinced me that they were indeed becoming more cognizant of their own learning and their needs as learners. As I took running records on the children, I began to see big changes; not only in terms of length of texts, but also the kinds of miscues being made and the efforts to make meaning by dramatically increasing their self-corrections (See Figure 4-2). It is not uncommon for a child to finish with me, walk over to a friend and say,

---

Figure 4-2   Running Records

Running records were developed by a New Zealander, Marie Clay. She observed good readers and the ways they approach text. The symbols used in running records map the route readers take as they work through reading material. For more information refer to *The Early Detection of Reading Difficulties* (1985).

Conventions

✓	= accurate
$\dfrac{\text{home}}{\text{house}}$	= substitution
$\dfrac{-}{\text{house}}$	= omission
$\dfrac{\text{and}}{-}$	= insertion
$\dfrac{}{\text{house}}\Big|\dfrac{\text{A}}{\text{T}}$	= appeal, teacher told the word
sc	= self correction
$\overline{\text{house}}$ R	= repetition

Note: The child's response is always on top

"Well, today I made four miscues; one was an omission, but the rest were substitutions. I reran and went back to self-correct. Not bad, huh?" When I first heard a comment like that, I certainly was surprised! I was hearing first graders use language that I would expect to hear from colleagues. Not only were they using the language, they clearly understood what they were discussing and were using appropriate terminology to convey their knowledge.

In addition, I see real changes as children work with one another. Sometimes following a guided reading lesson, the children like to reread the text in pairs to practice. I see very different kinds of behavior and activity as the children have more guided reading practice. I see children taking pride in helping their friends be successful as readers rather than making fun of the errors, or miscues, made. The individuals who do the oral reading begin to monitor themselves more carefully and effectively. The partners, or buddies as we call them, begin to take on the role I have in guided reading lessons. They ask probing questions to get at strategies rather than give all the answers requiring no thinking or work on the part of the reader. They don't really see themselves as teachers but more as facilitators or resources to guide the readers to get the message of the text.

In fact, the children asked me to reproduce the strategy list they had brainstormed as they could use it as a guide or checklist to remind them of the options they had made available. (See Figure 4-3) They also wanted to keep track of the work they did in pairs. "After all, Mrs. Giard, we know you like to take notes and keep track of everything." Many a debriefing session has been devoted to discussion about the value and use of the form in addition to the whole notion of working together in a meaningful, productive manner. The children found the form to be useful to meet the needs they had articulated. They were also intrigued by my running records and often asked to see the pieces of paper when I finished doing a running record. They were interested in symbols used and wanted to know what symbols represented what kinds of miscues. One day as I was roving around the room monitoring individuals and small groups, I happened upon a pair who had been with me earlier in the day for a guided reading lesson. There on their sheet was evidence that they had worked together to use some strategies to unlock some unknown text but as I watched the two children interacting, I saw the buddy turn over the sheet and make checkmarks on the other side of the recording sheet. The child was taking a running record of his classmate by ticking off all the words the child had correctly read! The miscues were noted by writing the word it should have been similar to the way substitutions are shown on a running record. Not only were the miscues noted in the running record, but the buddy turned over the recording sheet and marked the strategy used to correct the miscue. I stood back astounded . . . first graders understanding strategies, articulating what they needed, and using sophisticated language was one thing . . . taking a running record and understanding its purpose was

Figure 4-3

Reader:	Date:	
Partner:	Title:	
Strategies	Yes, it worked	No, it didn't
1. Does it make sense?		
2. Does it sound right?		
3. Does it look right?		
4. Finger Point		
5. Picture Clue		
6. Read something you know		
7. Use your experiences		
8. Reread a book		
9. Rerun, start over		
10. Find word, self correct		
11. Rhyming Pattern cat fat		
12. Repeating Pattern Brown Bear Brown Bear		
13. Skip it, Come back The black house		
14. Length of Word cat Caldecott		
15. Beginning Sound cat come		
16. Give a hint (It starts)		
17. Ask Someone (Help)		
18. Make predictions (What do you think?)		
19. Title The Very Hungry Caterpillar 0000		
20. Small Word in a Big Word		
21. Insertion The fat cat...		
22. Omission The cat is on the mat		

Did the reader understand the piece?
How do you know?

Giard, 1991

quite another! I was dumbfounded. Needless to say, I invited them to share their discoveries at that day's debriefing session. They readily agreed. The children were as impressed as I and all wanted to try it themselves. I talked to them about why they might want to do a running record and that they would need to learn a few simple symbols if they were going to attempt them. We learned the symbols for reading the right word, making an omission, doing a rerun, and self-correcting. The next day twelve pairs of readers embarked on a new adventure. They learned a lot from doing the running records as you can see from the following conversation held during reading.

Dan began our conversation.

"Aaron and I were reading *The Very Hungry Caterpillar* and I took a running record on Aaron. He made five miscues as he read. Aaron wanted to skip the whole first page because he wasn't feeling confident, but I told him that I would help him work through the page. He did have some omissions and I had to tell him a couple of words because none of the strategies seemed to help him."

Mrs. G.:   "How did you record the kinds of miscues he made on your strategy recording sheet?"

Dan: "I checked off number fifteen because I had to help him. I put more than one checkmark there because I had to do it more than once."

Mrs. G.:   "Dan, I noticed you wrote the word no on your running record. Why did you do that?"

Dan: "Because neither one of us knew the word so I wrote no."

Mrs. G.:   "Had you both read this book in guided reading lessons?"

Dan: "Yes, but it had been awhile so we weren't sure of the word."

Corey: "Rene made three miscues, well actually, they were omissions. I ended up telling him a little of a word, like a hint. He used predictions to figure out the words for sure."

Joel: "Well, me and Kirstin were working together and I got a few miscues. But look at the running record I did on her. She got five big rows with all checkmarks and no miscues! I was a little frustrated . . . she reads fast, that's for sure . . . she was reading so fast that I couldn't keep up with the checkmarks and follow the text too. She was reading *Frog and Toad* (1970)."

Kirstin: "Joel got a lot right too. I learned that the book he read is almost too easy for him now—at least for doing a running record because he only made one miscue and he self-corrected right away."

Missy: "Patrick only needed one strategy, he only made one miscue. He had had a guided reading lesson on the book and knew it well. I had read the book earlier in

the year so I was a good person to help him. I was able
to help him with strategies if he made any miscues."

The examples I have shared demonstrate the transfer children make
from guided reading to their independent work. They have plenty of opportunities to reflect on their understandings and practice what they know.

Conclusion

It is now February. Shannon, a new student, recently joined our class. I
talked to her classmates to determine how we could best meet her needs.
Their suggestions reflect the values we share as well as the issues I have
highlighted in this chapter. Their comments reflect what they understand
about reading and writing to others, reading and writing with others and
reading and writing by others.

Mike:	"I think having her join our writing and reading groups will be a good idea. It will help her practice more and learn from the rest of us. She might have some good ideas to share with us too."
Missy:	"I think it is important for her to know where she can get help. All of us can help."
Hannah:	"Shared reading and hearing books read aloud should help her. I know it helps me set my mind for reading."
Sarah:	"She will learn that we try books in different ways. By trying different ways to approach books, she'll see there are different ways to meet our needs."
Dan:	"She will learn about the different genres, like science fiction, nonfiction, mysteries, realistic fiction, and others. She will see how we approach different books in different ways."
Hannah:	"We have to show her how important strategies are. Her running record might be full of Ts (meaning the teacher had to tell her words) and other miscues. She might not self-correct much either."
Dan:	"Yeah, by doing the running records we can help her know more strategies and reading. It will help her know more words and more about herself as a reader."
Sarah:	"We couldn't have learned as much about reading without Mrs. Giard around. Like we learned from Mrs. G., Shannon will learn from us. She will learn how to figure out how to work through text even if she hasn't read much."

References

Clay, M. M. (1985) *The early detection of reading difficulties.* (3rd ed.). Portsmouth, NH: Heinemann.

Mooney, M. (1990). *Reading to, with, and by children.* New York: Richard C. Owen.

Reading in junior classes. (19485). (Department of Education, New Zealand) New York: Richard C. Owen.

Children's Books Cited in the Chapter

Carle, E. (1990). *The very hungry caterpillar.* New York: Scholastic Inc.

Carle, E. (1984) *The very busy spider.* (4th ed.). New York: Philomel Books.

Cowley, J. (1991). *Greedy cat.* (2nd ed.). New York: Richard C. Owen.

de Paola, T. (1973) *Nana upstairs and nana downstairs.* New York: G.P. Putnam.

Lobel, A. (1970). *Frog and toad are friends.* New York: Scholastic, Inc.

Noble, T. H. (1980). *The day Jimmy's boa ate the wash.* New York: Dial Books for Young Readers.

White, E.B. (1980). *Charlotte's web.* (2nd ed.). New York: Harper & Row.

5

Bringing Children to Literacy Through the Writing Process

MARY KITAGAWA

*K*itagawa presents an unusually thoughtful and scholarly examination of children and the reading process as she invites us into the writing worlds of four of her students. Mary values the writer as a spectator who chooses from whatever has his or her attention at the moment. She recognizes the power of inner speech—"almost languaged" thought as it is shaped into the language of the writer. Here the reader is helped to understand the role and value of "writer bias" in creating shape, authority, sincerity, and voice in writing. Kitagawa helps us understand how she creates the writing environment that assists students in writing from the leading edge of their perceptions, powered by inner excitement. Especially powerful are Mary's demonstrations of how to respond to student writing as a co-spectator thus empowering writers rather than limiting them.

Introduction

Last year Vita looked over her portfolio in June and highlighted one of her poems, "because I was right there when it happened." It was not really a "happening," just a streetlight seen from her window on a dark night. Yet, she was right. The scene had significance because a poet had noticed it. She served as its witness.

I treasure her comment as evidence that she sees with a writer's eyes and that she is her own primary audience. Yet such might not have been the case a year earlier. When I asked her in June how she thought she had changed as a writer during that year, sixth grader Vita looked astonished at such a question. "Before this year, I *wasn't* a writer," she explained.

Writing promotes a healthy egocentricity that is natural to active learners. It helps people integrate themselves into their perceptual, intellectual, and imaginative experiences. Language is one way we situate ourselves so that external events have internal meaning. Composing texts is a special way to orient oneself into situations because the texts can be formulated, examined, and revised.

Toddlers provide the model. Through egocentric and sometimes repetitive storytelling, often with no audience at all, they give shape to their perceptions. As older children and adults, because of our self-consciousness, we submerge such external babbling, but we retain a habit of "almost languaged" thought that sometimes nibbles its way to the surface in words. Vygotsky (1962) called it "inner speech."

Many sorts of composition promote discovery by shaping inner speech into language; as we mentally rehearse and review experiences, we see connections that we had not consciously recognized. A story emerges. Informal writing serves as a further rehearsal and review of experiences. A text emerges.

If an impersonal audience imposes itself too early, as in a product-oriented classroom or in a timed writing test, an author may have no chance to learn from the emerging text. What we call voice, or textual evidence of the writer situated within the words, may remain undeveloped as a result of premature audience concerns.

Contrast that with what James Britton (1975), after D.W. Harding, called the co-spectator role. By favoring the writer's agenda, the co-spectator is an audience that nurtures links between experience and experiencer, observer and observation, writer and text. The effect is similar to the way a rapt audience gently helps a storyteller shape a tale. Active listening is the best example of this. There is no formulaic way of achieving co-spectatorship; rather, there is a mindset that I call "writer-bias."

Writer-bias is a term my husband and I devised to describe a significant attribute of *seikatsu tsuzurikata* classrooms in Japan (see Kitagawa and Kitagawa 1987) that seemed to distinguish them from typical classrooms here. In subtle but consistent ways, the teachers of that small, grassroots movement use margin-written responses and class discussions to promote the self of each of their students.

Once the writer's personal connections are secure, a text naturally develops shape, authority, sincerity, and voice. Gradually, it takes on attributes that an audience can appreciate without knowing the writer. Teachers wait, because beginning writers need the security of time to foster first those connections, then that shape-making, authority, sincerity, and voice.

Professional authors are no different, but they often have internalized ways to read "from over their own shoulder," as a co-spectator would. Most of them also have a support system of friends and editors who are on call for that function. When texts are still emerging, and therefore writer-biased, authors are very selective about who may see them (c.f. Britton 1975 on the need for a trusted reader).

As much as possible, I expect my students to read and write in the same ways that accomplished, adult readers and writers do. As co-readers and co-writers, we also serve each other as co-spectators.

Children talk about books with authority and I join in. Children engage in the writing process and I listen and help in the same ways that my adult writing support group helps me. If what they read and write does not engage them fully, I try to help them find another book, another topic, another angle, genre, or strategy. I work hard, but my students work even harder under the driving force of their own sense of authority.

Writer-bias in Journals

Vita's last year before junior high was also our principal's final year. In a pre-retirement interview Michael Greenebaum told a reporter that he wants teachers to teach "from the edge of their knowledge and the center of their excitement" (Amherst *Bulletin,* May 15, 1991).

Similarly I want students to write from the leading edge of their perceptions and I want their writing to be powered by inner excitement. Therefore, on the wall of my fifth-sixth grade classroom I put a large array of cardboard gears to represent the writing process. In the center, as if turning and turned by the rest, is a fluorescent orange one labeled DISCOVERY, the impetus and the reward for writing. The complexity of the gears should be intertwined in ways only artist M. C. Escher could illustrate, and my more mechanical students and colleagues point out that this gear arrangement would actually lock, but I still like it as a way to symbolize the exploratory nature of writing. When children tell me where they are in the

Figure 5-1

writing process, their eyes go the labeled gears for descriptors, and it reminds them that each one turns the others but most of them are held together by discovery.

Students start with journal writing in September. I model writing in which "a small moment," as storyteller-teacher Marni Schwartz calls it, is a topic. We tell each other "small moment" stories. The purpose is to shrink topics to proportions that can be explored in small texts. Students cannot easily write in depth about "My trip to Disneyland," but they can write a focused text about getting lost there last summer, or how the family dog ate its dinner last night, or how they learned to recognize poison ivy last week.

As co-spectator, I cannot set the topic; the spectator chooses from whatever has his or her attention at the moment.

Students who must base their writing on story starters, classwide assignments of topic, and prepackaged gimmicks that take away their options are severely hampered, often by well-meaning teachers who think they are making the job easier. Teachers who are fellow writers with their students know that such constricting assignments are a specialized form of reader-bias that hinges upon the teacher as an evaluator and the classmates as competition. Those constraints would gag even experienced writers.

My role, instead of staging the writing, is to buffer students like Vita from audience concerns while they shape what it is they most want to say. Only when they reread a draft and sense, "Yes, that's it exactly," will they begin to care if the more general public gets it right. As in Figure 5-2, it is the solid connection, between the writer and the perceived experiences, that the writing process and the presence of a writer-biased reader fosters.

"Write whatever remains clear in your memory," is my September advice for a journal entry. "Even a small memory can be explored with your pencil. Let it surprise you as you write." I also read them examples from students of previous years or entries translated from those my husband and I collected in Japan. If the open-ended aspect of the task is intimidating, we talk a bit longer. Students hear other stories of some small moment of puzzlement or discovery until they say to themselves, "Oh, if that is a topic, I have one too" (c.f. Kikuchi, 1977).

Students fold back a wide margin on the right side of the page to leave room for my responses to be written alongside the inspirations in the text. Setting up that margin reminds them to anticipate a co-spectator.

Figure 5-2

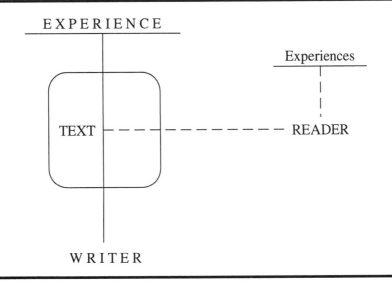

But, they do not need to impress a critical or unknown audience; they have the guarantee of my rapt, writer-biased attention. With that guarantee, writers can situate themselves in terms of both the topic and the text, measuring one against the other instead of prejudging how a generalized audience would accept their words. The guaranteed audience enables them to focus on mundane subjects, with the result that they learn to value, as Vita did, the small details that may fleetingly attract their attention.

Vita and her classmates wrote daily in their journals during class in September and then on a less frequent basis as homework. Her early journals were amusing accounts about her conflicts with a brother: ". . . no job no pay no pay no money no money no rent money no rent money Back With Mom." She told how they divided their bedroom into areas into which the other could not trespass. Then she would taunt him by putting up posters of rock groups he hated, at which he threatened to throw darts. "My mom is the ringmaster of the house," she concluded in one entry.

Most of my responses were the written equivalent of conversational backchanneling. Listeners nod, murmur, and otherwise show interest without taking the floor from the speaker. To backchannel in writing, the response typically mirrors the message as it comes through: "Oh, no, what a threat!" "Your mother has to keep the peace." Ideally, I succeed in creating an over-the-shoulder effect that symbolically leaves the pencil in the writer's hand. The rationale for that is to let the writer maintain ownership, unlike most school writing in which there is no taking back what has been turned in to a teacher.

I try to read spontaneously and intuitively, but there are also specific techniques, such as the following:

- Try to use present or present progressive verbs ("I see that you are recalling just how the kitten sounded").
- Avoid questions (Hmmm, my curiosity is raised about this").
- Use the child's name occasionally.
- Praise sparingly and always avoid unspecific praise. Your attentive responses are appropriate credit to an author.

To help yourself be writer-biased when the author's intention is not clear, some of the following strategies are helpful:

- Envision the child's probable posture or facial expression that comes through in the writing.
- Read the passage aloud as a performance; you may hear a sub-text that you had not noticed in straightforward reading.
- Look for unusual punctuation and capitalization as clues to the emphasis intended ("Back With Mom").

Responding to journals in writer-biased ways feels a bit awkward and I often cannot be as natural and spontaneous as I wish, especially if I am rushed or tired. Usually, however, it is my favorite homework. My goal is for children to be inspired to reread their own words, eyes linking the response in the margin to the expression in their text. Surprisingly, even responses that seem a bit phony seem to take away the loneliness for beginning writers.

Furthermore, these responses can be thought through and revised, unlike the spontaneous reactions we express in conferences. Writing in journal margins at home is like rehearsing for face-to-face conferences. Written responses are a tangible symbol of our co-spectator relationship. Children can review them anytime, and parents can see how we respond to their child's writing.

Sam's first journals were so restricted that I developed a code phrase in responding to his first few and then used it in talking over texts with him in class as well. "Tip of the iceberg" reminded him that he had a lot more to say. Soon he learned to go beneath the surface and produced fascinating journals from things as mundane as eating his brother's pancakes. Here is an example of a journal that reflects the fact that he is an avid reader. My response encouraged him from the margin, as shown.

Animals

Animals have different styles like a pig, horse or a dog. Most of these have a story book attitude.

Hmmm, different "styles."
I wonder how.
Oh, I read ahead to see what you mean, Sam.

The pig has been said to be dirty, selfish, greedy and moody, but it's not really that dirty and sometimes are very friendly.

You've done it again; you've found a most original topic! Here you are contrasting fictional traits with actual characteristics.

A horse strong, goes on forever, never stubborn, does what it's commanded to. The truth strong, can tire, sometimes stubborn, does not always do what it's told to.

You are really thinking this through to get from the stereotype to reality.

The dog dangerous to others loyal to the master. Fights other dogs. The mans best friend. Truth also man's enemy, Also a nice pet not an outlaw.

I'm wondering if it is deliberate that these sentence fragments sound like a list.

My conclusion is that animals are not always what books make them up to be.

Your organization is clear: an introduction, three examples and a conclusion. Are you going to develop this further in writing workshop?

For many years I taught in a school whose students not only came from a single cohesive neighborhood but who had spent so much time together since infancy that, at first, they resisted writing personal narratives. "Everybody was there anyway," they would complain. My challenge was to convince them that, because of each unique perspective, the narratives would be distinctive and therefore essential. A co-spectator role of attentive responses on the margins of their first tentative journal entries encouraged them to feel they had something to express: "It is good that you have noticed this." "This is the sort of thing that is often forgotten if no one stops to record it."

Even in schools with more diverse populations, children of our present media generation need help to realize the unique value of their own observations and contemplation. Writing on a regular but informal basis about what is directly experienced, children make connections that enable them to shape and be shaped by those experiences. Whenever I have discontinued my expectation that students will keep such informal writing as journals, the result has been that their writing remains fairly generic until I have them take part in some sort of writing that promotes their reality-connecting selves.

Vita wrote entries about her family all through the fall, winter, and spring of sixth grade. In January she extended one of these into a composition that went through the entire writing process including many drafts and a carefully edited final product for her portfolio. It was a "slow motion" description of the skidding and impact of a car accident she had recently been in. She stressed amazement over her mother's ability to remain calm in contrast to the thoughts going through her own head. Although the car was destroyed, Vita ended philosophically with ". . . but life will go on."

The two genres Vita usually chose were these personal narratives and poetry. It was the latter that she seemed to enjoy most.

Poetry

For some years now, I have used poetry in September as a launch for creative writing. There are a number of benefits. One is that, like journal entries, poetry seems easy for students to "own." Punctuation and style are often a matter of choice rather than rules. Texts are usually short enough that making revisions and multiple drafts is not a chore. Writers can toy with phrases, letting their ears guide decisions. Readers who claim not to understand a poem are easier to shrug off than if they complain of confusion about prose. Revision is often a matter of subtraction instead of addition, which trains poets to be incisive rather than expansive.

To start the poetry unit on the first day of school, I simply have lots of poetry books for students to browse through and enjoy. Over the next few days they select poems to perform as oral interpretation and/or chart for hanging on the walls. (Sometimes I videotape the performances to play at Open House.) Invariably, someone will ask to use an original poem. Others overhear my enthusiasm and begin to either compose poems or bring in some they have written in the past.

Within a few weeks, all the charted poems copied from books have been replaced by classroom poets' works. Yet, as "local" poets, we reserve the right to keep on perfecting poetry drafts; I'm especially pleased when I find a child pasting a few new lines over a bit of text on her verse already hanging on the wall. Having put up a few of my own, I know that my eye often goes back to them and I come up with wonderful revisions after many rereadings. We print the poems large, using colored markers on lined newsprint. I had the custodian line two walls with wire held in place by eyehooks. Clamps on the wires hold the charts until we run out of space and substitute more recent ones. Some students illustrate their poems. They create a decorative, literary milieu that enables us to eavesdrop on visitors who always take notice of them.

I provide poetry journals and show how, in mine, I date each draft so I can look back later and see how the poem grew. Often something rejected in a second draft proves useful after all in a fourth or fifth version (c.f. McClure et al, for more on poetry journals). Informally I use my poetry journal to show how writing new drafts without copying from the old ones results in discoveries and gradual refinements until I am well enough satisfied to go public with a poem. I also model my own search for words that fit "what *I* want to express." Then, when students ask me, as they are apt to do in the early part of our relationship, "Is it good?" I can remind them to judge it against what *they* wanted to express. It is their intention and their discovery that are measures of success.

Many preadolescents already write poetry at home, as a source of personal satisfaction and sometimes comfort. Writing and sharing poems at school seems to legitimize this form of self-expression, and poetry remains a favorite genre throughout the school year.

At the end of the year, Vita said of the following poem, written in school in September, "I like it because it was the first poem I ever wrote."

The Butterfly

The Butterfly lands on my butterfly blouse searching for a companion looking confused the butterfly flies away because she is alone in the world.

That poem launched a barrage of poems, mostly written at home at night, so we called her our Midnight Poet. Vita would rush to school the next day and find friends and teachers to listen to her creations. She did not seem ready for advice and rejected many suggestions that she take the poems through the editing process to final drafts for her portfolio. Only near the end of the year, perhaps in anticipation of the final portfolio review, did she choose about a dozen of these for recopying after getting help with editing.

One piece, a prose poem written in February, reduced many of us to tears. Vita had not been taught the terms metaphor and simile, but she built them in naturally starting from the coincidence of her sister living on Sea Street in Boston.

My Family

My family, the highlight of my life. The joy I feel when I wake up. My sister, my brothers, are what make me happy. Not money or anything manmade can make me love them less.

My sister drifted out over the sea never to come back for she has her own life now, living on Sea Street somewhere faraway. I see her face but only in my mind. She's like the wind over the sea!

My brother, like a worm lugging his way around, finding new worlds for himself, not wanting to cross the sea!

I have family on my father's side; sisters, brothers, but only by name for they have crossed the sea too many times. I feel nothing for them.

My father never came, so I am as cold as winter to him.

My mother, always in bloom. Her warmth covers the cold my father left. She is the source of my life. The source of laughter and tears, most of all my love.

I love them all.

This sort of writing works best for Vita and next best for those of us who know her; yet, it also contains the sort of voice that makes it work for strangers. Her success was linked to her discovery of topics in which "I was there when it happened."

Vita began to define herself as a writer in that context. The fact that she rarely displayed her poems on charts probably indicates that she was very writer-biased herself, more than many of her classmates. Yet she was also more engaged in the writing process than many students who readily charted their poems.

Writing in Workshop

Every year's schedule has its own constraints, but I try to carve out a large block of time, averaging five hours a week, for writing workshop. Writing occurs in other parts of the day, but usually it is workshop where the choices are most open. Other writing occasions during the day typically involve assigned writing, such as learning logs, reading response journals, research papers, and so forth. Only in writing workshop are the writing process "gears" (Figure 5-1) turning so much at their own speed.

Because of high numbers of special needs students, I co-teach with a special education teacher every morning. This eliminates pullout sessions for all but beginning ESL students, because special needs can be met by the lowered student-teacher ratio and my co-teacher's specialized help. Students are not differentiated by any grouping or variation in assignment. We try to keep most lessons open-ended so that we can accommodate individual differences. Writing was one of the easiest parts of the curriculum in which to accomplish that diversity.

Once a format of writing support groups (heterogeneous and periodically reshuffled) and whole class appreciation sessions is established, the students usually write independently. Borrowing an idea I heard in a workshop with Dorothy Watson, my co-teacher and I make conference notes on wide address labels we carry about on clipboards, trading clipboards if we happen to confer with a student not in our own writing support group. When a child's address label gets full, we stick it on that student's card in a recordkeeping book. In that way, no recopying is necessary.

Writing workshop involves little daily preparation. Occasionally I make up a mini-lesson or exercise to emphasize a skill or strategy, but often my class preparation is just showing up ready to be a co-spectator. Regular homework is responding to journals. Several times a year, I do spend a lot of time for evaluative tasks like portfolio reviewing or assessment of spelling and language mechanics skills, but most of the time, the writing process itself spells out how we all spend our time.

Routines include signals for a whole class meeting at the beginning, if there is to be a mini-lesson on language mechanics or writing strategies. Another routine is meeting for about fifteen minutes with a writing support group to listen to bits of each other's texts and reply to requests for advice.

We borrowed from Calkins (1991) the term "bubble of silence" to remind students to give each other a concentration level of quiet when not doing group work. I used to call it "going into our private studies" but the term "bubble of silence" seems to work better. Under these conditions, only our soft-spoken conferences are allowed. Peers who get permission may share in parts of the room where no one is busy writing.

Drafts in process are kept in the students' own folders. Their portfolios are hanging files in an open crate on a low shelf. All final drafts, including tape recordings of raps, cartoon drawings, and other variations of text, are kept there.

In January and June, portfolios are self-examined and teacher-evaluated. The midyear reflection includes a lengthy written analysis that I do on five of the pieces the student chooses for that purpose. Students explain why they have chosen the ones they offer for evaluation. Then, including my written comments, a "portable portfolio" (manila folder with large paper clips) is sent home for student-parent reflection upon all that the portfolio contains. There is an open-ended form inviting parents, students, or both to write whatever they choose about the portfolio contents. This response becomes part of the portfolio.

In June, students look at the entire portfolio and write open-endedly about any aspect of it. There are optional prompts such as "The piece I treasure most is . . . because . . ." or "The hardest to write but it was (wasn't) worth it is . . . because . . ." and so forth. I heard of this sort of categorization from Donald Graves at a convention and it does help children to evaluate their work specifically. It was under such prompting that Vita wrote about liking "The Butterfly" because it was her first poem and the poem about the streetlight because she was right there when it happened.

I also made up a survey to use twice a year. It lists many descriptors such as "I frequently come up with topics with ease" or "I am usually relieved when I finally come up with a good topic." (For one version of this that I have since refined, see the supplement to the *Whole Language Catalog* on assessment, in press.) I fill out the same survey on each of the students before I look to see which descriptors the students marked for themselves. We compare our results and then both sets go home in the same temporary portfolio. Our results are usually amazingly similar, or we generally find mine to be more flattering. One benefit besides assessment is that the survey focuses attention on goals peculiar to a process-oriented writing curriculum; it indirectly informs students and their parents about expectations that might not be a part of their previous experiences.

The survey also acknowledges developmental growth in writing prowess and gives a clearer perspective about strengths and weaknesses than grades do. If any child marked more than one or two of the somewhat negative ones, like "I can never come up with a good topic, so I just write about anything," I would worry. So far, by midyear, no child has had such a low self-image in more than one or two categories.

My district has no procedures yet for portfolio assessment beyond the classroom level. Ways to pass them on to junior high have not yet been developed. I am glad to be able to experiment with classroom-internal portfolio use. For now, I simply send the contents home in June.

Writing Across the Curriculum

Our first science unit for Vita's class was the study of crayfish. For six weeks we paired up to study and care for fourteen of them. Students spent both free time and science class documenting their habits and capabilities. We shunned secondary sources and let the crayfish show us the range of their eating preferences (lettuce, school pizza, or worms? food offered underwater, on dry carpet, or while being held? if held, horizontal or vertical?); maze running abilities (speed of learning, effect of visual clues or scent); social interactions (dominance, sex differences); strength variations; and so forth.

Vita's partner happened to be the only class member with no interest in crayfish but she was a naturally glib writer who could have turned their collaborative research paper into a precise, albeit generic, report. Vita compensated for her partner's disinterest by taking leadership in all but the mechanical aspects of the final draft.

Having a partner who was almost a secretary rather than a collaborator provided Vita with a way around her own discouraging spelling and handwriting obstacles while giving her responsibility for the content of their report. Doing primary research on an animal her partner was even loathe to handle encouraged her voice of authority.

Seeing Vita's unusual involvement brought to mind a conversation with a physicist, Carl Tomizuka, of the University of Arizona. Carl had been a student of a skillful *seikatsu tsuzurikata* teacher in Japan during fifth and sixth grades. He credits that experience with making him a scientist. Since the movement stresses the rather subjective writing of journals to record everyday life, I asked him how it could have helped him with the objectivity of science. Carl insisted that scientists cannot make sense of any observation unless they remain aware of their own perspective. That is how writer-bias plays itself out in science.

The children working with the crayfish had to be constantly aware of variables their own behavior might contribute to interactions with crayfish. They had to keep themselves in the picture. The reports were detailed with fairly accurate firsthand information, and they were vivid accounts at the same time.

What came together for Vita that September was the writing up of this primary research on crayfish, her personal narrative journal, and our poetry unit. It may have been this fortuitous combination that seemed to awaken the creative scholar in this bright girl. Her attendance and scholarship improved greatly all through the year.

What remained after all those topics with the advantage of immediacy was to learn to write with confidence about more remote, less personal topics, as in history, geography, and more abstract science units. In assigned writing, as opposed to the flexible choices during writing workshop, students had to search out a position of spectatorship.

One antidote to the generic writing that often accompanies school reports is to delay beginning the text until ideas have simmered for awhile. The worst writing happens when students panic over forgetting something, and, being unskilled in notetaking, plunge directly into their text, hoping it will make more sense on paper than it does in their heads.

Gradually Vita and most of her classmates could hold off writing when they were not yet immersed in topics in relation to our thematic unit studies. If I found them overly anxious to begin a draft, I would remind them of the ease with which they wrote about crayfish once they had educated themselves by taking care of them.

A task more abstract than observing crayfish was to make a comparison of desert and tundra areas. I wanted them to have a reinforcement of their ability to write without having done text-driven research, but this time the data came from films, slides, filmstrips, visual imagery exercises, and mini-lectures. I made sure there was never enough time for more than scanty notes. They were surprised at the parallels they could find between the physical and biological characteristics of such seemingly opposite settings. For example, snowshoe hares have tiny ears to prevent heat loss while jackrabbits have large ears for the opposite effect. After the information blitz through the various media, the children groaned that they "knew too much." I asked them to freewrite on a set of papers they first labeled with the broad categories they might want to use as subtitles, like precipitation or birds. In thirty minutes of scribbling, no pencils had run dry! They were ecstatic: "Look how many sheets I filled." "I can't keep up with myself." That experience helped them realize how absorbent their brains really are.

Our unit of study for the entire second semester was the broad theme of immigration. We used many of the over 70 books written by Milton Meltzer, such as *The Hispanic Americans* (1982), and *The Chinese Americans* (1980). We were fortunate in having a visit from Meltzer himself. Since many in the class had Latino roots, we all stopped in February and took on some aspect of an Hispanic culture as a topic for which the type of presentation was to be their choice. Children wrote and shared reports, poems, puppet shows, and visual displays. Vita described and demonstrated dances from the Caribbean that she learned from her mother and an uncle.

Vita's crayfish study partner interviewed her and many other Puerto Rican acquaintances to gain their perspective on prejudice and discrimination. She wrote a long poem that rang with the voice she adopted on their behalf.

In literature study we read a variety of books about immigrants. These books served to personify the reasons why people emigrate and the conflicts that may occur after immigration.

Students were taught some interviewing strategies and sent to find interviewees with direct or indirect experiences of moving into this country. In some cases, parents' long distance phone bills soared that month. Ben's paper described the hardships of his grandfather who almost lost ties to his family in Mexico when he took on the precarious existence of an illegal alien in the early part of the century. Ben learned about it from phone conversations with relatives in New Mexico and from examination of photo albums that his mother said he had never shown an interest in before.

Another student's paper came from an interview with a family friend who had traced her ancestry through records in the library; from her report we learned about local resources for genealogical searches. A paraprofessional in our school shared the difficulty of separation she and her parents felt when she followed her husband here from Germany. Vita wrote about her mother's mixed feelings in leaving Puerto Rico, which, though not technically international immigration, was clearly within the bounds of our study and an important research experience for Vita.

Writing in *Persona*

Sometimes I encourage students to write in the *persona* of a character in a book. Since this had seemed to be a popular reading response, I decided to have our immigration unit conclude with adopting the *persona* of an imaginary immigrant. In order not to rush the process, I set aside six weeks. In the first two weeks students chose a country or origin and a time and reason for emigration. They studied nonfiction to get accurate historical and geographic information and they read fiction to get a sense of immediacy.

We found the money to take a five hour bus ride to New York for a day at Ellis Island. Students were to look at the huge mural photographs and, whether the country of origin was precisely right or not, to find "their" immigrant's face; they were to read into the face and eyes the story that immigrant would have told. In fact, they were to view the entire museum through their immigrant's eyes, finding luggage and personal effects among the displays, and seeing the Statue of Liberty as if after two months at sea.

By the time they began to write, students had spent three weeks merely taking on their *persona* on both intellectual and emotional levels. They began to write either a diary or a series of letters in that *persona*. Vita relied mostly on fiction to put herself into the Englishwoman she chose to portray through letters. Sam had the most authentic resource of any student, his own great, great grandfather's diary. Although most of it was barely legible, his grandmother supplemented some of the family lore and he filled in the gaps:

> . . . My father, William Knipe, was a Captain in the Queen's army, but he died. My mother, Jane Hall Knipe, had had a burden of eight children.
>
> It was July 10, 1853. It was a fine sunny day in Ducklington. In the house of the late William Knipe, levels of extreme excitement were being shown.
>
> We had received news that we had seven bookings for the ship Staffordshire. It would be leaving on July 23, 1853 from Liverpool.
>
> Although our family had eight kids and a widowed mother, we had already decided that the two eldest were staying behind. They that stayed behind would tend the grave and house of the late William Knipe. . . .

And on and on went the story, many pages long, with a strong sense of his ancestor's voice. Sam had clearly recovered from his tendency to write only the "tip of the iceberg."

Lawren also had access to an actual ancestor. Through conversations with a relative, he was able to incorporate some family history and some

notions he had about Ireland. Excerpts from the eleven entries of "Patrick's
Personal Diary" indicate the sort of intensity which Lawren invested in his
topic. What was most important was the sense of connection he accomplished, at his own level of understanding of the conditions in Ireland and
the immigration experience.

Sunday, March 17, 1875

Hi, I'm sixteen years old as of today, Saint Patrick's day. I live in
County Monahan in the town of Limerick. I have straight red hair.
I'm five feet and eleven inches tall, and I weigh over 100 pounds. . . .

I'm going to America where my Uncle Andrew is. He wrote that I
could earn as much as one dollar a day there. I'm lucky to earn two
pence here. We've been saving up for the 150 pounds I'll need for
the trip for almost five years. . . .

I want to make a better life for the generation after me. The Potato
Famine was the biggest reason of all.

I decided that I wanted to go, because Ireland never recovered
from the Famine. My family has never been able to get out of
poverty. We thought Ireland was under a curse. . . .

(My friend) Hugh went through third grade with me so we could help
each other with the homework. We hated the mosquitoes in the hedge-
row school. We were always worried that we would get caught. It's
illegal for Irish to go to school, and the British soldiers could come at
any time. That's the reason we were in the hedge-rows. . . .

Monday, April 19, 1875

I got half a shilling for bringing a package with money in it successfully to somebody's house. That's the most money I've earned.

Tuesday, July 16, 1875

This is the day. I'm in the boat. For five and a half years I've been
dreaming about America and now I'm on my way. The ticket cost
one hundred pounds. I have fifty pounds in my pocket. American
Immigration requires it. I'll have to change it when I get to Boston.
Uncle Andrew will be waiting for me when I get there. Everything's
planned out to the most pinpoint detail possible. I feel so grown up.
Oh gosh, we're moving. It feels as if I'm on a log near my house
trying to shake Hugh off. . . .

Wednesday, July 28, 1875

I FEEL SICK! I've decided that this is *not* a game with Hugh. This
is a torture chamber. It seems like half of the people have died and
this place smells like a dungeon. . . .

Monday, August 5, 1875

We're close enough to see the dock, but we're not moving. . . .

I'm in the terminal. They gave me a number and said they would call it in a few hours. I thought they were kidding, but wow, I was wrong. It's been five hours. I counted 687 tiles on the wall. That's how desperate I am. . . .

Tuesday, March 17, 1948

Hi, I was going through my trunk that I hadn't opened for a long time, and dug up the Diary. I decided to write in it. I'm eighty-nine years old. I retired a few months ago. I got a job as a Dock Laborer a week after I got off the boat. I lived with Uncle Andrew for about a month until I had enough money to rent my own room. Then I worked my way up to a First class Hoisting Engineer. When I got my job, all the jobs that were high paying or needed some brains had N.I.N.A. or No Irish Need Apply, signs. . . .

The students' diaries and letters written with the voices of immigrants all carried varying amounts of information. Although they were not always factually accurate, they were a measure of what the youngsters believed to be true and they contained whatever emotional content they understood about immigrant experiences. These were, of course, pseudo-observational writings, but most students seemed personally invested in the experiences they concocted.

Fifth grader Hector read from one of Meltzer's books (1980) and from a *Cobblestone* magazine dedicated to Chinese Americans (March, 1991). He "translated" factual information into a first person account that came out rather formal but was clear, accurate, and informative in its depiction of a Chinese immigrant in the 1800s. He had just transferred to our school as this project started and I was pleased that he could so quickly adapt to an unusual assignment.

. . . Like other immigrants, most of us came to the United States to earn our fortunes. When I came I planned to stay only as long as it takes to make enough money to improve life for my family back home, where I would return.

. . . I have spent many hours telling long stories about when my relatives came to the U. S. in the 1800s. Gold was discovered in California in 1848; and by 1852, twenty-five thousand of us had come to the gold fields.

Many men like myself lived in boarding houses and we met at family and clan headquarters for conversation to receive news from home. . . .

Fiction

Writing in *persona* is a form of fiction that epitomizes first person voice, probably the clearest voice for beginning writers to use. I find that, without a base of extensive, reality-connected writing, students are frequently disappointed in the fiction they create. Perhaps because they read more novels than short stories at this age, they often tackle complexities of plot that are beyond the scope of their time and energy. Hence, in exhaustion, they finally "punch out" the climax of the story *and* the antagonist in quick resolutions: "He punched out four monsters, found his way through the rest of the maze, rescued the princess, and earned her hand in marriage." Or, having hopelessly trapped the protagonist, they resort to cop-out finales like, "and then she woke up" or "If you want to know what happened, read the sequel" (which never gets written!).

My students' most successful stories, in general, have been fictional extensions of personal narratives and stories built around a moral, in the manner of folktales. Vita simply chose not to write fiction in sixth grade.

I had not discovered the benefits of a storytelling unit the year I was her teacher. The next year, however, storyteller-teacher Marni Schwartz convinced me to give some writing workshop time to storytelling. The class and I spent five weeks trying it out. Most of us chose stories from books or family lore, but some wrote their own. I noticed that many children who had previously been bogged down in their own fiction were immediately more able to bring closure to their own stories. Now I am trying to also incorporate more oral tellings into writing support groups meeting during writing workshop. Before a rapt audience of co-spectators, a story will often emerge.

Conclusion

The writers quoted in this chapter all had been students whose writing processes were matters of concern, and yet all four achieved remarkable success that year. I think it mattered to them that I had a writer-biased attitude that they were able to achieve also for themselves.

In most sixth grade classrooms students range from active and self-motivated learners to passive and uncooperative. Along the continuum are some who are industrious but robotic and others who barely put up with school. Even seemingly model students who stay on-task out of a sense of diligence are learners at risk, in the long run, if they do not see themselves as a part of what they are learning. What helps them all is to learn to situate themselves in light of their emerging worldview. They do this by having time and opportunities to elaborate upon their own perceptions, especially in writing.

It is especially satisfying to be a teacher of students who, like Vita, Lawren, Sam, and Hector, activate a natural learning mode. They learn to read their drafts with a sense of inquiry: is that what I wanted to say? And, on reading the final draft over, they enjoy surprised satisfaction: So that is what I wanted to express. Yes!

References

Interview with Michael Greenbaum. (1991, May 15). *Amherst Bulletin.*

Britton, J. (with T. Burgess, N. Martin, A. McLeod, & H. Rosen). (1975). *The development of writing abilities* (11–18). London: Macmillan Education, 1975.

Calkins, L. M. (1991). *Living between the lines.* Portsmouth, NH: Heinemann.

Cobblestone. (1991). (entire issue) Peterborough, NH: Cobblestone Publishers, Inc., *(12)* 3.

Kikuchi, K. (1977). Keikaku-teki taikei-teki shidoo no jissai (Application of planned and systematic guidance). In *Seikatsu tsuzurikata no kiso kooza (Lectures on the fundamentals of seikatsu tsuzurikata),* pp. 77–119. Tokyo: Shinhyooron.

Kitagawa, M. M. & Kitagawa, C. (1987). *Making connections with writing.* Portsmouth, NH: Heinemann.

Meltzer, M. (1980). *The Chinese Americans.* NY: Thomas Y. Crowell.

Meltzer, M. (1982). *The Hispanic Americans.* NY: Thomas Y. Crowell.

McClure, A. A., Harrison, P. & Reed, S. (1990). *Sunrise and songs.* Portsmouth, NH: Heinemann.

Vygotsky, L.S. (1962). *Thought and language.* Cambridge, MA: MIT Press.

6

Bringing Children to Literacy Through Theme Cycles

DONNA BYRUM

VIRGINIA LAZENBY PIERCE

As Donna and Virginia describe how they organize for theme cycles, we see the real meaning of "empowerment" emerge. In these classrooms children are truly empowered to take responsibility for designing and conducting their own learning. These talented teachers view the use of theme cycles as an organizational device—a way of involving students in learning experiences through research on topics identified by the children. In many classrooms using themes as an organizational device, the theme is used to teach the curricular areas. In these classrooms the traditional curricular areas are used to investigate the theme. This is not merely a semantic difference. It is a significant difference in organizing for instruction. Byrum and Pierce help us see how students have helped them evolve in their understanding of learning and move away from direct teaching to a combination of facilitating and mediating (similar to Porterfield's coaching from the side). One of the most difficult issues in thematic teaching is tackled in this chapter—grading procedures that are consistent with wholistic beliefs— especially the role of student self-evaluation.

Prologue

It is the first day of a new school year. Eagerly the children transfer to their chosen desks their reams of notebook paper, freshly sharpened pencils, and carefully selected notebooks of just the right pattern and color. The children seem pleased to select their own desks, but a little surprised by this unexpected privilege.

As the teacher moves to the pad of chart paper placed at the front of the classroom and invites the class to list the things they want to find out more about this year, the fresh faces of the fifth graders take on puzzled expressions. After an awkward period of silence a couple of children respond in a hesitating manner: "Dogs". . . "Frogs" . . .

It is clear that this departure from the expected—the barrage of "do's and don'ts" the fifth grade students have come to expect on the first day of school—has left the students confused. They appear reluctant to commit, or uncertain about making a choice. The teacher emphasizes that these are merely options, just a working list to give the class an idea of what they might choose to investigate. A few more suggestions are uttered: "Antarctica". . . "Trains". . . "Sharks". . .

The teacher waits and then nudges, "What are some of the things you haven't had a chance to study yet, or things you want to know more about?" More responses come forth: "Dinosaurs". . . "Crickets". . . "Black Holes," . . . "What are fingernails made of?". . . "Pirates,". . . "Jets,". . . "Pandas,". . . "What about other galaxies?"

Then it is as though there is no end to the identification of possible areas of study. Students' ideas fill the chart: "Why different people's hair is different." "How fast can a motorcycle go?" "What is ozone?"

The teacher tapes another page to the bottom of the first to accommodate the now abundant suggestions. She comments that they will use this list to guide them during the year and notes that it can be changed—ideas may be added or deleted as the class sees fit. A couple of children add the final possibilities for this initial list: "Why don't we feel the earth move?" "How do satellites work?" Another school year has begun.

While this particular scenario describes the beginning of a fifth grade class, we have used this approach in our first and second grade classes and in a summer program with students from kindergarten through grade nine. Similar scenarios could occur in any classroom at any grade level in which there is a focus on *learning*—students making connections and constructing meaning—and which builds off the students' interests and curiosity.

Theme Cycle: An Overview

First, let us describe what we mean by theme cycle. We use theme cycles as an organizational device—a way of involving the students in authentic learning experiences through research on topics they have identified themselves. By authentic learning experiences, we mean those experiences that represent activities which people use to survive in and interact with the real world. In real life we read and write to find and organize information, to learn from and communicate with others, and for pleasure.

Isolated facts and details are not as important as knowing how to learn—having a variety of strategies for identifying and locating print and non-print resources, interacting with text, organizing and presenting information, and thinking critically. It is through the theme cycle that our students engage in the construction of meaning and utilize life-long skills of problem-solving, effective communication, and collaboration.

Our theme cycles take place during large daily blocks of time—as big a block of time as can be managed within scheduling constraints of lunch, PE, and other programs. This time could be labelled as reading/writing/language/grammar/handwriting/social studies/geography/science/health/critical thinking and study skills. It is definitely not a free-for-all, hodge podge time of *laissez-faire* learning, but rather the students use these curricular areas as tools for learning and, in so doing, demonstrate their mastery of specific skills.

The theme cycle is an ongoing form of organization in which the students:

- collectively determine a general topic of study;
- work in groups formed by common interest;
- engage in mini-lessons with the teacher and/or peers;
- evaluate themselves daily in respect to individual and collaborative success;
- determine the information they will share with the class and the methods they will employ;
- participate in active listening as other groups present information;
- write a summary of what they have learned from all the presentations;
- write an evaluation of their overall learning experience in this unit of study; and
- begin the cycle again by determining the next topic of study.

Theme Cycle vs. Thematic Unit

We must emphasize that we are describing theme cycles in which the traditional curricular areas are used for investigation of the current theme. We are not using the theme to teach the curricular areas as in thematic units. As Edelsky, Altwerger, and Flores (1991) note, "in theme cycles subjects and skills (science, math, reading, etc.) are used for investigating the topic. . . .", whereas in thematic units, "the topics are used for teaching subjects or skills." (p. 64–65).

We first encountered the term "theme cycle" in *Creating Classrooms for Authors: The Reading Writing Connection* (Harste, Short & Burke, 1987) just as our classroom organization was moving in that direction as a natural step beyond our earlier thematic units. We were excited to see that others were drawn in that direction as well.

The theme cycle moves beyond the neatly packaged dinosaur and bear units with their thinly disguised and artificially integrated activities and worksheets into more authentic learning experiences that follow a pattern or cycle both daily and over the course of a topic of study. The time frame for the units is determined by the students and the teacher, so one unit might last three days or three weeks depending on the depth of the study.

The theme cycle as the overall organization for our classrooms evolved naturally from our interactions with and observations of the students. Placing the children first, instead of the material to be covered, is fundamental to a successful program. We agree with Margaret Mooney (1988), reading educator from New Zealand, who states:

> A child-centered programme is more concerned with how children learn, and with helping children to learn how to learn, than with instructing. This requires a shift in focus from the traditional concern with imparting knowledge to ensuring that the conditions that have fostered and nurtured natural learning during the child's early years are the foundation of the school environment. These conditions focus on the child as the learner, and not on the adult as the teacher. The learning has occurred and been accepted as a natural part of living. All attempts have been accepted without strings attached. (p. 2)

> The natural results of a child-centered program are children using math, reading, writing, science, and social studies as tools for finding out more about the world around them.

Theme Cycle and the Curriculum

While the lines between traditional curricular areas are blurred, our classrooms do not reflect an eclectic approach but rather an instructional program consistent with how children learn and with what we consider to be the purpose of education—enabling individuals to respond to the changing world of the 21st century as empowered individuals with the skills, attitudes, and knowledge necessary to function as responsible citizens.

Such a purpose for education requires a rethinking of its elements. The traditional curricular areas of literacy, language, mathematics, science, social studies, and fine arts become tools for understanding and interacting with the world rather than ends in themselves. Characteristics of responsible citizens, such as life-long learner, problem-solver, effective communicator, collaborative worker, quality producer, and involved citizen, become the skills on which we focus, while at the same time developing attitudes of positive self-esteem, inquiry, reflection, negotiation, critical response, empowerment, social awareness, and wellness. These skills and attitudes combine with the tools (the traditional curricular areas) to foster the construction of meaning of one's world, and the larger world in which the student participates. The diagram below (Figure 6-1) represents this shift in focus.

The theme cycle is an effective curricular scheme in which the students use the tools and skills, and develop the attitudes associated with being a responsible citizen.

Theme Cycle at Work

To return to our scenario of the first day of school, following the listing of possible topics, we discuss the advantages of engaging in study on the same general topic versus students working independently on unrelated topics.

Figure 6-1

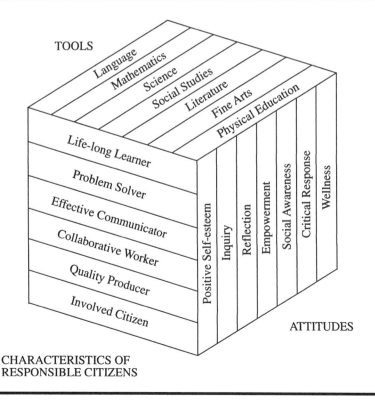

Quickly the students recognize the potential of working on the same general topic and begin to express their insights. "We can tell each other stuff we find." "Maybe we could work together on some research." "We could have displays in the room to go along with what we are studying." "We can learn from each other by reporting what we know."

This sharing of insights is important for a number of reasons. First, it provides an opportunity for the students to assume ownership of the process that will be carried out in their class and naturally serves to motivate the students. Second, the dialogue demonstrates that learning is a social process; and, third, shows that the teacher values the input of the students. On the second day of school, and on the first day of subsequent topics of study, the students write "What I Know" and "What I Want to Know" about the given topic. This writing is not intended as a pre-test, but to encourage the students to record their thoughts. It is important to acknowledge the students' experience base before moving into a theme. The sharing in class discussion of this information, or sometimes misinformation, helps the students begin to see the variety within and complexities of the topic and most importantly helps them focus on what they want to know more about.

It is around these interests that groups are formed to work collaboratively in finding out what they want to know. If students have chosen a subject for study that no one else has chosen, they can work independently or, given a little time, the students usually find a group into which their topic will blend. The allure of working with others is very strong and becomes stronger as the children learn and practice specific skills in group dynamics.

Yes, there are those who are not initially enthusiastic about a chosen topic, but they soon learn that there is a wide range of possibilities and are able to locate their own area of interest. In conversations with students having difficulty finding an area of interest, we offer a variety of invitations to the students to find their own area of investigation and at the same time affirm their interests or questions as valid. By the second or third topic of study, individual curiosity and enthusiasm play an important role in keeping everyone involved.

Organizing Daily

The daily schedule follows a definite pattern. The students first take a few minutes to look over their research folders and get organized for the day. The class comes together for "status of the class," (Atwell, 1987) a calling of the roll with the students stating what they will be working on during research time that day. We record that information in an abbreviated form on a grid sheet so that we have knowledge and documentation of what each student is doing. Examples from our status of the class include: taking notes from a source read yesterday, labelling a mural, going to the library, writing a letter requesting information from a source found during research, or finishing preparation for the group presentation. This takes no more than a couple of minutes as the students have had time to prepare and are accustomed to doing this daily.

Their responses provide a focus enabling students to begin work quickly. In addition, the commitment serves to hold them individually accountable while working in a group. We use the status of the class as an overview to know how things are going so that we may gently nudge those who are stuck or not budgeting their time wisely. For example, "Joey, I see this is the fourth day you have been taking notes on the piece you read. You must be finding a lot of information. Would there be a time today you could share a bit of what you have found in a teacher conference?" Or, "Dee, I see this is your third day to be searching for resources. How is the rest of your group helping you on this?"

Once status of the class is complete the students quickly move together in groups and begin their work. Classroom observers often note the speed and ease with which the students settle in to the task at hand. We feel there are several reasons for this, primarily choice, ownership, and an identified sense of direction. Choice and ownership are important aspects of the theme cycle as the children participate in planning and are given the responsibility for choosing the work in which they will become engaged. The students have chosen a topic of interest to them, and they have made decisions of what to do that day so they are ready to work. The teacher and students both have high expectations for what will transpire.

Creating the Environment

The environment, both physical and social, is an integral part of our theme cycles. We utilize the classroom environment as a learning tool arranged to build on the children's natural curiosity and to support the learners in their development. The environment serves to pique a learner's curiosity about new topics or questions to investigate, and provides resources to support the students in making their own connections. In assembling resources for units of study we include a variety of materials ranging from those intended for primary students to magazines, books, and reference books for older readers. Coupled with the materials the students include, this array exposes the children to more complex texts offering more opportunity for growth. Because the students are seeking information about a topic of their own choosing, have the support of their group members, and have a broad foundation of skills, more difficult texts are not so intimidating.

By using a variety of materials we can also create more opportunities to examine the multicultural aspects of our world. As Dorothy King (1991) states, "Multicultural education is predicated on the concept that all learners can be enriched by perceiving different ways of viewing the world." It is our task as teachers, "to promote understanding, appreciation, and acceptance of cultural differences" (p. 161).

The organization and arrangement of materials as well as the collection of resources is not the sole responsibility of the teacher. The learners are encouraged to contribute to the environment so that they can experience the joy of discovering related materials, of finding materials from within the classroom, and of bringing in materials from home to extend the current theme. Above all, the environment provides powerful invitations to the students to engage in learning. The following excerpt from *Reading in Junior Classes* (1985), the New Zealand teacher's guide, describes the environment we strive for.

> The ideal classroom is an interesting, lively, and accepting place, where children are encouraged to ask their own questions and find out things for themselves, and where their efforts are valued by both the teacher and the other children. Here, mistakes are seen as steps towards independence, not as errors to be instantly corrected. Here, what they have learned at home exists comfortably alongside what they learn at school. (p. 54)

Establishing a Learning Community

Just as the physical environment supports the theme cycle so does the social environment. Our classrooms function as communities in which all members assume roles as teachers and learners—depending on the nature of the interaction—with the teacher functioning as the more experienced member of the community. The teacher is not the only source of information in our classrooms, nor is our role limited to imparting knowledge. We participate as readers, writers, and learners. In their daily research the children seek support and feedback as well as share their new knowledge with community members. Fundamental to this is an appreciation for each other as learners and teachers, and a respect for risk-taking. As the students become experts through their investigations, and we acknowledge the new information we are gaining from them, we are modeling life-long learning as well as affirming the children as successful learners and teachers.

A teacher conference is an option the students can exercise. Teacher conferences can be to seek clarification or just to touch base as to how the student's or the group's research is progressing. Sometimes the students require immediate feedback from the teacher, however they are encouraged to work within their group to find solutions to problems. The students soon come to realize that in our classes the teacher often does not have all the answers. Teacher conferences are requested more frequently, both by the teacher and the students, during the beginning of the year, but the conferences seem to phase out as the students become more capable of assuming responsibility and more comfortable in using peers as sources of information or feedback.

Attention must be given to developing the skills necessary for effective group work. Some of these skills include sharing resources, compromising, taking turns, and challenging ideas not people. As with any learning, these skills are learned by doing—by using them. On the first day students work in groups we listen and watch as the groups first grapple with group dynamics. From these observations we learn about their past experiences of working in groups, as well as gain information about each individual, and then identify a group skill on which to focus.

While our group work is not as structured as described in "cooperative learning" (Johnson & Johnson, 1984), in that we do not always assign groups or jobs within the groups, we do zero in on a particular group skill at the beginning of a session. We lead the class in a brief discussion of what that skill would look like and what it would sound like. Then, during the debriefing, the daily reflection, we discuss that skill and how it was exhibited in their group work. This procedure helps the students build their repertoire of techniques to work successfully with each other.

Searching for the "Wows"

The guiding principle for research is—don't tell us what we already know, tell us the "wows," the "ahas," the surprises. The world around us holds an abundance of "ahas" for our students whatever their age, and it is while searching for those "ahas" that we are surrounded by content material.

Research skills needed for authentic inquiry include note taking, alphabetical order, skimming and scanning, chunking (working through content a small piece at a time), reconciling conflicting information, using the table of contents, index, and bibliography, finding appropriate sources, and reading charts and graphs, to name just a few. These skills are not taught to the whole class as isolated skills, but rather demonstrated to small groups on an as needed basis. So when a group is at the encyclopedias thumbing through page by page, that is the teacher's cue to offer help. By thinking out loud, "Let's see 'lightning,' that's 'l,' you have the right book, now let's look for 'li,' here's 'la,' 'le,' ah 'li,' now let's look for 'lig'" and so on. This immediate hands-on demonstration, when they are earnestly wanting to use this skill, is the most efficient use of our teaching time. It takes only a few minutes and serves a real purpose for the students, thus the message is absorbed and they can call upon that skill again and again. Later they can often be observed helping someone else to "see how the encyclopedia works." It is through these teachable moments we can best meet the needs of our students.

The Teacher's Role

During our big blocks of time we have the opportunity to work with small groups of four to six students for direct reading instruction. By direct reading instruction, we are referring to the New Zealand model of reading instruction which incorporates shared and guided reading as part of a balanced reading program. Shared and guided reading are used with small groups of students to assist them in developing effective reading strategies. (For further information see Chapters Three and Four.) Early in the year appropriate materials for shared and guided reading are selected by the teacher, but as the year progresses the resources the students use for their research can be utilized for shared and guided reading.

The need for this instruction is based on our observations of the students. As the students are engaged in their work, we note the strengths they are demonstrating in reading strategies, research skills, and group dynamics. Along with the strengths we identify "next steps" that we can focus on in shared and guided reading or in our discussions of group dynamics. We have found that a small clipboard holding $3'' \times 5''$ cards or address labels that we will file later, works well for us. In the beginning we let the students know we will be making note of their strengths, and at the end of the class, we read a few of the cards without names to give the students an idea of what we are writing so that they will be comfortable with our ongoing note-taking throughout the year. Once the students are secure in the fact that we are writing strengths, not weaknesses, and that these notes will be shared with them individually at later conferences, they become less conscious of our presence and our note-taking.

Instruction determined in response to our observations of our students allows us to value the uniqueness of each learner and support their individual development. Fundamental to facilitating learning in children are the beliefs that all children are valuable and capable, and that all children can learn. We firmly believe all children want to learn, to improve themselves, and to assume an active role in a learning environment. Our strong positive expectations play a crucial role in helping the students succeed. When students enter our classrooms, they are all regarded as the very best readers and writers with unlimited potential. We have a deep respect for them and use every opportunity to convey that respect. Treating students as individuals does not mean we must teach them individually, but rather we must know them as individuals and tailor specific learning situations for their needs. So, as mediators we use our informed professional judgment to determine next learning steps.

Insights gained from our observations of our students caused us to move from text-driven to interest-driven curriculum, from teacher-directed to student-directed choices, from individual and competitive to collaborative and supportive group work, from product-oriented to process-oriented emphasis, and from looking for the one right answer to understanding the field of possible answers. In essence, we have come to value the learners as the determiners of what transpires in our classrooms.

Evaluation

Since the majority of our class time is spent in theme cycle research, we must find valid ways to determine grades in language, reading, and the content areas. We have endeavored to develop a grading system consistent with our wholistic beliefs. Even in the content areas we are not looking for the memorization of isolated facts, but rather a basic understanding of the principles, a familiarization with the terms, and a meaningful connection with the subject. We are also looking for demonstrations of growth in the skills and strategies that make up reading, writing, research, and social interaction. Again, we have looked to the students as our guides to design a workable grading arrangement.

We feel very strongly that the students' reflection and self-evaluation are the best basis for our evaluation. We agree with Short and Kauffman (1992) that

> Through reflections and self-evaluation, students learn to think about their learning. They reflect on what they are learning (content), how they are learning (process), why they are learning (purpose) and where they want to go next in their learning (goals). When they are able to evaluate their own and others' assumptions about the world, they are able to act on those assumptions and make their own meaning about the world. (p. 1)

For our students to be able to do this kind of valuable reflection, we must build into our theme cycles abundant opportunities to initiate and practice this kind of dialogue. We begin by making oral, critical reflection a part of everything we do. At the end of our big block of time every morning the students come together to discuss with the whole group how the day's learning went and how the group worked—to take a step outside the learning experience and look at it as an observer rather than a participant.

The most valuable result of this daily reflection is the development of metacognition (thinking about thinking) by the students. They come to understand their personal learning styles: "I need to see an example sometimes before I really understand something." They can acknowledge personal preferences: "I would rather read by myself and then talk it over with someone than take turns reading with a partner." The students can determine personal learning strategies and abilities: "I have to read something and think about it awhile before I can talk about it." These insights can be the most important aspects of the process because these discoveries about their personal learning will serve them well into their adult lives. The constant exchange of this kind of information will expose the students to a variety of learning strategies. The teacher, as a fellow learner, can join in this dialogue and demonstrate even further the wide range of possibilities. The students must be engaged in this type of reflection so much that it becomes an integral part of the act of learning. Once the students have accomplished that, they can use this reflection in written form as a part of their more formal self-evaluation.

The basic reason for self-evaluation is to increase the learning, not to generate a grade, but since we live in the real world of accountability, grades can be seen as one product of self-evaluation. Students can grade themselves on process, content, and/or conventions. They can develop simple rubrics or checklists to aid them in determining a letter or number grade. It is important that the students have a role in the development of these systems as well as seeing them as merely devices to get a grade—not as the sole means of valuing a piece of work. It is also important that these devices are seen to change over time as growth in learning takes place. So at the beginning of the year we might look at capitals, periods, and complete sentences; as the year progresses we might focus on varying sentence structure, use of adjectives, and figurative language. Grades can also be generated by collaboration in conferences with the teacher as they note the student's strengths and identify next learning steps.

Grades are not seen as a motivation for learning in our classrooms because we feel intrinsic motivation is most powerful. Stickers, rewards, prizes, and free time are not dangled before our students as reasons to learn, but rather the students take responsibility for their own learning and are encouraged to see learning itself as fulfilling and rewarding.

Students sometimes choose to use textbook tests or worksheets and then laugh at how much *more* information they know about a given subject, as seven-year-old Beth does at the completion of her study of weather.

Clearly Beth has discovered the joy of learning as shown in Figure 6-2.

Questions Often Asked

As we have shared our interpretation of theme cycle with other teachers, we are frequently asked these questions. It is our hope that including our responses here will prove helpful.

1. How do I begin?

Begin your move to theme cycles by discussing with your class the particulars of the new design. Try to allow as much time as you can every day for the students to become immersed. (This is not a Friday afternoon fun fix!) Keep in mind that the purpose is not to cover material! or use contrived activities to teach isolated skills, but rather to offer an abundance of opportunities to use reading and writing as tools to learn. Because the teacher or textbook "says so" is not the reason children study a topic—but because their own interest or curiosity leads them into a topic. It is this shift in thinking by both your students and you that will get you off to a good start.

Remember also as you begin that an effective theme cycle evolves with time. The students will need to be engaged for a while before everything runs smoothly. Taking responsibility for their own learning may not be easy for them at first, just as allowing them to take that step may not be easy for you either. You cannot and should not be the solver of all problems. Fight the urge to intervene, but be watchful as the students work through

Figure 6-2   End of cycle of reflection.

Beth H. Feb. 12, 1991

Everything I know Now About
→ Weather
I know now how snow is
formed. I think it was real
neat learning about snow it
was terrific! I also learned
that snow has six sides. I
know Now ~~that~~ some of
the names to snowflakes.
A real neat thing I learned
is how to save a snow-
flak. I also learned in
weather what makes a tornado. And I learned how fast
a tornado can go that was
real exciting! I learned all
about rainbows too. And I
also learned about how a
rainbow is formed. And the
colors of the rainbow plus
I know now that there
can be twin rainbows, triple
rainbows and one hole big
rainbow. I learned about
hurricanes also. When, I
was learning about the
hurricane it was very
intrasting because I learned
what to do. And how fast
that was real neat! And
I know now how danger-
us. And I also learned about
wind. They told us how to
~~me~~ mesure wind and the
name of the intraments.
Called anomonator. The ligh-
tining group, told us how
dangerus lightning and
that the lightning makes
thunder. Plus ~~wha~~ they told
us what you should do
if lightning comes near
by. And they told us about
the lightning rod. When
we did the tests about
weather they ~~were~~ were
so easy because we
learned about weather!

issues on their own. You will sometimes see surprising spurts of growth and independence as they assume the role of genuine learners.

2.   What happens during the debriefing time?

Use the daily debriefing time at the end of each class session to highlight successes and work through difficulties. This is not a time to share content information—that will come later. It is during this time that students can briefly share the discovery of new sources of information, or a useful research technique. They can also discuss problems they have encountered as in the following example from a second grade class:

Teacher: So how did your groups work today?

Gary: One of our people just didn't do anything at all. (Notice we don't use specific names.)

Sherry: We kind of had trouble with that too at the first of research time today.

Teacher: How did your group handle that, Sherry?

Sherry: We just told him what to do.

Teacher: How else could we handle such a problem?

Becky: We asked her what she wanted to do when that happened in our group.

Gary: I guess that would be better than just griping about it like we did!

Teacher: Let's hear some more suggestions and make a list in case we need to remember these tips.

As the class discussed a variety of suggestions, the teacher stressed the importance of involvement of all the group members and called attention to the positive solutions such as, issuing invitations rather than mandates, allowing for personal preferences but understanding individual responsibility, and the necessity of compromise on everyone's part. By clearing the air and offering workable solutions daily, problems do not escalate and we all learn from the experience.

3.   Tell us some more about the presentations at the end of the cycle.

The purpose of the presentations is merely for the children to share what they have learned since we are not all able to study every topic ourselves. Because we are looking for the "ahas"—the interesting parts—it is very natural to want to share, and sometimes it is even difficult to contain our excitement for very long. This adds an extra element of anticipation to our presentation days. The students decide when they have exhausted their topic and through status of the class make known their readiness for presentation. Usually within two or three days, often less, the rest of the class is ready to present as well.

A few rules for the presentations apply:

1. Everyone in the group should be involved in the presentation itself.
2. Don't tell us what we already know, just tell us the "ahas."
3. Be prepared and willing to answer questions from the class.
4. Spend no more time than absolutely necessary preparing the presentation itself.

We feel very strongly that the emphasis should not be placed on the finished product, but rather on the content and techniques employed. While we do stress pride in a job well done, and celebrate the various forms of presentations, we remain cautious that precious learning time not be spent on superficial decorations. Often the students work at home or collaborate on the phone to supplement their group creations. Our students have created posters, murals, television shows, question and answer panels, live interviews, demonstrations, role plays, readers theater, and music to add to their presentations—all of their own design.

Because we value the learning foremost in our theme cycle, we choose to have no other audience than our own class for the presentations. It is very time consuming to present for other audiences, and they would not have the same investment in the topic that we would have. Also as the students become more comfortable operating within the theme cycle they start looking forward to the next unit with some urgency and expectation and sometimes have their new group and topic organized and waiting.

4. *How do we use theme cycle with beginning readers and writers?*

Educators have long acknowledged the benefits of themed studies in the early grades because it makes use of a child's natural need to make connections. It is in the early grades, however, that teachers have often engaged the children in cute, artificial activities rather than authentic experiences with a real purpose. We must first look at the wealth of knowledge and experiences the children bring and build upon their background.

We must orchestrate an abundance of situations daily for the students to be involved in reading and writing for real purposes. They can write letters to seek information, notes to each other, memos to school personnel, newsletters to parents, and posters, poems, and songs to highlight a unit of study. We can help these children to begin by using shared reading to create meaning; to gain information by using illustrations, captions, and headings; to learn to read charts and graphs; and to learn to group things by categories or qualities. Jane Baskwill (1990) suggests making topic books and "all about" books with emergent readers by sorting, classifying, and organizing pictures from magazines into books. By encouraging the students to label and supplement the pictures with their own text, the children can begin to see the value of print.

The most important aspect of working with young children is viewing them as readers, writers, and learners and convincing them that they are readers, writers, and learners.

5. *What about required content?*

Yes, we are required by our school districts and the state (Texas) to teach and test specific content area material. But rather than making the required content an end in itself, the required content becomes a means of learning about the world. Our students have shown us that whatever topics the class decides to pursue, we find ourselves immersed in the required content area subject matter. For example, a closer look at pirates led us into Texas, United States, and world history; maps and geography; and the history of coins.

Yes, there are the times when the list of ideas may have a gap in terms of reflecting the required curriculum. On such an occasion we orchestrate a situation to head us in that direction. This can be done by carefully selecting just the right book to share with the class; by creating an inviting display such as an empty aquarium with a note: "Amphibious tenants only"; or by using the direct approach of discussing with the class the required content and asking their help in devising a plan for study.

6. *What about incorporating the arts?*

Children have the inherent ability to make connections in their world of experiences. It sometimes seems that education has imposed an artificial separation of subjects to facilitate things other than actual learning. We have witnessed several examples of students making connections between content areas and the more aesthetic areas of art, poetry, drama, and music. It is our responsibility to make sure our classrooms offer a variety of invitations for our students to explore the arts and experience the richness they contribute. We can encourage our students in this direction by making sure they have a variety of art materials available to them, that the books and displays include fiction as well as nonfiction, and that the students value these natural connections. We have looked at the types of clouds represented in classical art as we learned the names of the different cloud formations. We have sung the songs of slaves as we learned about the Civil War. We have read and written poetry expressing our feelings about insects. All these extensions were a result of our own discovery and delight in the connections of our world.

7. *How do I put this all together?*

It is important to note that a delicate balance exists that necessitates inclusion of all of the elements we have discussed for a successful theme cycle. The students must have ownership, responsibility, respect for each other, high expectations, and a clear understanding of the task at hand. Students need instruction in group dynamics, research skills, reading strategies, writing process, and presentation procedures. But rather than plowing through these areas in traditional, whole class lessons and textbook exercises, the students can learn while they are engaged in meaningful and purposeful experiences. Another important component is trust. You must trust your students and firmly believe that they will want to learn. Perhaps the traditional teaching methods of the past have removed some of the joy of wonder, discovery, and the satisfaction of learning for all but a few of our students. It is our job to bring this to all our students and experience it for ourselves as well.

Epilogue

As teachers we were once passive practitioners, but as we began to focus more on our students, they provided the catalyst for us to move to more authentic learning experiences. Rather than abandon our role as professional educators to external sources such as state mandated curriculum and teacher guides, we began to assume more responsibility for the curricular decisions in our classes. Our child-centered approach allowed us to make the old adage, "A child is a candle to be lit not a cup to be filled," more than rhetoric.

Our classrooms became rich environments inviting and supporting the children in discovering the joy of learning. As Margaret Mooney (1988) explains:

> The teacher's role is to awaken the interest and power within children to enable the fire to be lit, and to enable children to become aware of what they already know, are able to do, what they need to know, and where they can get the appropriate help. (p. 2)

And what are the benefits to the students? To answer this question let us move to the last day of the school year of the fifth grade described at the beginning of this chapter. Tricia writes in her Legacy Letter that she will leave in her desk for next year's fifth grade occupant, ". . .You will make a bunch of decisions. You will decide on the things you want to learn about. . . It will be different than the years before. . . .You will have a terrific year!"

References

Atwell, N. (1987). *In the middle*. Portsmouth, NH: Boynton/Cook Publishers, Heinemann.

Baskwill, J. (1990). *Connections: A child's natural learning tool*. New York: Scholastic.

Department of Education. (1985). *Reading in junior classes*. Wellington, New Zealand Available from Richard C. Owen Publishers, Inc., New York.

Edelsky, C., Altwerger, B., & Flores, B. (1991). *Whole language: What's the difference?* Portsmouth, NH: Heinemann.

Harste, J., Short, K., & Burke, C. (1987). *Creating classrooms for authors: The reading-writing connection.* Portsmouth, NH: Heinemann.

Johnson, D., Johnson, R., Holubec, E. & Roy, P. (1984). *Circles of learning: Cooperation in the classroom.* Alexandria, VA: Association for Supervision and Curriculum Development.

King, D. (1991). Assessment and evaluation in bilingual, multicultural classrooms. In B. Harp (Ed.), *Assessment and evaluation in whole language programs.* (pp. 159–175). Norwood, MA: Christopher-Gordon.

Mooney, M. (1988). *Developing life-long readers.* Wellington, New Zealand: Department of Education. Available from Richard C. Owen Publishers, Inc., New York.

Short, K. & Kauffman, G. (1992). Hearing students' voices: The role of reflection in learning. *Teachers Networking—The Whole Language Newsletter*, 11, 3. Katonah, NY: Richard C. Owen Publishers, Inc.

Bringing Children to Literacy Through Reading and Writing Demonstrations by the Teacher

KITTYE COPELAND

Copeland invites us into her classroom to see how she handles reading and writing demonstrations by the teacher. Most teachers seem very comfortable with reading demonstrations and very cautious about doing writing demonstrations. This might be because so few of us ever had a teacher demonstrate writing for us! Kittye appreciates the differences in life with and without authentic reading and writing events when she says, "What a pity I have wasted so much time for myself and for my students." In this classroom time is wasted no more! At all times reading and writing are valued for the purpose of creating high levels of thinking and communicating with others. The reader will find helpful the questions Copeland says we must address as teachers when we are considering assuming the role of demonstrator. Without question, this teacher works not just to teach but to share how she uses and values language and communication.

Several years ago I read a story in *Reader's Digest* about a little girl. When the principal came into the classroom to give the teacher her pay check, the little girl inquired about what he had given her. The teacher replied that it was her pay check. The little girl asked, "Oh, do you have a job somewhere?"

This story may alarm some people, but I see a wonderful difference in the perspective this child has of the role of the teacher compared to what most students have of teachers. The teacher was so much a part of the classroom that the child didn't see her as someone working at a job.

In contrast when we played school as children there were no doubts that the teacher was in charge of the students every move. The teacher stood in front of the classroom and no one was allowed to talk. The teacher would direct our lessons from memorizing the alphabet to practicing forming our letters by writing them numerous times. If we did well we got a gold star. If we were quiet enough then we got a recess. After recess, we would round robin read the stories in our "see Spot run books" and then we would take our spelling test. Nancy always got a gold star.

When I got to kindergarten there were no surprises. Well, maybe one, the teacher didn't have a white tea towel on her head. That's when I learned I was the only non-Catholic on the street. We had played school just as my neighborhood friends had seen the nuns (with "tea towels" on their heads) teach. We had valued all the instruction that the school valued and worked hard to memorize those lessons so gold stars would be ours. Nancy always got a gold star.

Actually, I didn't like school. I hated copying things out of books to practice writing. At home, I would write letters to my grandad like my Mom was doing. Using my inventive spellings, I would ask for things that always found their way to my house. Because of my bad speech impediment, I dreaded round robin reading. The other kids laughed at the simple "see the ball fall" that I tried to articulate. At home when reading Hardy Boys with my brother, I had no fears of failure and could read with understanding and fluency because he demonstrated how it should sound as we partner read. No wonder my parents were confused when the teacher said I couldn't read because I didn't know my short vowel sounds. Mom just wanted me to keep reading *Gone With the Wind* with her. I didn't get gold stars. The teacher never read or wrote, only gave out gold stars to students who formed their letters neatly, had 100% on spelling tests, and knew where to read when it was their turn in round robin reading.

I grew up thinking the classroom should look more like my home where everyone was involved in various uses of writing and reading such as writing letters, making lists, and sharing reading. As a graduate student, I relished the information I finally heard in whole language courses, that children need to have authentic demonstrations to learn how to read and write in classrooms as well as in homes. It became clear that one of the teacher's major roles is to demonstrate his or her own reading and writing processes to students. Students that have teachers that are real readers and writers in the classroom will see how reading and writing are used to learn and to communicate instead of discovering the use outside the classroom. I knew in my learning that I learned processes that I had seen demonstrated. I became engaged through purpose and choice, but because of the lack of teachers demonstrating their uses of reading and writing I thought I was an exception.

The rewards I have found in the last ten years of being an active, involved reader and writer in the classroom are incredible. I know the difference of classrooms with and without the teacher engaged in authentic reading and writing. What a pity I have wasted so much time for myself and for my students with nonsense curricula. The knowledge of the power we hold as thinkers when we use reading and writing to better ourselves as learners must become all our students' curricula. To reach such a goal, we have to have teachers who value themselves as readers and writers and who share their processes and enthusiasm with their students.

The classroom I live in is multi-aged for children from five to twelve years of age. It sits on the edge of Stephens College campus in Columbia, Missouri. I have been at this school for ten of the twenty-five years I have taught. Our classroom looks nothing like the play school that the neighborhood kids had imitated, or the ones I had before viewing myself as a reader and writer with firsthand knowledge to share with my students. This is a community of language users that are using language for real purposes in school. We don't need gold stars.

Teachers as Demonstrators

When looking at the role of the teacher as demonstrator, teachers need to consider the following questions:

- What theories of learning and of language underlie my own reading and writing processes?
- How can I share my processes with my students to promote positive attitudes toward learning?
- Does my demonstration show learners the internal rewards of literacy so that they will want to become literate?
- Do I give children the opportunity to develop their own interests and styles instead of forcing mine?

- Is the atmosphere in the classroom one of cooperation?
- Does the curriculum take into consideration each child's needs, strengths, backgrounds, and interests?

I ask these and other questions to help me become a better teacher, a teacher who sees the importance of demonstrating my own reading and writing processes to my students as a part of the curriculum.

Engaging in Authentic Reading and Writing

My goal is to have children realize, appreciate, and use language in a variety of ways to learn about themselves and others. At all times reading and writing are valued for the purpose of creating higher levels of thinking and communicating with others.

As the teacher in the classroom, I value my role as the one who provides the authentic reading and writing opportunities for the students. However, instead of being in charge, I'm collaborating with students, helping them decide their needs and purposes to learn about the uses of language. As a teacher, I demonstrate and share with them the possibilities available to them.

Children will develop positive attitudes toward using reading and writing to communicate when they are in an environment that treats writing and reading as natural processes. Children learn language as they use language in order to negotiate meaning and to interact with others at a very young age. They also learn written language as they read and write for their own purposes.

Importance of Atmosphere to Nurture Demonstration

As children developed oral language, they were encouraged by adults who accepted them without judging them. The adults demonstrated their use of language through interaction with the child as language users, not monitors. When inviting students to use language at school, they must feel the same acceptance. The importance of accepting their approximations of conventions is essential to giving them the assurance and support that they need to develop as confident, successful readers and writers. The teacher is the adult that demonstrates how language is used and refined. Teachers must share their own struggles to gain control of language by working through processes in view of the students. The atmosphere of risk taking in the classroom is a necessary one for both teacher and students. Children must learn language knowing mistakes are inevitable and welcomed. The students must know that their questions of refinement will be dealt with at the appropriate time, allowing them to move ahead in their endeavors.

Environment and Curriculum that Nurture Demonstration

For the teacher to be free to demonstrate that the classroom is a place that language is learned and used by the teacher, the physical aspect of the classroom is as important as the atmosphere. The environment becomes a major factor that invites students into a world of literacy that includes the teacher as a student and user of language. For the teacher to become engaged in reading and writing activities, students must be self sufficient in what they do. The structure of the environment needs to be such that students are independent and self directing so that the teacher is not wasting time directing students' movements. The physical nature of the room alone must tell the students that the teacher feels "this is your living space as well as mine." To establish the environment, the year begins by children receiving letters from the teacher asking that they bring posters, animals, plants, books, magazines, brochures, and decorations to help make the classroom a students owned environment. The students feel the respect that they will have as a member not a guest in a community of learners.

When the children arrive, they help the teacher arrange furniture and set up areas that will aid the group's function as a community. The teacher points out ways that will make their classroom one that invites the teacher and students to engage in communicating with each other. Areas that the teacher will use to manifest ways of learning about language through using language are established. Such areas include: reading areas, writing labs, literature discussion areas, experiment centers, large and small group areas, game areas, listening centers, research areas, and so forth. These areas help children know what spaces will be used for what activities. Predictability, consistency, and rituals help the students become independent.

As the teacher uses mailboxes for each learner, message boards, class magazines, writing journals and writing notes to communicate to members of the class, the students in turn experience the benefits they will receive when using each of them. Encouraging children to make decisions about how and when to use them shows the learners that the teacher values their choices.

Teachers who want to be engaged readers and writers, just as the students are, must create a community and curriculum that is a vehicle for authentic language. The idea of an active, engaged learning environment is based on three principles of learning theory. We know that learning is enhanced for a student by 1) playing active rather than passive roles in learning situations; 2) by real as opposed to vicarious experiences; and 3) by participating in decisions about consequences he or she will bear.

Teachers who encourage students to go beyond the known answers and to question the authorities, stimulate learning how to learn, thus assuring that students will become active participants in their own learning. This attempt to move children out of taking in information to questioning the known is accomplished by becoming a reflective teacher. Teachers must demonstrate to students how they are active learners, encouraging students to do the same.

Time to Work

Teachers who are engaged readers and writers have an understanding of the importance of not being bound to time constraints that interfere with their momentum. A major way for teachers to support students' reading and writing is to have the students' input into planning the schedule. As adults we realize that we must have a schedule to manage what we want to accomplish; we can support students by helping them develop workable time tables.

A schedule should respect the need for each reader and writer to be able to set personal agendas.

A typical day's schedule may look like this:

8:30	Class meeting to decide what is needed for that day.
8:45	Writing and reading and math related activities
10:30	Recess
10:50	Continue work
11:30	Read aloud
11:50	Clean
12:00	Lunch
1:00	Research, experiments, and making visual aids
3:00	Meeting
3:20	Home

Physical education and music meet twice a week for 30 minutes. There is one hour of swimming instruction each week for twelve weeks. The meeting is to discuss the day, current events, personal sharing, problems, and the like.

During reading and writing each child determines what he or she needs to do within the class schedule. For example, one child's list could look like this:

Poem for the magazine

Pen pal letter

Magazine story

Special contest entry

Conference with Ms. Copeland for revision suggestions or final editing

Conference with another student for suggestions on writing problems

Literature study book reading

Literature discussion group meeting

Literature study projects

Math related projects or math folder

Math conference with Ms. Copeland

Math concept group meeting

Computer time

After lunch, the class shifts to either research on special topics chosen as a group or individually. Within their research students find information to share with their classmates in the form of a written, oral, or center report.

The day closes with a class meeting to discuss events of the day, solve problems, share work, or discuss work needed to be done at home to prepare for the next day.

The class has structure within this schedule. I'm there as a resource person as well as a learner. I have the responsibility to keep the flow of the creativity going and the communication and process moving. Children need time to work at their endeavors. Teachers who are engaged in their own work recognize the time it takes to develop quality work, so they are willing to give the time and support it takes.

Literature and Demonstration

Read aloud is a time to share print as a whole group. The teacher demonstrates how different reading materials are handled, sound, and valued. Big books, chapter books by a favorite author or specific topic, poetry, illustrated books, student authored works, teacher authored works, newspapers, and magazine stories are examples of materials that can be shared at read aloud time.

Teachers who honestly share their own feelings about literature as a member of the community help learners feel the connection that literature holds for the reader when the situations in books reflect our lives and feelings. Our class had a moment of connection with each other and literature when we were reading *Racing the Sun* (1988) by Paul Pitts. The story is about a young boy helping his grandfather die. We had talks at length about older members of families, family members dying, my mother and father and brother passing away, how hard it is to lose those we love and how reading other stories about loved ones dying helps us know things that will support us in similar situations. The children knew how hard this book was for me to read at times. When we came to the last chapter, I said, "I just don't think I can read the last chapter. We know he will die tomorrow. I just don't think I can get through it." "It's okay," Lara spoke up, "I will take over." Lara was a shy reader who hated even to partner read, much less read to the whole group. The next day the children gathered in a circle to hear the ending. I dug my nails in my hand as I read, hoping I could do it. Then not one sound would come. Not realizing Lara was sitting by me, I felt a hand take the book from me and she read on. As I looked around the room each of us shared our hearts, emotions, and trust in each other as we let the story carry our feelings in dealing with death. After she finished we just sat in our circle for a long while. Literature had connected and changed us all. A teacher didn't need to explain the components of what makes a strong ending because we were experiencing the impact of a story. We lived through and shared feelings as people who have events in our lives that hurt.

Because of sharing that moment, a year later, the children in my literature study group understood my reaction to *Charlotte's Web* (1952) by E.B. White. "Charlotte was alone when she died." I couldn't silent read anymore. I closed the book as tears rolled down my face. Two students looked up from their silent reading, "Was your friend alone when he died? Did he have children?" They knew why I felt so much pain. The day before, my forty-year-old friend had suddenly died of a heart attack. They didn't need a lesson in how literature was affecting me and connecting to my life. They reached for some hope for me to carry on. "Did he have children too? You could be like Wilbur, try to be there for them, for him." They saw that literature held an answer to help me in a real life situation.

One way I can demonstrate my reading is sharing personal reactions, strategies, and questions that I have recorded in a literature study log such as I ask the children to do. Following are two examples of how the entries in my literature log demonstrate to students concrete reactions as well as some of my strategies which they will be able to relate to when they are reading.

Sept. 13

As I started reading *Daddy Long Legs* (1986) I wasn't sure of the depth that a book could have in a letter writing format; however, as I kept reading the letters drew me in. The letters were descriptive allowing me to envision the setting and also to know the main character as a person. She is a delight. I wonder how she can be so together and have only lived in the orphanage. I wasn't sure how to say her name, Jurusha so I have been just calling her Jay. I don't think she will ever find out who Daddy Long Legs really is. I have a feeling it is her real father.

Sept. 16

I was wrong about the real dad idea, now I think it is Master Jervis. I was not sure what Misanthropes are. I hope in discussion I can find out. Who will take care of the other children when she is gone?

I would hate to live in an institution all my life or even a day. I go to visit the children at the Fulton State Hospital and it makes me really glad I live in my own home. Could you believe she never had been in a house? I found out I certainly can't read French.

Students need to understand that readers have specific reasons for what text appeals to them and why.

When we were asked to select our favorite poems for a book that a group of children had decided to compile, I chose the following:

Off to school, I'm now college bound
    looking for my future that's waiting to be found.

A new home, a new world, an unknown place
    Around every corner is a new smiling face.

In control of my life, so many things to choose
    Exploring and taking risk, I have nothing to lose.

In the hub of excitement and important tasks
    There's an uneasiness I sense, something that lacks.

It's hard to pin down, I can't really describe
    The essence of missing deep down inside.

In search of confidence in a maze of stress
    Wanting security; nothing more, nothing less.

The realization hit like an enlightening bomb
    What I'm missing is. . . .

                . . . I'm missing my Mom.

After I read the poem. Monica asked, "Who was the author?" The students smiled when I told them that it was my daughter, Dana. They immediately understood. There was no need to explain; through my demonstration these students knew why readers value certain texts. We write to our special friends and family using text to let the readers know how we connect.

Some of the theorists that have guided my thinking about reading include Ken and Yetta Goodman, Louise Rosenblatt, Jerry Harste, Frank Smith, and Dorothy Watson.

Miscue analysis, a procedure to evaluate a reader's reading process, has been the strongest vehicle to show me how readers bring their background knowledge to the reading process which affects their interpretation and understanding of the text. Once I started using miscue analysis, as Dorothy Watson has said, "I never heard a reader the same way again." My belief of the reading process changed from a decoding theory to one of a transactional theory with the potential of meaning between the reader and the text.

Writing

I find participating is the most powerful form of demonstrating. What I want the children to engage in, I engage in also. If I am involved, I am lost in demonstration. I wonder at times if the reason I'm still in the classroom is because I finally get to learn. I value the explorations into the unknown, the time to read and write with interest, the intensity of my investment, and the knowledge gained.

I share with the children my processes as a genuine writer. I am not just a person there to teach them but to share my use and value of language. Many times as I write, I seek help from my students. I ask them for revision suggestions or editing needs. It is not a set-up situation, I really want their advice and the students know it. Students must see their teachers' efforts when writing as well as their products. They need to observe teachers as they write, to see all that is involved when engaging in writing. The times students observe and interact with teachers in the role of writers are an enormous benefit in their understanding of writing.

Our class had decided to write "family stories" as the major theme of one of the issues of our class magazine. This piece was to be about a family event that we would remember always. As other times, we started our pieces by talking out our ideas with a partner to help focus on the theme or to develop a plot. My partner saw me shift my idea of a piece about my mother to a specific incident that focused more on my brother. We free wrote after our oral brainstorming, then in response groups the writer got advice for making the writing clearer or more descriptive.

My piece changed because of my group members' suggestions for vocabulary, sentence structure, ideas, and questions about clarity. I accepted the students' suggestions with honesty. During this time I was able to point out the important components such as unity, sequencing, specifics, and voice. Many times students saw that I needed to focus on areas by elaborating and also by deleting ideas that went in another direction.

The students were able to see that my drafts were not tight, neat work, something all new writers do not realize. They saw how I pencilled in, crossed out, wrote marginal notes, referred to another sheet of paper to be inserted.

As we sat in our circle I read my first attempt. The children giggled, smiled, and looked confused. The questions flowed: Where were you? Why was your brother being bad? What happened to him next time? Then because I was not sure I had made a point clear, I ask if they understood about the neighbors' reactions. Through demonstrations, students see that a writer has to consider the readers' reactions and understandings.

The students also became my editors and helped with such things as spelling, verb-noun agreement, singular-plural agreement, and punctuation. They observed me using reference materials such as dictionaries, a thesaurus, and an atlas.

"The teacher appears lost in her thoughts as she writes," as Jack cautions Eric not to interrupt to wait, "I think she has a flow of ideas coming, she'll answer when she gets it down." Some observers may see this as an irresponsible instructor, however when analyzing the impact of a teacher being an active writer that is working within a classroom, one will see the teacher is demonstrating writing as a process that is used and valued.

Teachers who are writers know that writing takes time, patience, work, and commitment. Writing can bring joy, pain, and perhaps, a miracle. Teachers who write learn about their own struggles, making it possible to share their understanding with their students. In fact, I have now begun to envy some of my gifted young writers who can just sit down and write their flowing ideas.

Teachers must give real invitations to students for them to decide what is useful, enjoyable, and successful for themselves. Just because a teacher likes a certain kind of writing and has made that available to the students, that doesn't mean that the children will accept or should accept it as useful or valuable. I still hate writing poetry. I have written only a few poems because I find it almost impossible for me. I resent being given an assignment to write a poem, therefore I understand the difference between an invitation and an assignment. The students in our classroom do too. They need to be given information, models, demonstration, and suggestions for many kinds of writing, but never forced to do any of them, only encouraged and supported.

To let the students know that writing is a way of giving directions and information, I write the children many notes and make signs for the room, even when it would be easier to talk to them. Children then begin to use writing to work with each other in the classroom. Anything from asking advice, telling someone off, asking for supplies, or making plans becomes routine writing. Most children are hesitant to put up signs or to pass notes because these activities are not usually viewed as part of a writing curriculum. The notion of sending messages is to me critical to get students to value writing as something they need to use in life. Messages happen many times in many different situations: "Warning leave this project alone!" "Do not touch," and so forth. Notes give children power. A good example occurred last year. Each night after the children left, I turned off the bathroom light, wondering why the security guard always left it on. One night the guard was late so we arrived at the door at the same time. When I turned out the light, he said," Oh I thought the sign said to leave that on." When I looked in by the light switch, there in functional spelling, a note read "Lev Lit on fr plnt xprimnt" (Leave light on for plant experiment).

We ask that children use writing for real purposes that will help them organize their lives, to understand something, to remember—anything that is meaningful to them as humans.

Teachers should feel comfortable writing for personal and meaningful reasons when they are demonstrating the way they approach the writing process. When one of my students asked me which of my pieces that I had written was my favorite, I realized that my favorite piece was not part of the work I had written in the classroom. I realized that my writing in class had been on a surface level only, to demonstrate writing, not to really write for my own personal reasons. I realized that to demonstrate the writing process that I needed to write for my own real and meaningful purposes, as I was asking the students to do.

The class observes that I use a journal to record my ideas and feelings and also that I have a learning log that serves as a way to record questions that come up when I research. I always make a point of reading possibilities from my journal or log, asking my students which they would advise me to pursue. The children see that when keeping writing journals, writers can look back at entries that they felt they wanted to work on as a piece. Students who see this as a good strategy then begin to keep their own logs and journals.

All the students and the teacher in our classroom engage in research that is important to us; we take the responsibility of being in charge of a topic to give information to the entire class. Students need to realize that writing allows us to discover what we know as well as what we don't know. Therefore, when starting research, I first have the group write what we know about a topic, then what questions we want to answer. Soon the individuals use this procedure to guide the researchers to take notes on what they are investigating.

> "The encyclopedia doesn't tell me how the cool down affects the turbine in the nuclear reactor plant. Do you know, Eric?"
>
> "Well, here is a pamphlet from my text set on nuclear power that I think you'll find the answer to that question. If not, here is a phone number of the Callaway power plant. Some one there could tell you. By the way Ms. Copeland do you know if a presidential candidate has to have held a public office to run for president?"
>
> "Yes, here it is in this book."

We both are involved in our own research. Neither of us cares who is getting or giving support at the time. We are two researchers trying to answer our own questions; two learners seeking information with the help of the expert available in the community.

When looking at writing, the theorists and researchers who influenced my theory about reading also influence my theory about writing. Two other theorist who contributed to my understanding of writing are Donald Graves and Donald Murray.

Conferences: One on One Demonstration

Conferences held with individual students enable each student to talk about what he or she is doing and thinking about during the reading and writing

Figure 7-1   Valuing Writing: Mine/Ours/ Analysis

Name _____ Date _____

I.   Topics and Ideas

II. Language and Clarity

III. Organization and Design

IV. Mechanics and Conventions

V.   Other: Personalization, Socialization, Intertexuality

processes. The teacher has an opportunity to give new information or clear up misconceptions that the student may have by consciously sharing what he or she is doing during those processes. Simply thinking out loud illustrates to learners that all readers and writers can bring the process to a conscious level to help themselves figure out anything from spelling, punctuation, syntax, word meanings, or why one reads or writes a certain word.

Students can't be expected to discover all the ways of dealing with print such as taking notes, reacting to text, or revision without an experienced language user sharing ways that they take notes, interact with texts, or revise. During conferences I show individual students various ideas and strategies that I feel would be of specific help to that individual. I can do this because I know the students' needs, style, abilities, and strengths. Strategies I use as a reader and writer are shared with certain students because I have found them helpful for purposes that this student is needing at this time. Many of the ideas I use come from personal discovery; others come from resources produced for teachers such as *Creating Classroom Authors* (1988) by Jerry Harste, Kathy Short and Caroline Burke and NCTE'S *Ideas and Insights* (1987), edited by Dorothy Watson. The strategies and suggestions are valuable possibilities if they help or fit that learner's needs and style. The form illustrated in Figure 7-1 was developed by Dorothy Watson to help inform teachers and students about what the writer needs to focus or build on during writing conferences.

Evaluation: A Powerful Demonstration

Evaluation that nurtures language use and growth must be based on the teacher viewing evaluation as another way to demonstrate. The teacher uses evaluation as a way to support the student learning how to refine and evaluate their own work. Through interacting with the students, the teacher gives guidance, information, and suggestions to help the student become proficient. The major stance the teacher must always take when dealing with evaluation is trusting the students as being capable of evaluating their own growth in using language for different purposes.

Evaluation is a part of the curriculum instead of being a separate time set aside to test. Evaluation is a way for students to reflect on their own processes. They analyze their own reading and writing with others' input and by themselves. They fill out forms such as the following (see Figure 7-2) to think about what they are doing and how they are doing. A strong way to demonstrate to children that you see them as active, self-motivated learners is by having them set personal learning goals and record activities that will help them reach those goals (see Figure 7-3). After two weeks, the children evaluate how they did meeting their goals then find other ways to meet their goals or establish new goals.

A major factor of students' success is their being able to share their processes with others. Children that have had the demonstration of trust in

Figure 7-2   Students Evaluation on Peer's Reports

Date _____

Name _____

Evaluation on _____   Report

Topic _____

What I liked best:

What I think would have improved the report:

I learned:

I learned:

I would like to learn:

Figure 7-3   My Personal Goals

Name of Lit set book: _____

READING:

Activities:

How I think I did:

MATH—Concepts Studied _____
Activities:

WRITING—Types of Writing _____
Activities:

SOCIAL:

Activities:

SOCIAL STUDIES AND SCIENCE RESEARCH UNIT
Topics_____
Activities:

TEACHER COMMENTS:

PARENT COMMENTS:

STUDENT SIGNATURE _____

TEACHER SIGNATURE _____

PARENT SIGNATURE _____

their judgment of their own products begin to read like writers critiquing any works they read. Caroline was somewhat disturbed when one of her editors told her she had too many "ands." She exclaimed, "So does Gary Paulsen." I was not surprised with her self-defense in the form of writing Paulsen the following letter:

Tuesday, February 25,1992

Dear Gary Paulsen,

You youse to many ands in the book called the Winterroom. You even use 3 ands in one sentence. I am a little girl that writes stories and I don't use as many ands as you do if I do, I cross them out of my rough draft and then I do my final copy of my story. I think you shouldn't use that many ands in your books or talk about manure so much either. I don't write about gross things like that in my storys.

Sincerely yours,

Caroline

Students who have input on evaluation become articulate about writing and reading. When children are asked what their best or favorite pieces are, they have real reasons. Tracey liked the cat story she composed, because, it was a true story about my own cat. A true story is easier for me to write because I have the experience to come alive on the page. Caroline liked "The Monkey That Came Alive" because "it was so creative. It became creative because I let my imagination run, remembering other stories that had a similar theme." Nick liked "Bad Billy." "It was funny and I liked my reindeer character. I used funny human traits of people I see on TV or kids in school to develop my character." Matt chose his limerick because, "it was the easiest because poetry is the easiest to write because I love to play with rhymes." Each student has very real and different reasons for choosing the topic and genre best suited to them. Evaluation that works is a kind of demonstration that aids students in finding their strengths.

An important kind of evaluation looks at what is being used by the learner as a way communicating. I have found you must solicit information from the students to help develop the curriculum that ensures you are including all the possible uses of reading and writing. I ask my students questions that help me assess if the environment and curriculum are nurturing all the uses of written language. When I see an area that is not being used in our curriculum, I find ways of illustrating that type of writing or reading that will demonstrate to the students how it can be used to communicate. For instance, after interviewing the children about why we write, I noticed that no one mentioned to persuade or to change opinions. To give students a purpose to do so I set up a situation that would warrant such a need. The class had just voted in some new laws which were found unconstitutional by our supreme court (judges include a student, another teacher and myself). I then suggested that the students write letters to try and persuade the judges to change their opinions. It was then decided that their parents would vote on the final outcome. You can be sure the children wrote letters to parents to encourage them to vote yes.

Conclusion

Teachers interacting authentically with students make it possible for the teacher to value the learner as a person, not just a name to judge in a grade book. When I entered education, I had visions of being a positive influence to children, helping each of them become positive, self-sufficient learners. It is not that I didn't try to know each child personally, but I just didn't get to the learner as a person in a textbook-driven curriculum. The learner was looked at as a receiver of my information not as an active, responsible individual, a transmitter as well as a receiver. The interactions I have when working with readers and writers is a way to get to the child as a person. When I moved from a teacher giving information to a teacher engaged as a reader and writer, it allowed students to become engaged themselves. When children encounter teachers who see themselves as real writers and readers instead of instructors, they see the benefits of how written language can enhance our lives. The teacher's demonstrations encourages students to become learners that use reading and writing to enhance their lives and no gold stars are needed.

References

Harste, J., Short, K. & Burke, C. (1988). *Creating classrooms for authors.* Portsmouth, NH: Heinemann.

Pitts, P. (1988). *Racing the sun.* New York, NY: Avon Books.

Watson, D. (Ed.). (1987). *Ideas and insights: K-6 language arts.* Urbana, IL: National Council of Teachers of English.

Webster, J. (1986). *Daddy-long-legs.* New York, NY: Bantam Books.

White, E.B. (1952). *Charlotte's web.* New York, NY: Harper.

8

Bringing Children to Literacy Through Drama

SHERYL MCGRUDER

I suspect that teachers who have been reluctant to use drama in their classrooms will be much encouraged by reading this chapter. McGruder distinguishes dramatic experiences from free play as she offers many examples of how to implement drama in the classroom. Sheryl helps the reader appreciate the value of drama in assisting students to develop autonomy, gain a deeper understanding of language, refine concepts of story, and improve social structure in the classroom community. We see how McGruder places an emphasis on process rather than product and how this results in improved products. Many of the suggestions Sheryl makes here could be coupled with the ideas of Shelor's and Porterfield's chapters.

My introduction to drama happened slowly over a number of years. My husband and I have always been terrified of speaking before groups and wanted to make sure our son didn't suffer the same malady. So when my friend, Nancy Helland, opened The Creative Place, a school that encouraged creativity through drama, dance, and puppetry, we enrolled our son Matt as a student. Matt attended The Creative Place for several years and during that time Nancy and I visited often about how the wonderful experiences that worked so well with small groups of children could be adapted for classroom use. I learned to interpret the meaning of the word drama to include creative dramatics, puppetry, movement, and vocalization. She recommended readings (many are listed in the bibliography), and invited me to help with productions at the local library. Finally, in exchange for my volunteer work at The Creative Place, Nancy came into my second grade classroom to demonstrate her teaching strategies and to see if they worked in a public school setting. I am not a quick study, plus it was lots of fun having Nancy in the classroom, so she visited for several years. We worked on creative dramatics exercises and developed pieces of literature and music into plays without script for puppets or live actors.

Any time a teacher brings a new activity to the classroom he or she must consider its impact on the curriculum, and how it will fit in with the beliefs he or she holds about learning. I soon realized how useful drama could be in helping children develop autonomy, while at the same time enriching the total learning experience. The evidence of my own son's growth and development along these lines encouraged me to bring dramatic experiences to my school children as well. Using drama in school also has a powerful impact on the social structure of the classroom community. Creative dramatics and other dramatic activities are a wonderful way to help children develop a strong self-concept, gain a better understanding of language, and to come to grips with the concept of story.

As all teachers know, there are some activities we choose or the children choose that are more conducive to the development of community. Many teachers I've known through the years pick learning events in which they themselves are interested. They become known as the cooking teacher, the science teacher, the book making teacher, the juggling teacher, or the rapping teacher. Sometimes the children are the ones to generate special interests. For example, one year we were into classroom pets in a big way, both short term and long term. Our class was given a pair of baby guinea pigs that lived for nine years. These shared interests contribute a great deal to the development of community. The last ten years I've been known as the drama teacher, or the puppet teacher. Several times throughout the year Room 107 gets involved in dramatic arts projects of one kind or another. Through these social learning events the children and I cooperate, problem solve, communicate, create, and in every way exercise the functions of community.

Millie Greimann, in her book called *Creative Dramatization* (1973), explains like this:

> Everybody is bones, skin, senses, feelings, ideas, imagination, spirit. Grown-ups are all of these, sometimes. Kids are all of these, always. Each child is a special mixture of sensitivity, spontaneity, energy. How many times people have said to me. The magic of childhood— how soon it is over. Where does it go? It doesn't go anywhere. Everybody's got it; the trick is to use it. Most grown-ups keep it captive. Why? Kids spin out this magic into an endless, complex weave of color and movement. Creative dramatization provides the pulse and the impulse which make happenings of this magic.

Greimann's co-author Katrina Van Tassel, feels

> Creative dramatization provides opportunity for language: the language of the body, the senses, the emotions, and the language of words. Like love, it is a bridge, a communication from me to you, involving the whole being.

In their book called *Creative Drama for the Classroom Teacher* (1981), Ruth Heinig and Lyda Stillwell explain how a teacher might incorporate creative drama into a full curriculum.

> Creative drama, then, need not be considered a special subject area. Since it incorporates so many desirable educational goals, it can be used in conjunction with many subject areas whether they be the language arts, science, social studies, or the fine acts.

Understanding Dramatic Experiences

Early creative dramatic experiences are not to be confused with free play or with children's theater. Creative dramatics must have rules that are understood by everyone in the class. Procedures and limits must be set so that everyone, including the teacher, feels comfortable. Unlike free play, creative dramatic play is stimulated by the teacher and/or the literature so that an environment for the creative play is set. But like free play each child responds to the stimulus out of his or her own imagination and experience in an individual way. In contrast to children's theater, creative dramatic experiences do not entail memorized lines, choreographed movements, or director initiated feelings or plot. The activities should be fast-paced and of a wide variety. The children's spontaneous ideas are valued and accepted. For example, if a child is trying a cat-like movement with his or her body or puppet that is especially good, this is a time to stop the whole group and have them observe. Sharing ideas and experimenting with a variety of ideas is encouraged. Through this activity the spirit of fun and creativity becomes part of the curriculum.

Later when everyone knows the rules of creative dramatics and puppetry and the reasons for them, the children will be able to work comfortably in small groups with student leaders. These rules or working structures can be developed with the children in the same democratic manner as the classroom rules. We all need rules to live by, to guide our actions. Children, like everyone else, need limits to be set and consequences to be understood and agreed upon. There will be more about the working structure in the Getting Started section.

In creative dramatics a leader guides the group in a variety of ways. The first is through example, followed by an invitation to join in a new activity. Heinig and Stillwell offer teachers these encouraging words,

> The leader need not be skilled in playing; in fact, one could intimidate some children by being too accomplished. Participation should, instead, emphasize the spirit of play rather than the skill. If one is enthusiastic and appears to enjoy the experiences, the children are encouraged to participate and to relax and enjoy themselves also.

The value of using drama with children is found in their improved self-confidence, ability to express themselves creatively, positive social attitudes and relationships, emotional stability and self-control, and bodily coordination. In drama, an activity or exercise presents a confronting idea that may be either vague or clearly defined. The teacher or leader presents the stimulus and sets the stage, which might include ground rules for the activity and a setting for the story. One child or a group of children then encounters the idea and begins a problem-solving process which enables them to invent and create dialogue, action, and staging which makes it possible for the story to emerge.

Side coaching, when the teacher moves through the group offering encouragement and honest praise, is also important. In the beginning everyone works together, or at least in groups. I certainly feel safer in numbers when doing something that is potentially embarrassing. The children will feel safer, more willing to try out a voice or movement, more willing to show an emotion when a sense of trust has developed. All of these events must take place in a warm environment free from ridicule or this sense of trust will not develop and the children will be hesitant to participate.

It has always been my feeling that children of school age would benefit greatly from the opportunity to express themselves freely in a wider variety of ways than the usual art projects and writing activities found in most elementary classrooms. They also need opportunities to make use of the five tools of creative expression: emotions, body, voice, imagination, and control. There is another very important outcome of creative expression. Pretending, being other than who we are, helps us become more adaptable, more able to accept people and other beings as they are. Being other than who we are enables us to comprehend what might be.

The leader must believe that he or she is free and extend that freedom to the children. There is really no right or wrong answer here. There are simply expressions of the inner self. We all must believe in our selves, adults and children. One's inner self is a most precious commodity because it is the basis of inner strength. Pride in our individual heritage is an integral part of this inner strength. People who are taught to please, to follow orders, to do what others have decided is right, bypass their inner selves. They become other-directed. To help them develop their inner selves, invite the children to begin seeing with the mind's eye, listening to their inside ear and hearing their inside voices, making pictures in their minds. This is imagination, but it is more than imagination. It is mind stretching, considering all the possibilities before making choices or solving problems.

The purpose of creative dramatics and puppetry is to promote the personal growth and educational development of the participant, not entertain an audience or to train actors. They do however help children become more comfortable when they are in front of an audience.

Are You Having Questions?

You might think, "But this has no academic value." Emphasis is placed on development of self-esteem, a sense of uniqueness and ability to create, to problem solve. It has been my experience that children who have been encouraged to express themselves creatively, using all of their body and mind later go on to do a better job of expressing themselves in more academic forms. For example, once the concept of story is understood in a dramatic sense through creative dramatics or puppetry, teachers will be pleasantly surprised at the exciting changes that occur in creative writing.

You might wonder, "Would drama-related activities fit into a multicultural curriculum?" The cultural background of drama is extremely diverse. Every culture celebrated its history, current events, and even religion through dance, puppetry, story telling, and dramatic presentation, long before written language made it possible to record such events. By sharing culturally unique stories and experiences, children can connect with each other on a human level without losing their own identity.

You might think, "There may not be a finished product to show, no art piece to hang up, no performance to give." It is true that the emphasis is on the process and the experience itself and not on the finished product or the performance. However, when you do choose to involve your children in a major project, writing their own books, preparing a favored piece of literature for a performance, I can guarantee an improved product.

You might also feel that you could never overcome your own inhibitions. I always think this. Just go ahead and do it anyway. Stick to your feelings, your beliefs. Decide for yourself if your students are happier, feeling better about themselves, and if you are all having fun.

Moving Forward With Puppetry

Since first beginning drama I've tried all kinds of dramatic arts activities with my children. Before creating a story in any form, children need to become familiar with all forms of stories. At the beginning of every year I invite children to retell familiar folk and fairy tales using finger puppets. Sometimes I tell children old stories from all over the world and the children join in with variations they have heard. They are able to demonstrate their knowledge of the elements of a story, the sequence of events, and character interaction in the stories. Sometime the children become interested in changing one element in the tale to see how the story will be affected. I call this the "what if" factor. By manipulating stories in this way, children learn that they can control the story; they can be authors.

The next thing I usually do is ask the children to make up stories of their own to tell using easy-to-make stick puppets. Again we talk about what constitutes a story, what makes the story fun to hear and what is interesting to watch. Later when the children write stories of their own, I refer to these experiences when we talk about ways to make our writing more interesting. These experiences are the roots of story revision and critique.

There are many books in print on how to make and use puppets with children. My favorites are listed in the bibliography. Most teachers I know watch expenses when choosing projects to do with their children. One of the best and most inexpensive projects is stick puppets. A number of materials may be used as sticks: paint stirrers or yard sticks for larger puppets, popsicle sticks, drinking straws, pipecleaners, and bamboo skewers. Tag board, construction paper, pom-poms, bits of felt, and other cloth can be used to make the body of the puppet. Little wiggly eyes, buttons, or small beads can be used for eyes. Students' families are usually happy to contribute other trimmings for a "bits and pieces box" to add sparkle and personality to the puppets.

Some of the oldest and most failure-proof puppets children can make are shadow puppets. This idea was given to me by April Koonse, a puppeteer working in Columbia, Missouri. Shadow puppets may be made with scraps of construction paper, tissue paper or colored acetate, and bamboo skewers. The child cuts the shape of the puppet out of construction paper, then punches or cuts holes that can be covered with colored tissue paper or acetate. The finished puppet is then fastened to a bamboo skewer with a masking tape hinge that allows the puppet movement and makes it easier to work. Use a piece of tape about two inches long and stick about half an inch of the end of the skewer through the center, press the tape together around the skewer, and leave the ends open to be pressed to the back of the puppet.

An old white sheet stretched on a frame or large piece of white paper taped over a good sized opening cut in a large cardboard carton will serve as a shadow screen. All that remains is the light source—an overhead projector works very well. The puppeteers stand behind the shadow screen with the light source behind them. Holding the ends of the skewers they move the puppets across the screen as the story unfolds. If a tree or some other puppet needs to be stationary the end of the skewer can be stuck into a large piece of styrofoam to hold it still and free both hands to move other puppets.

Sometimes the end of the year project is a puppet project call Fingerkins. The children begin by creating a world in which the story will take place. The children draw pictures, make lists, and jot down possible adventures for their Fingerkin characters. The next step is to create a story. I've tried this several ways: generating the whole story orally and then presenting the story with the puppets; or writing the story first, then performing it with the puppets. The best dialogue between characters comes from the oral stories. When the stories were written first, the children became narrators, and the puppets said very little. The very best presentations developed from stories that began orally, were presented with puppets, and later written down so the children would not forget the story. Many of the children included dialogue in these stories, but others wrote stories that were basically outlines for the actual performance. These stories were bound and pockets included for the puppets. The final step was to create box stages for the puppet plays. The scenery is not large, no taller than the distance from the child's finger tip to arm pit, because they must be able to reach over the scenery to manipulate the puppet on the box stage. A great follow-up activity is to let the children work in pairs, combining their puppets to create new stories. I try to time the Fingerkin project to end in May. It's a wonderful way to end the year and keeps the children happily engaged to the very last day.

Unlike the puppets mentioned earlier, Fingerkins are not inexpensive or easy to make, but they are very durable. The blank puppet is made of felt with a popsicle stick spine. Parents have always been willing to sew the fifty to eighty blank puppets that are required for each child to have two or three characters for their plays. I always send a pattern home with the children so more puppets can be created at home. Once the children know what the characters will be, we begin construction. We use a glue gun to decorate the puppets, especially to attach the wiggly eyes. The children design their puppets and attach things to them with straight pins, then bring the puppets to me for gluing. While a few of the children and I are involved in the gluing process, the rest of the group is working on stages and scenery (tag board), perfecting the stories, helping each other cut pieces of fabric, wrapping yarn for hair, and so on.

It is not necessary for children to make puppets to benefit from their use. A collection of puppets from past years may be kept in the classroom for the children to use in stories of their own design, so that the class doesn't spend the time and expense necessary to construct new puppets every year.

Moving Ahead with Creative Dramatics

The bibliography gives a list of resources which contain quick activities for working on the isolated skills of creative dramatics that involve the use of emotion, body, voice, imagination, and control—mini lessons if you will. Only a few minutes are needed to snap on a tape of music containing mechanical sounds and to invite the children to stride around the room as robots or giant earth moving machines for a movement mini-lesson. Creating sound pictures while everyone sits in their seats is a good voice lesson. After reading *A Story, A Story* (1970) by Gail Haley, we might creep around the classroom like Anansi the Spider, searching through the jungle for a leopard. Or we might work on concentration and control while waiting in line for lunch by having the children pair off and gaze into each others eyes without giggling or looking away. These activities are loads of fun and at the same time build confidence and prepare the students for more involved experiences later on. The books listed in the bibliography and many others found on library shelves will offer other mini-lessons or creative dramatics exercises that use body, voice, and imagination.

If a teacher wishes to dramatize a piece of literature, after everyone is familiar with the story, the group needs to discuss the voice, movement, and motivation of the various characters. When I read aloud to the class I use different voices and the children quickly try some of their own. If you have ever seen a good story teller, you have been as thrilled as I have by the way he or she uses her whole body and voice to excite our imaginations. This use of voice and movement helps the children understand who the characters are and what they are doing in the story.

There is an activity I call Quick Drama, that takes about 30 minutes from beginning to end. This is a super introduction to dramatizing literature. The teacher takes the first step, which is to select a good piece of literature, one with lots of action, and two or three very different characters. My favorite story for this purpose is *The Funny Little Woman* (1972), by Arlene Mosel. I do the first reading using voice and some body movements for the characters. The first time children see me do this they usually think their teacher is really crazy. Once they get into the fun, the shock quickly evaporates. For the second reading I pass out copies of the book and invite the children to read along. Some of the children will join in with the "Tee, hee, hee" of the Funny Little Woman and make up a few disgusting feeding noises for the Wicked Oni. If the children have already had creative dramatics experiences and feel comfortable and safe within the group, they enjoy developing the voices and movement for the characters in the story. After the second reading the group selects a section of the story to act out. The class divides itself into three groups: the Little Woman, the Wicked Oni and the Jitsu Sama. I begin to read the story again, inviting the children to recreate the action in the story. If children are shy or seem unsure, I move from character to character to help them get started. In the next step I separate the children into small groups of five or six and ask each group to choose an event in the story they would like to present. I must be prepared to lend support if needed. Because several children are playing each character, there is seldom reluctance to participate.

I'm sure there is a time and place for scripts, but drama without scripts is lots more fun, and much more freeing. When the children know the story, the characters and the sequence of action, it's not necessary to repeat the exact words each time for the actors to keep to the story line. Every child knows what is needed and what must be done to move the story along.

This activity is of short duration and fits very well into a theme cycle. If the class is studying habitats, for example, I would choose a set of books that roughly fit that topic. This year we chose several titles including two Bill Peet books, *Farewell to Shady Glade* (1966) and *The Wump World* (1970). I divided the children into groups of three or four and asked them to choose one event in a book to present to the class. After each presentation we discussed what happened and how the audience felt about what they saw. We had the same sort of discussion that arise from literature study. In a way this was a literature study event, except the parts of the stories the children dramatized were held up for closer examination. The actors especially had a different view, because they were inside the story.

A related strategy involving small groups makes use of situation cards. At first I compose the cards. Later the children contribute situations. Habitat theme situations might include: being caught in a strong wind storm; finding a blackberry patch on a hot summer day; a huge bear rises out of the blackberry patch as you are both reaching for the same juicy berry; catching a really big fish; mice being chased by a cat; and soon. The children dramatize the event using only body movement. The rest of the class, which makes up the audience, tried to guess the situation. The situations can also be dramatized with sounds. After participating in this activity children begin to make it their own. Last year one group of boys began their presentation on Colonial America by dramatizing a friendly meeting with Indians. After this silent drama they went on to explain how later meetings became unfriendly and why.

Using creative dramatics and puppetry is part of our classroom life throughout the year. We try to take something to the production level with an audience from outside our classroom twice a year. This step requires much time and energy on everybody's part, but the amount of pleasure it brings and what's learned by working through the process makes it all worthwhile. We usually select pieces of literature that lend themselves to dramatizing. Folk tales are my favorite, especially African folktales. For primary grades stories with repeated phrases are very good. We have masks, costumes, and scenery from past plays which speed things along. We begin these big projects in easy steps, using the techniques described earlier to develop characters, movement, and voice, then gradually refine the process to gearing up for the big production. In this way the children prepare for what lies ahead and have ideas about what might work in their roles. Another good reason for working on all the characterizations and situations as a group is that just in case the class is struck with chicken pox the week of the presentation, another child can quickly step into the role. Because there are no scripts to memorize, but rather a well-structured story that all the children in the class know very well, the actors say and do what is needed to move the story along. It is true that, like other language arts, the greatest value in drama lies in the process, but a final product is also very satisfying.

Drama and Children as Authors

Several years after integrating creative dramatics activities into my classroom, Dr. Nancy Knipping from the University of Missouri came to me with an idea for helping children revise their own writing through drama. Primary age children believe that once something is written on paper they are finished with it. In fact some children do not even reread to see if they left anything out. Because I wanted to encourage children to revise and edit their work, I thought drama would be a wonderful way to engage the children's interest in this important life skill. We began by inviting the children to write the rough drafts of stories in their writing journals. This strategy was different from the single draft stories, complete with illustrations that they often chose to write. It also proved to be difficult for some children who draw first and then write, so we were flexible on this point. One child said he would write his rough draft on the left side of the paper and leave space on the right in the event he might want to add something.

When some of the children had written their first drafts, we asked if they would like to invite their classmates to help them dramatize their stories to see if the drama gave the author any ideas about changing something in the story. The author came to the front of the group and read his or her piece to the audience seated on the carpet. The children who wished to participate in the drama raised their hands and were called upon by the author. We encouraged the children to pick boys and girls who had not had turns recently. The rest of the class worked on some project of their own, while the author directed the cast and the actors offered suggestions and asked questions of the author. Many times the actors asked if they could add something they had thought of during the first reading. Some authors agreed to major changes, while others wanted the story acted out primarily as they had written it.

When the actors were ready, usually in about ten to fifteen minutes, the audience was called back and the drama began. Some authors kept very tight control of the story and actually fed the actors their lines, and the actors performed as directed. Other times the author would begin to read and the actors would go on alone. Sometimes the author would just read the title, then step back and allow the story to unfold. After the drama, the author and the actors would take seats in front of the audience and the whole group would discuss the story, the drama, or the acting. We talked about what we liked, what we wondered about, some children picked up gaps in logic. The children quickly learned the role of audience in this context and took their responsibility seriously. I helped keep the discussion going and also took notes.

As a member of the group I also made comments and asked questions. In the beginning I tried to model appropriate comments about real concerns. "I wondered about . . . ," or "I didn't understand . . . ," "What did you think about the dialogue added by the actors?" were some examples of comments I thought might focus the authors attention on the drama. Occasionally, if a child made a comment like, "I think the boy should say more." I would ask, "What do you think he should say?" In some cases if the comments were too general and not much help to the author, I would ask for more information. As time passed the authors would ask the students making suggestions for more information. Most of the time the speakers could give more information, but sometimes they couldn't.

The way the children were seated seemed important during the discussion. After some trial and error we felt the best way was to have the children seated around the large area rug. When the children could easily see and hear everyone, they spoke directly to each other and stayed focused on the task.

We also tried various methods of taking notes on the discussions and saving the children's comments in order to have them available if and when the authors decided to revise their stories. What seemed to work best was for me to sit in the group circle next to the overhead (turned off) so I could jot down a few names or key phrases. Then when the discussion seemed to be over, I flipped it on, and with the help of the audience and the author wrote down the most important points from the discussion. This way the author could tell us what was the most helpful, and at the same time, we could all review what had happened.

The story dramas took place once or twice a week, with two children dramatizing their stories. We began with children who had a revision ready to read, and moved on to the new stories ready for dramatization. Not every child wrote a story to be dramatized, and some children wrote several.

Information pieces with no action were read and discussed, but not drama-tized. Several times the children asked questions of the author which en-couraged the author to find more information or to clarify something.

Our original purpose was to help the children "resee" (Graves, 1983) their stories to aid the revision process. As usually happens with children, you don't often get what you expect. Many of the children did use the information from the drama and discussions to revise their writing, clear-ing up questions their classmates asked, adding dialogue for characters and taking out things that did not fit with the story. Alison's story, *The Little Old Lady Who Loved Ham*, is a very good example of this type of revision.

Alison's Story

The Little Old Lady Who Loved Ham

There was once a little old lady who loved ham. In fact, the only thing she ate was ham, and the only thing she drank was ham juice. But one day when she went to the store to get some more ham (because her supply was running low), she got her purse and got into her little Corvette and drove into town. When she got to the store and went to the section where there were usually tons and tons of ham, but when she got there, there was only one pack of ham. Then she turned around and there was a little old man with all the ham that was usually there except for one pack! She got so mad she went straight home. The next day when she went out to get the paper, she discovered that the little old man was her neighbor. Five years later. After five years of the whole neighborhood having to hear them fighting, they finally figured out a plan. They would send a fake love letter from the little old man. When they finally got up enough never to send it, the little old lady got so happy that she invited him over to have some lunch. While eating, they de-cided to make friends. "Let's be friends, shall we?" asked the little old man. "Why, I guess we shall," said the little old lady. And the neighbors never had to hear them fight again.

During the discussion that followed the dramatization, Alison's class-mates made the following suggestions for her story:

Sunni: I think the lady should be even more surprised when she found out that the man who took all the ham was her neighbor.

Michael: I think she should be even madder when the man took the ham. She just went (pounded fist in air) and walked away.

Katy: She could faint because she was so mad.

Morgan: I think it should tell what they said when the man took all the ham.

Mrs. M.:   So, more dialogue at the store, you think?

Troy: I think they should eat ham when they make friends.

Sunni: I think you should say something about what they said when they were fighting.

Mrs. M.:   Well, you didn't have anything about their fighting, did you?

Alison: I just said they fought for five years.

Troy: Let's act it out.

Mrs. M.:   All right, let's have the characters work through a short fight scene.

Jessica (OLD LADY):   How dare you take all that ham?

Michael (OLD MAN):   Well, I needed it!

Jessica: Give some back!

Michael: No, I got there first!

Jessica: Selfish!

Alison worked on her story periodically for several months. This is her final version:

The Little Old Lady Who Loved Ham

There was once a little old lady who LOVED ham. All she ate was ham and all she drank was ham juice. One day the little old woman decided to go to the store (because her supply was running low). So, she got her purse and went to her little Corvette and drove off. When she got to the grocery store and went to the ham section, she saw a little old man grabbing all the ham he could see! So, the little old lady got the manager. She told him what the little old man was doing and made him put most of it away. So the little old woman only got twelve packages of ham. The next day when the little old lady went to get the mail, she saw the little old man. She figured out that he was her neighbor. They got into a fight. First the little old lady, "How dare you move in next door to me?" Then the old man, "Oh, yeah, well it's a free country!" In the maddest way they could, they both ran in their houses and slammed the doors behind them. Five years later. After five years of the whole neighborhood having to hear them fight, they got together one afternoon. An hour after they got there one of them said, "I've been thinking, why don't we make a prank phone call to the little old lady and say that she won a trip to the fanciest restaurant in town. Then she'll ask all of us and we'll say "no" and she'll be forced to ask the little old man and he'll surely say "yes". "Hold it, hold it," said another neighbor, "Where are they going to get the money?" We'll give it to them! piped up another one. So the next morning they all got asked and guess what they said. "NO!" And she was forced to ask the little old man. Guess what he said? "YES!" Just like they had planned. Over dinner they decided to be friends. Guess what they ordered? HAM!

Some of the children used their classmates' suggestions, but more often something that happened in the drama would appear in the story. The thing that we didn't expect was that ideas from the drama and discussion that were not used by the author whose story was being shared, were used in other children's stories later on, much later in some cases. Occasionally wonderful improvisations would occur when something one actor did caused the other actors to react in ways not expected by the author. The authors reacted differently: some would reread the part of the story misacted; others would laugh, obviously enjoying the changes happening in their stories, but often chose not to include the changes in their revision.

Many experiences affect childrens' writing. In the case of Alexa, many influences are reflected in her story. I believe drama was the catalyst which allowed these experiences to come together and work for Alexa in her writing. When Alexa was Star of the Week, she invited her father to school to tell stories of his childhood in the Caribbean. He told the class of an experience with a shark that Alexa later wrote and decided to dramatize. Here is the first draft of that story.

Alexa's Story

Once my dad was fishing. He waited and waited and waited and waited and waited and finally he caught something, a rock. So he put on his scubbadiving gear and went to get his hook. And as he approached the rock a shark came the other way. He swam away and thought, boy that was close.

The drama was very good and the actors and the audience had a wonderful time. The child playing her father added "Mom, did you see that big shark?" The discussion was long and several good suggestions were made that would lengthen the story. Someone asked where the story took place and what did the people say to each other. Several children remembered things her father had said in the original telling. Dialogue was suggested between the boy and his mother. Alexa waited a few days and began work on her revision. She decided to rewrite the story from each character's point of view, her dad, his mother, and the shark. She ended up combining her dad's and grandmother's version. This is the final draft.

Dad

Once my dad was fishing on the beach. He said, "So Mom, how did your operation go?"

"Fine, but my hip is killing me. I think you caught something! A fish, a fish!"

"No, Mom. I caught a rock. I don't want to break my new hook! I'll get my scuba gear." Dad swam over the rock.

He saw the shark and turned around and said, "Mom, Mom! Did you see that shhhhhh!"

"Calm down Dear, you're safe now."

"I know buttttt it would have eaten me if I diddddn't swim to shore."

"Okay, okay. I get the point!"

Shark

Hi, I'm Deadly Fin the shark, call me Deadly. Well, as you know a guy came trespassing in my territory. So by instinct I chased him away. And do you believe it? He was scared! Boy, was he scared!

I asked Alexa why she decided to write the story from two points of view and she said, "It seemed more fair to tell both sides, like in *The True Story of the Three Little Pigs* (1989)."

The drama/discussion strategy proved to be more valuable that just an aid to the revision process. It changed the way my second graders thought about writing. It seemed they considered their audience more. I also noticed they reread more often during the writing process. The other outcome that grew out of this strategy, and the sense of community that developed in my classroom, was that children frequently asked to dramatize incomplete stories so the audience and the actors could offer the help they needed to bring their story to an interesting conclusion. Many times seeing the story unfold gave the author the ideas they needed. Ownership of the stories always remained with the authors; they decided whether and how to use suggestions and where to make changes.

We also noticed changes in children who never or seldom wrote a story to be dramatized. Some of the children who wrote less often were favored as actors and were frequently recognized for their creativeness and their ability to improvise dialogue and content. This was a great boost to the ego of children who did not write as much as others. It would be interesting to see if this experience helped them to use their unique ideas in their own writing in the future.

On one occasion, we began the story drama strategy very early in the school year, before the children had much drama experience. This told us that experience with creative dramatics was not necessary for the story drama strategy to work. It may have helped, in that the dramas themselves were better, but the affect upon the childrens' writing remained the same. The story drama activity is able to stand alone. However, the control that children develop through experience with creative drama helps to make the whole process work more smoothly. A strong sense of community is required for this strategy to work. The children must be able to trust the teacher and their classmates to not make thoughtless comments before they will be willing to take the risk of presenting their work to an audience.

Getting Started

When considering activities in the classroom that involve lots of movement, and vocalization or student responsibility for group work, you might be thinking, "I'm afraid I'll lose control. How will the children react to all that freedom? It's going to get too noisy in here." As with anything you choose to do with children a certain structure is required or chaos will result. It is necessary to create balance—balance between freedom and discipline, between giving and taking, between concentrating and relaxing, between being free and being restricted, between imagination and reality. My friend Nancy Helland calls it the working law. What is needed is a way of working, a carefully constructed set of directions crafted with the help of the children and well understood in advance of beginning the drama activity. The working directions provide the framework for a creative environment. No teasing, no running into each other, and there is no right way to portray a character. The rules for working in a group are always there and allow us to create in an accepting environment.

Working directions vary according to the teacher's and students' tolerance for noise and movement in the classroom. If children choose not to follow the rules, they expect a logical consequence to follow after a warning. The children are usually having so much fun that simply having them "sit this one out" is enough. If someone is sitting out too often, going over the rules and the reason for the rules is helpful.

Modelling and side coaching are very helpful, in fact necessary for success. In the case of the mini-lessons, many of the activities you might choose to do are silent, the only rules are not talking, no touching. Here are suggestions for working in a group. Some are directions and some are environmental and social strategies.

Freeze—(as in Freeze Tag) or any agreed upon signal like a tambourine, that will stop all sound and movement immediately, focusing all attention on the leader.

Relax—relax muscles and listen quietly follows freeze, focus remains on the leader.

Focus—concentrate on specific activity, person, or sound.

Working space—child is visible and not touching anyone else. Sometimes it is necessary to work with half the group at a time to have enough space.

Sharing circle—a time and place for everyone to share ideas, to think about and discuss what happened in the activity.

Sharing and accepting ideas—no negative comments, questions for clarification are fine, willingness to deal with an idea, to try, to experiment, save unused ideas for another time.

Audience—how to be a good audience and behavior before an audience is carefully taught as we change from audience to performer. Understanding why and how we react, applaud, and laugh.

Suggestions to Consider Before Beginning

Be confident.

Remember always that the process of creating should be enjoyable.

Set up the environment. You need a large open space. In the classroom we push the desks back and half the class works while the other half observes. It might be best to begin in the classroom until everyone understands the working directions. Later when it's not being used for P.E., the gym is a large enough space to work with the whole group at once. A quick review of the working directions helps to ensure a pleasant experience for all. Working in bare feet also creates the mood that this is a special activity and saves stepped on toes. (No socks, too slippery.)

Use your voice for side coaching.

Music can be used to set the atmosphere and helps the children to become involved.

Begin with activities in which all the children you are working with at the moment participate simultaneously.

There is no right or wrong answer; emphasize imagination and creativity.

Never force a child to participate. Have a place in mind for a nonparticipant to sit quietly and watch.

Do not allow disruptions. Remove children who are having difficulty following rules to the resting or time out spot.

Adapt activities in accordance with your own ideas and experiences. Just use what you already know about children, learning, and life. Exercise your freedom of expression and allow the children the right to express themselves.

Do it your way, but don't hesitate to collaborate. Sometimes the best things come from the minds of two or more people working together.

The strength of drama in the curriculum is social and personal, academic, and imaginative. Drama allows children to take risks in a safe environment. It provides a socially acceptable way for children to get attention. Drama builds self-confidence. It allows children and teachers to find and appreciate the uniqueness in others, and perhaps more importantly, in themselves. Drama requires cooperation and group effort. It requires a balance between freedom and self-discipline. It helps children develop the ability to relax, to concentrate, to remember, to focus and to imagine. Drama provides children with a broader means of creative expression. And finally, because children are encouraged to use all the tools of language, body, voice, and mind, they become better, happier learners within an academic setting.

References

Brooks, M. Curriculum Development from a Constructivist Perspective, *Educational Leadership*, Dec. 1986/Jan. 1987, *44*(4), 63–67.

Dewey, J. (1938). *Experience and education*. New York: Collier Books, Macmillan Publishing Co.

Gartrell, D. (1987). Assertive discipline: Unhealthy for children and other living things, *Young Children*, *42*(2), 10–11.

Graves, D. (1983). *Writing: Teachers and children a work*, Exeter, N.H.: Heinemann.

Heinig, R. & Stillwell, L. (1981). *Creative drama for the classroom teacher*. Englewood Cliffs, NJ: Prentice-Hall.

Helland, N. (1983–1987). Personal interviews.

Hunt, T. & Renfro, N. (1982). *Puppetry in early childhood education*. Austin, TX: Nancy Renfro Studios.

Kamii, C. (1985). *Young children reinvent arithmetic*. New York: Teachers College Press.

Nicholls, B. (1974) *Move*. Boston: Plays, Inc.

Noblemann, R. (1979). *Mime and masks*. Hartford, CT: New Plays Books.

Peck, J. (1979). *Leap to the sun*. Englewood Cliffs, NJ: Prentice-Hall.

Renfro, N. (1982). *Puppetry and the art of story creation*. August, TX: Nancy Renfro Studios.

Sims, J. (1988). *Puppets for dreaming and scheming*. Santa Barbara, CA: The Learning Works.

Stewig, J. (1983). *Informal drama in the elementary language arts program*. New York: Teachers College Press.

Van Tassel, K. & Greimann, M. (1973). *Creative dramatization*. New York: Macmillan.

Children's Books Cited in the Chapter

Allard, H. (1977). *Miss Nelson is missing!*. Boston: Houghton Mifflin.

Aardema, V. (1977). *Who's in rabbit's house?* New York: Dial.

dePaola, T. (1975). *Strega Nona.* New York: Prentice-Hall.

Haley, G. E. (1970). *A story, a story.* New York: Macmillan.

Lobel, A. (1970). *Frog and toad are friends.*New York: Harper & Row.

Mosel, A. (1972). *The funny little woman.* New York: E.P. Dutton.

Peet, B. (1966). *Farewell to Shady Glade.* Boston: Houghton Mifflin.

Peet, B. (1970). *The Wump world.* Boston: Houghton Mifflin.

Scieszka, J. (1989). *The true story of the three little pigs!* New York: Viking Penguin.

Steig, W. (1969). *Sylvester and the magic pebble.* New York: Simon & Schuster.

Steig, W. (1985). *Soloman the rusty nail.* New York: The Trumpet Club.

Steptoe, J. (1987). *Mufaro's beautiful daughters.* New York: Scholastic.

9

Bringing Children to Literacy Through Technology

DENISE DEFRANCO

*D*eFranco's work with five- and six-year-olds in an
ungraded primary classroom is a wonderful testimony to
the power of expectation on the part of the teacher. Denise
believes that children come to literacy through active
participation, self-directed play, and manipulation of learning
materials. She further believes that computers are among the
tools of literacy. Here she explains the role computers should
play in literacy learning, describes the equipment she
recommends for creating multimedia stations, and describes
the physical arrangement of the classroom that fosters
literacy growth with computer technology. I think you will
find Denise's tips on scheduling techniques very helpful. The
instructional strategies described here using the computer
could easily be integrated with ideas presented in all previous
chapters.

As an early childhood teacher I believe that literacy learning is a congruent and interrelated process that begins in infancy and continues as children use language to explore the functions of speaking, listening, reading, and writing. It is a process that emerges naturally as children interact with their environment. Young children learn through active participation, self-directed play, and manipulation of learning materials. Materials such as books, paper, pencils, markers, crayons, and computers are the tools of literacy. I believe that in order to become truly literate in an increasingly technological society, children must begin meaningful, developmentally appropriate interaction with technology at an early age. Computer and related technology should be as fully integrated into our classrooms as they are in the rest of society.

> It has become banal to say that computers *will become* a lifelong learning tool. Nearly 80 percent of the workforce now use computers every day. Libraries, banks, and grocery stores are giving clients direct access to services through the use of computer terminals which bypass clerks. Learning how to use computers, about how they work, their limitations, what they can and cannot do, and about their impact on society are essential knowledge and skills to enable lifelong learning. (Ray, 1991)

By providing opportunities for interaction with a variety of literacy learning tools, an effective early childhood program supports literacy learning and promotes independence, responsibility, and self-direction. It focuses on growth in all developmental areas: social, emotional, physical, and cognitive. Conditions that support emerging literacy in early childhood are:

- Immersion in a print rich environment
- High expectations and positive responses to literary approximations in a risk-free environment
- Sufficient time for hands-on exploration and practice
- Opportunities for student planning, choice, and decision making
- Effective models of literacy behaviors.

Natural literacy learning is facilitated when young children are immersed in a print rich and risk-free environment. Research suggests that children expect print to be meaningful and therefore seek its meaning (Goodman 1987, Smith 1982). Young children learn to recognize environmental print at an early age. For example the golden arches of McDonald's and the Coca Cola logo are recognizable to most American toddlers. At the age of two, our daughter Lauren was a "reader." Upon arriving at the shopping center where we did most of our daily errands Lauren read:

"D-A-R-T D-R-U-G, Dart Drug, Mommy!"

Many young children enter school with a vast knowledge of environmental print. Teachers can capitalize on this knowledge and extend it by creating a classroom environment that literally comes alive through meaningful print posted throughout the classroom. Children's self-esteem and comfort level both rise when they begin to recognize and use meaningful environmental print. How exciting it was for Terrell to be able to help a new student find his cubby. "This is your cubby, Songkane. See, it starts with an 'S.'" Classroom centers, cubbies, furniture, and materials are all labeled; rules and routines are posted; songs, poems, and collaborative stories are charted; children's table work and computer work is displayed throughout the classroom; daily message boards invite children to communicate with others through writing; big and small books in a variety of genres are available throughout the classroom; print is everywhere! When writing materials are available throughout the classroom and children have free access to computers as a writing tool, they spontaneously create signs, labels, and messages and post them throughout the classroom.

High expectations and positive responses to approximations encourage children to take the necessary risks to grow as readers and writers. When teachers focus on *process* rather than *product* they begin to see approximations as natural and essential behaviors of language acquisition (Fisher, 1991). Early attempts at reading and writing are celebrated rather than corrected. On the first day of Kindergarten I write a message to the class in a special place on our board that is designated for our Morning Message. The Morning Message is a strategy that I first saw modeled by Dorothy Strickland at an inservice in Fairfax County, Virginia in 1989. It is a short and simple message that follows a predictable pattern and is written with and for the children each day. My morning message usually looks something like this:

Good morning. We will read a story about a little boy that was made of gingerbread today. We will bake gingerbread boys and girls today.

After working with the children to read the message I ask if one of the children would like to write a message on the board. There is usually at least one child that says, "BUT WE DON'T KNOW HOW TO WRITE!" My response communicates my high expectations in a way that lets the children know that I value them and what they can do.

We are all writers! In Kindergarten we write the Kindergarten Way. We write the letters we know or the sounds that we hear. The letters are like magic. They will say whatever we want them to say.

The children know from that moment on that I see them as writers and will allow each child to begin writing in his/her own way. Many hands go up into the air and there are several volunteers to choose from. As Aimee comes up to the board I tell the children that every one will get a chance to write a message when we go to our tables. Aimee completely fills the message area with random letters and letter like symbols. When asked to read her message to us, Aimee touches the letters and *reads:* "I Love Kindergarten."

When our group time is completed and the children begin their writing there are usually a couple of children who are still hesitant and need additional encouragement. Often these are the children that have the most knowledge of sound/symbol relationships and can spell several words correctly. These children are inhibited by what they know and may be unaccustomed to taking risks. By the end of the first week even the most reluctant writers get caught up in the wonderful process of writing. They will still feel proud of the list of words that they know how to spell conventionally but will no longer be limited to these words alone. When expectations are high and approximations are valued children are able to take the risks necessary to grow. Roland Barth, founder of the Principal's Center at Harvard University believes that risk taking is essential if we are to improve our schools:

> In my vision of a good school, students and adults are encouraged to take risks, and a safety net protects those who do. Considerable research suggests that risk-taking is strongly associated with learning. (Barth, 1990)

Sufficient time is allowed for hands-on exploration and practice. Just as very young children learn to talk by talking, they also learn to read by reading, and learn to write by writing. Children must be given daily opportunities to pursue reading and writing for a variety of purposes and in a variety of ways. During center time Lakeisha loves to interact with books at the computer using the CD ROM (Compact Disk, Read Only Memory) and *Discus Books* (interactive electronic books with sound). Sophia likes to sit on the floor pillows in the Reading Cave (classroom library) and "read" books to the stuffed teddy bears. Alexaundra often chooses to "re-read" and listen to the story that was read during shared reading at the listening center. Likewise, Charles does most of his writing at the computer and Kyle usually chooses to write messages on small pieces of paper and post them throughout the classroom. Each individual child feels comfortable taking the time to explore literacy in his or her own way.

The flow of the classroom schedule should be flexible and allow individual children to engage in an activity for as long as necessary and then move on to another activity of choice. This type of schedule encourages self direction and allows children to take responsibility for their learning. My daily schedule begins with an interactive, integrated group lesson that is teacher directed. The children go from the lesson to an extension activity based on the book that was shared during the group lesson. The focus begins to shift from a teacher-directed activity to activities that are child-directed. From this point on the children determine how much time is needed for a particular activity. A child can take as little or as much time as needed to complete the extension activity and then move on the an extended free choice center time. The children will be called back as a group before dismissal.

In our half day kindergarten program the children are given approximately an hour to an hour and a half in which they make choices from a large number of available centers. There are just two rules for center time, which are posted prominently in the integrated lesson area and are consistently reinforced:

- When we finish a center we raise our hand and wait for the teacher to mark our center card before going to another center.
- If a center we want to use is full, we use our time wisely by making another choice.

The first rule helps me keep track of how children are using their free time. I use a "caterpillar card" system developed by Lena Goreski at Lake Anne Elementary in Reston, Virginia (Figure 9-1). All of the available centers are coded on the card with a letter or a number. When a child completes a center the appropriate code is circled. Subsequent uses of the same center are marked with caterpillar legs and hairs. When a child completes an entire row on the card we ring the bell so that the class can applaud and celebrate each child's progress. The second rule helps the children become self-directed and keeps classroom traffic running smoothly. *All centers are free choice!* Young children are capable of taking responsibility for their learning and will make choices that are appropriate to their individual developmental level (Elkind 1986).

Figure 9-1

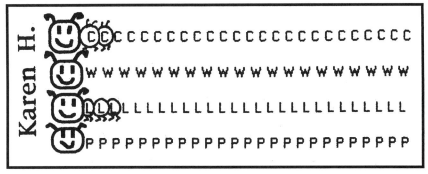

Some of the main learning centers that are available to the children for free choice during center time are:

- Art
- Blocks
- CD ROM/*Discus Books*
- Computers
- Creative Dramatics
- Dialogue Journals
- Housekeeping
- Listening
- Library

- Message/Letter writing
- Painting
- Publishing
- Puppets
- Sand/Water
- Science/Exploration
- Snack
- Reading/Writing/Drawing

Every effort is made to adapt all centers to reflect the current thematic unit of study. All centers are *literacy centers* that are fully equipped with paper, markers, crayons, and the like. In addition to the three computers in the Computer Center two computers are placed strategically throughout the classroom to encourage integration of concepts and spontaneous extensions from other centers and classroom activities.

Opportunities for student planning, choice, and decision-make occur throughout the day. The teacher prepares a stimulating environment and acts as a guide and facilitator by modeling appropriate behaviors and working with children when assistance is requested.

> There is no better system to control the complexities and intricacies of each person's learning than that person's own system of operating with genuine self-determination within reach of humane and informed help. (Holdaway, 1979)

When children self-select activities and repeat acquired skills by choice they are given opportunities to fully assimilate their learning (NAEYC 1989). Children's choices are respected and supported by the teacher.

Children need to see a variety of effective models of literacy behaviors in a variety of settings. Parents, teachers, siblings, and peers can all serve as models of literacy in action. Teachers should establish open and positive interactions with parents and should provide opportunities for parents to volunteer in the classroom. Parents can read with children, help with classroom publishing, work with individuals or small groups at a computer, help as facilitators during center time, share a special interest or hobby, or help with the preparation of classroom materials. In today's society many parents use computers either at home or in their work. There is a growing opportunity for involving these parents innovatively in the classroom. Parents who have not had experience with computers are often excited about the opportunity to learn along with the children. Volunteers are a valuable resource to help fully integrate both literacy and technology in the classroom.

Computers in the Classroom

Technology is not likely to have a qualitative impact on education unless it is deeply integrated into the purposes and activities of the classroom. (Sheingold, 1991)

COMPUTERS BELONG IN THE CLASSROOM! If a school has a limited number of computers the first priority should be to begin by putting one computer in as many classrooms as possible. Computer labs can actually impede integration by keeping technology on the edge of the system (Sheingold 1991). Putting all of a school's computers in a lab situation is analogous to putting all of a school's books in the library. The idea of keeping all books in the library sounds absurd because there are more than enough books in most schools to adequately stock classrooms and a central library. If there were a severe shortage of books where would they be kept? In the classroom of course! Both book and computers are tools of literacy and both should have a prominent place in the classroom.

Technology in Action

Hunters Woods Elementary has actively pursued the acquisition of computer technology through grants, county supported pilot programs, and PTA funds. Consequently, the school currently has approximately ninety-five computers which include IBM, Apple IIE, Apple IIGS, and Macintosh computers. As a teacher of an ungraded primary class for five- and six-year-olds my room is equipped with four Macintosh LC computers, an Apple IIGS connected to a large screen TV, a CD ROM, and three ImageWriter II color printers. This configuration provides for a student/computer ratio of approximately 4:1. In addition, the school library houses two multimedia stations on rolling carts that are easily wheeled into classrooms. Each multimedia station is equipped with a Macintosh LC computer, an Apple Scanner, a CD ROM, a laser disk player, and a large screen television. All of the Macintosh computers have a 40 megabyte hard drive, an Apple IIE card and 5¼″ external disk drive, a mouse, a keyboard, and a color monitor.

Multimedia in education is an approach to instruction and learning that incorporates multiple tools for gathering and presenting information.

These tools can include, but are not limited to:

* computers
* laser disk players
* VCRs
* CD ROMs
* Scanners
* books

* tape recorders
* still cameras
* video digitizers
* TVs
* music digitizers

A full description of each of these tools is outside the scope of this chapter. However, a brief description of each of the components of the multimedia station at Hunters Woods follows:

Apple Scanner. Conceptually, scanners are very much like copy machines. An image can be copied from a piece of paper and stored in the computer. Once an image has been scanned into a computer file it can be manipulated through the use of graphic and word processing programs. The file can then be stored on a disk. A copy of the file can be printed if a hard copy is desired.

CD ROM. CD ROM stands for "compact disk, read only memory." The CD ROM plays disks that are identical in appearance to audio CD's. The difference is that the disks that are played on a CD ROM also store visual images. CD ROMs are used primarily in education for interacting with electronic books and encyclopedias. The CD ROM enables the reader to manipulate the size and font of the text, the rate at which the text is read, and sometimes the language in which the book is read. As the reader comes to an unfamiliar word a simple click of the mouse will allow the user to hear the definition of the unknown word.

Laser Disk Player. A laser disk player is similar to a VCR. A laser disk is like a large version of a CD. Each disk is capable of storing up to 54,000 visual images. These images can be accessed instantly through the use of a special remote control.

By using computer software specifically designed for multimedia these individual components can be used interactively. A program called *Hypercard* enables the user to program instructional windows called "buttons." By clicking the mouse on one of these buttons the user can activate a video clip on a laser disc or move throughout the Hypercard stack for additional information. The user controls how each of these multimedia components will be linked. The benefits for students are multidimensional. Children learn to manipulate the latest technology as they utilize a hands-on approach to exploring content area materials.

Physical Arrangement

The physical arrangement of the classroom has a powerful influence on when and how computers are used. In a multiple computer classroom at least one computer should be placed in the area where the children and teacher gather for integrated lessons. This computer should be booted up and ready to go at all times. During a lesson a well-provisioned teacher would have the option of choosing from a number of writing tools at any given moment. It should be as easy for the teacher to use the computer as it is to pick up a marker and write on chart paper. Integrating the computer into daily lessons is the first step in the process of integrating the computer throughout the total program. The proximity of the computer allows children to interact naturally with technology within the context of daily lessons.

If a classroom is equipped with more than one computer, additional computers should be placed throughout the classroom in a manner that facilitates integration and extends learning. The Computer Center in my classroom houses three Macintosh LC computers and is located between the Library Center and the Reading/Writing/Drawing Center (Figure 9-2). The fourth computer is located between the Puppet Center and the Block Center and the fifth computer is in the lesson area. The placement of computers among the other centers serves as an invitation to the children to extend their learning to include technology. Research shows that both the quality and quantity of children's writing increases when children have ready access to computers as a writing tool (MacDonald 1991).

During a thematic unit on dinosaurs, Kyle and Dean played together with dinosaur puppets in the Puppet Center. After about twenty minutes Dean raised his hand to signal that he was ready to choose anther center. I circled the "P" on Dean's card to record his center choice. When I asked Dean if he had decided which center he was going to go to next he said, "Oh yes, I am going to write a message about playing with Kyle." Dean proceeded to the computer center and typed his message on a Mac LC computer. When he was finished he printed his message and went to a work table to illustrate it (Figure 9-3). After completing the picture he asked if he could share his writing with the class at group time.

> (Children) share when they feel good about what they have done, when growth has occurred, and when learning has taken place. (Fisher 1991)

The proximity of the computer facilitated the ease with which Dean was able to plan his activities and extend his learning in an individual, self-directed way. Dean's eagerness to share was evidence that learning had occurred in a way that was meaningful to Dean.

Computer Management and Scheduling

The need for rigid scheduling is more acute in classrooms with a high pupil/computer ratio. Managing a rotating schedule in a single computer classroom can be difficult. In this situation a single computer is best used as a tool for teacher productivity or group instruction. In a multiple computer classroom the scheduling is more natural because children are not restricted to unrealistically short periods of time at the computer. The educational flow is easily maintained when there are multiple computers available for student use in the classroom.

In addition to giving students free access to computers during center time I use a rotating schedule to facilitate maximum use at other times of

Figure 9-2

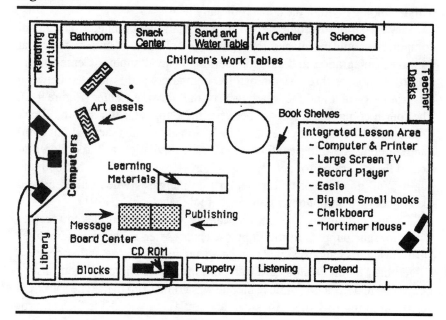

the day. This schedule allows some students to work at the computers while others participate in a group lesson. The four computers that are located outside the lesson area are color coded to match the colors of the four student work tables: yellow, red, blue, and green. Each computer has a pocket chart containing the names of the children that are assigned to that

Figure 9-3

Figure 9-4

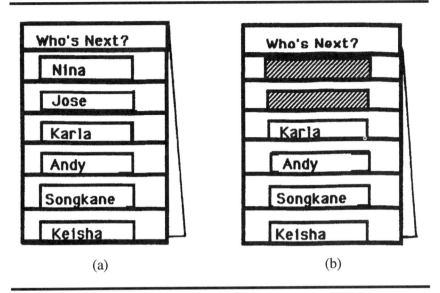

(a)   (b)

color table (Figure 9-4a). Upon arriving at a computer to work, each student will turn his/her card over in the pocket chart. A quick glance at the chart will show who has had a turn and who's turn will come next. Figure 9-4b shows the pocket chart after Nina and Jose have taken their turns. Upon leaving the computer center Jose would go quietly to Karla to let her know that it is her turn. This system allows the children to function independently as they move between the computer center and the lesson area.

At times these computer learning sessions are preplanned for a specific purpose by the teacher. At other times they arise naturally from student interests and desires. During a large group integrated lesson that included a shared reading of the big book *Hairy Bear*, Nina excitedly announced to the group that *Hairy Bear* was her favorite big book. Nina bubbled with enthusiasm as she went on to tell the class about specific parts of the story. Other children began raising their hands and were eager to share their favorite big books. Nina seemed a little frustrated; she obviously had more to say. Sensing this, I asked Nina if she would like to go to the computer to write a message about *Hairy Bear*. She beamed as she left the group and headed for the computer. Nina followed our normal routine and went directly to the computer that was assigned for use by students at the "yellow" table. As she sat down to begin her work, Nina took her name card out of the pocket card, turned it over, and returned it to its slot. Nina could see from the chart that it was Jose's turn next. Upon completing her writing Nina knew that she would go quietly to Jose and ask him if he would like to have a turn at the computer. In the event that there was not enough time for all the children to have a turn the rotation would pick up at the same place the next day.

When children are working at the computer while a lesson is being conducted it is necessary to have a routine for them to follow if they need assistance. The following procedure is posted and modeled for the children before the class begins using a rotation schedule.

- First ask a friend at another computer for help.
- If you still need help put up the "HELP" flag.

The "HELP" flag is a signal to the student computer helper to go to the computer area to lend assistance (Figure 9-5). If the children still are not able to figure out the problem the instructional assistant or parent volunteer will go to the computer area to give assistance. Usually the children are able to figure the problem out among themselves and without adult assistance. When adult assistance is required, however, the teacher can take advantage of the teachable moment and have the entire class brainstorm to help find a solution.

Children are also invited to use the computers when they first come into the classroom in the morning. The children begin to arrive in the classroom approximately twenty minutes before the morning bell. A computer icon is hung above two of the four tables each morning. The children at these two tables are free to choose someone to work with and to go to any of the five computers in the classroom. The computer icon will be rotated to the other two tables on the following day.

By utilizing these simple scheduling techniques, computer availability and use are maximized. All students have daily access to computers. Stu-

Figure 9-5

Figure 9-6

dent motivation to work with the computer has always been high in my classroom. Students who are otherwise reluctant to write are often eager when given the opportunity to write at a computer.

> Using a computer will not in and of itself, change or improve the nature of children's writing. If writing strategies are or are coming to be parts of children's writing then word processing can enhance them and make it easier for children to use the writing strategies within writing. (Cochran, Smith et al., 1988, in Katzer & Crnkovich, 1991)

Instructional Strategies

Pre-writing strategies such as *Webs,* (Figure 9-6) *Story Maps,* (Figure 9-7) and *K-W-Ls, (What I Know; What I Want To Know; What I Learned)* (Figure 9-8) are excellent computer activities for elementary students. Webs can be produced on the computer with word processing software programs that have drawing capabilities like MacWrite or Kid Pix. In a large group lesson we used the Kid Pix program to create a web on insects. The story map in Figure 9-7 was created using Kid Pix after a shared reading of *The*

Figure 9-7

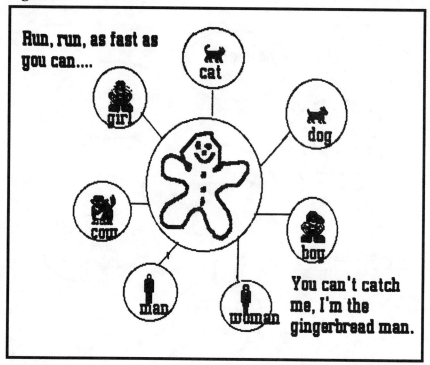

Gingerbread Man. Lakeisha used the mouse to draw the gingerbread man in the center of the map. The other characters were stamped by individual children at the computer using the stamp mode in Kid Pix. Each time a child came to the computer to stamp a character in one of the circles the entire class repeated the story pattern:

> Run, run, as fast as you can. You can't catch me, I'm the Ginger bread Man.

The template used for this story map was saved and used for other stories such as *I Can Fly* (Krauss, 1992), *Joshua James likes Trucks* (Petrie, 1987), and *Brown Bear, Brown Bear, What Do You See?* (Martin 1983).

The children love to use the computer for K-W-L's. I usually use the Apple IIGS computer for this activity because of it's large screen projection capabilities and voice synthesized speech. The children enjoy hearing *Talking Text Writer* repeat their messages as they are entered into the computer. A great deal of excitement is generated at the culmination of a unit when we enter messages in the "What We Learned" section of our K-W-L. After all the messages are entered the computer goes to work printing page after page in one long continuous strip. When the printer stops the children rush over to the computer to see their messages. The children laughed and cheered when

Figure 9-8

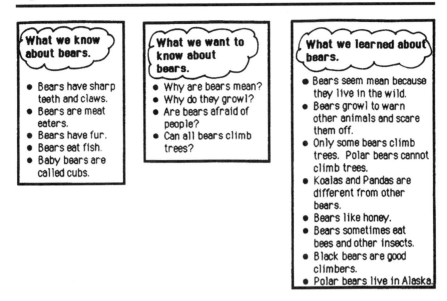

I had to stand on a chair in order to stretch out the long computer print out of what the children had learned about bears (Figure 9-8).

Another instructional strategy that has been particularly enjoyable for my students is *Electronic Dialogue Journal Writing.* I use Bank Street Writer/Mac software because of its capability of storing recorded messages and sounds into the computer file. When I begin writing to a child I write the child's name in a bright color and very large print size (48 point) on the computer screen (Figure 9-9a). Then I choose a smaller size print (24 point) to write a message to the child. After typing the message I use the format menu to record a sound button (Figure 9-9b). Once the message is recorded

Figure 9-9

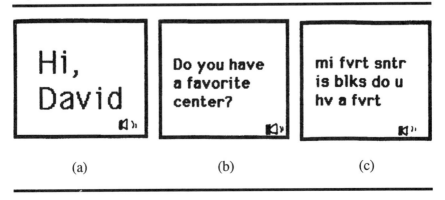

a small megaphone serves as a visual icon to indicate that sound has been recorded in the file. A double click on the icon will play the message. Readers and pre-readers alike enjoy hearing my voice as they "read" the message on the screen. The child types in a response and can record a message back to me (Figure 9-9c). I usually correspond with five students a week. At the end of the week I print two copies of the dialogue; one for the student and one for my files.

Webs, Story Maps, K-W-Ls, and Dialogue Journals are just a few of the many instructional strategies that are enhanced through the use of computer technology. The effective use of technology, however, must go far beyond the implementation of specific strategies and activities. Technology for technology's sake must be avoided. In a child-centered, developmentally appropriate classroom all practices reflect a philosophy that is based on a whole language perspective. Specific strategies and instructional practices are valuable to the extent that they support children's natural literacy development. Isolated uses of technology will do little to enhance natural literacy learning. Rather, it is through full integration into a developmentally appropriate, child centered classroom that technology becomes meaningful and useful as a tool for bringing children to literacy.

References

Barth, R. S. (1990). A personal vision of a good school, *Phi Delta Kappan,* March.

Butler, A. & Turbill, J. (1984). *Towards a reading-writing classroom.* Portsmouth, NH: Heinemann.

Brendekamp, S. (1986). *Developmentally appropriate practice in early childhood programs serving children from birth to age 8.* Washington, DC: NAEYC.

Elkind, D. (1986). Formal education and early childhood education: An essential difference, *Phi Delta Kappan.*

Fisher, B. (1991). *Joyful learning.* Portsmouth, NH: Heinemann.

Graves, D.H. (1983). *Writing: Teachers and children at work.* Portsmouth, NH: Heinemann.

Hansen, J. (1987). *When writers read.* Portsmouth, NH: Heinemann.

Held, C, Newsom, J. & Pfeiffer, M. (1991). The integrated technology classroom, *The Computing Teacher.* March.

Humphrey, S. (1991). The case of myself, *Young Children,* November.

Katzer, S. & Crnkovich, C. (1991). *From scribblers to scribes.* Englewood, CA. Teacher Ideas Press.

Maehr, J.M. (1991). *Language and literacy.* Ypsilanti, MI: The High Scope Press.

Strickland, D.S. & Morrow, L.M. (1989). *Emerging literacy: Young children learn to read and write.* Newark, DE: International Reading Association.

10

Bringing Children to Literacy Through Integrated Basic Skills Instruction

BILL HARP

*I*n this chapter I attempt to answer the question of the role played by basic skill instruction in whole language classrooms. The "great debate" over phonics is settled. Learning to manipulate the graphophonic cueing system is tremendously helpful in becoming an independent, fluent reader. Only one of the four cueing systems, graphophonics, must be viewed from the perspective that it is not the first cueing system to be mastered, nor the most important. Creating meaning using syntactic cues, semantic cues, and schematic cues is the first objective of the reader—and the first lesson of the teacher. Use of the graphophonic cueing system must be taught in the context of real reading and real writing events. Here we pull examples from preceding chapters to illustrate the integration of basic skill instruction with authentic literacy events, and offer specific steps for bringing this integration about.

A graduate student with twenty-plus years of elementary teaching experience sheepishly approached me after a class one afternoon. With head bowed, in a voice that only I could barely hear, she said, "I teach phonics. Does that mean I can't be a whole language teacher?"

The question amazed me at the time, has stuck with me since, and illustrates the deep confusion that exists in our profession. It is as though **whole language** is a secret club that this and other teachers want to join, but are afraid that some of the trappings of the past will cause them to be excluded or dismissed. One of the great myths of whole language instruction is that we don't teach skills. Let's set the record straight.

Whole language teachers teach basic skills. By basic skills I mean all of the subskills that comprise fluency in reading and writing. Examples are phonics, word meanings, sentence structure, spelling, punctuation, subject/verb agreement, plurals, and the list could go on and on.

The difference between basic skill instruction in whole language classrooms and basic skill instruction in traditional classrooms is that in whole language classrooms the instruction is always contextualized. In traditional classrooms it is separate from real literacy acts. Another significant difference is that in whole language classrooms such skills are taught and reinforced when the teacher sees that the child or children need the instruction. In traditional classrooms a given skill is taught because it is the next in the workbook or the next in the teacher's guide.

Let's look at an example to compare the two views. Suppose a teacher working with emerging writers wants to focus on ending punctuation. In the traditional classroom the teacher would probably teach a lesson on the overhead on ending punctuation and then give the children a worksheet with ten sentences to which they are to add the punctuation. Notice how far removed from any use of literacy by the children this is. The lesson is separated, isolated from the act of real writing.

Contrast this activity with the way such a lesson might be handled in a whole language classroom. Knowing that ending punctuation is to be a focus, the teacher might first have children examine ending punctuation when she does shared reading from an enlarged text or the overhead. The children might then be asked to pull a recent sample from their writing portfolios to determine the extent to which they are using ending punctuation in their writing. Some children may elect this as a writing goal and enter in on the "Things I Need To Do Better" list in the portfolio. Ending punctuation would later be a focus of writing conferences with the teacher for those who have not yet mastered the skill, and a subject of celebration for those who have.

The essential differences between the two scenarios above is that in the whole language classroom the basic skill instruction is contextualized—embedded within real reading and writing experiences in which the children are creating and communicating meaning. Skill instruction is not done in isolation.

One of the areas of greatest concern to many teachers is how phonics instruction is to be handled in a whole language classroom. The great debate over phonics vs no phonics is over. **Over.** The questions today are what kind of phonics, when and how. Whole language teachers certainly teach phonics. They just do so differently than teachers with other philosophies. Let's deal with the questions of what kind of phonics instruction should we design and when phonics should be taught. Then we will look at how basic skill instruction looks in whole language classrooms.

What Kind of Phonics?

There are essentially two ways to approach the teaching of phonics. One is with sounds in isolation (the sound of /m/ is "mmmmm"). The other is with sounds in the context of words (the sound of /m/ is the sound you hear at the beginning of "mother, man, maybe"). Before reaching a conclusion as to which of these approaches is best, let's consider four principles that should guide our instruction in word identification (Harp and Brewer, 1991).

Principle 1

Instruction in word identification should be seen as an aid to constructing meaning, not as an end in itself. We do not teach children the sound(s) represented by a certain letter because that knowledge is important as such. We teach the sound-letter correspondence so that the process of constructing meaning may go on as effortlessly as possible.

Principle 2

What we do in skills instruction should be as much like the reading act as possible. In skills instruction we should use examples taken from meaningful texts.

Principle 3

While engaging in skills instruction, we must respect the reading process. Having broken the process down in order to examine individual pieces, we should put it back together before ending the instruction, so children can see the relationships between the parts and the whole.

Principle 4

Word identification is useful only when the words identified are in the reader's listening or speaking vocabulary. The use of graphophonic cues will not be effective if children cannot recognize miscues when they make them and self-correct.

How then do these four principles help us answer the question of "What kind of phonics should we teach"? Principle 1 requires that phonics be taught in a meaningful context. This requirement is met by teaching phonics when a child asks how a word is spelled (How do you think it is spelled? What sound do you hear at the beginning? How do we spell that sound?). This requirement is met when we notice that a reader is having trouble decoding a word and we intervene *during the reading process* to teach a sound/symbol relationship that is needed.

Principle 2 requires that phonics instruction be as much like the reading act as possible. We do not read isolated sounds. We do not even normally, naturally read isolated words. This requirement is met when we teach sound/symbols relationships in the *context of words within a meaningful context*. No longer would we walk into a kindergarten classroom having an "M Day" and find children writing lines and lines of m's, reading contrived texts that highlight "m" words. Basic skills will be taught as children need them within the context of meaningful literacy experiences.

Principle 3 requires that skills are taught while children are using the reading (and writing) process. Skill lessons are not separate, contrived settings in which we drill on isolated sound/symbol relationships. Skills are taught as children are struggling to create meaning in reading or produce meaning in writing. While we may well take the process apart to focus on the skill, Principle 3 requires that we put it back together again so that we help children see the relationships between the parts and the whole.

Principle 4 requires that skills be taught in the context of meaningful words. It does a reader no good to decode a word that is not in his listening or speaking vocabulary; meaning will not be created. To meet this requirement we must always assure that children are focused on the creation of meaning and not simply on the isolated skill.

When Should We Teach Phonics?

The answer to this questions is really quite simple. *When readers and writers need it.* However, this answer applies to all basic skills, not just phonics. Let's expand our discussion to include all basic skills. This means that no longer will we see a basic skills lessons of any type taught because it is the next lesson in the workbook. Instead, whole language teachers are knowledgeable enough of the basic skills themselves and know their students so well, that they are able to design skills instruction on the basis of need. The curriculum is student driven rather than text or test driven.

How Are the Basic Skills Taught?

The answers to this question rest in the activities described in the chapters you have already read. Let's revisit each of the teachers whose classrooms we have seen, and consider the nature of basic skill instruction in each of them. At times I will paraphrase what they have said; sometimes I will use their words exactly.

Debbie Shelor—First Grade

Debbie described eleven areas she set up in her classroom. Consider what basic skills can be integrated with instruction and activities in some of these areas.

Check-in Center
✓ decoding skills
✓ new vocabulary
✓ following directions
✓ left to right orientation, sequencing

Listening Center
✓ auditory acuity, discrimination
✓ following directions
✓ listening to well done models of reading
✓ reinforcement of previous lessons
✓ left to right orientation, following text, turning pages

Conference Center
✓ teaching and reinforcement of all basic writing skills in the context of a current writing piece
✓ teaching and reinforcement of all basic reading skills in the context of a currently read text

Computer Center
✓ composition skills
✓ pre-writing, rough drafting, revision
✓ reinforcement of basic skills
✓ simulations

Building Area
✓ cooperation with others
✓ eye-hand coordination
✓ creativity
✓ problem solving

We have only scratched the surface in identifying basic skills that may be taught or reinforced in some of the areas in Debbie's room. She identified other activities that readily lend themselves to the integration of basic skill instruction. Let's consider some of them.

When her children read *The King Who Rained* (Gwynne, 1970) and *Chocolate Moose for Dinner* (1976) there were wonderful opportunities to deal with decoding, drawing inferences, dealing with double meanings, and examining humor.

Rhiannon's explanation of how she **interviewed** *Papa, Please Get the Moon for Me* (Carle, 1986) provided a rich opportunity to talk about previewing, skimming, predicting and relating background knowledge to a text. How much better to visit these basic skills in this *context* rather than to create isolated lessons.

Shelor's "Buddy Reading" is another time for dealing with basic skill instruction. When her students buddy read with their kindergarten buddies they become mentors and teachers "quite seriously." If the old adage that "the best way to learn something is to teach it to somebody else" is true, then a great deal of basic skill instruction may go on in buddy reading. Let's move back to Kathy Porterfield's room and see what contextualized basic skill instruction we found there.

Kathy Porterfield—Multi-age Intermediate

Kathy talked about the importance of tone setting in her classroom. She acknowledges that classroom tone is an important matter, and her students know that the business of their classroom is to read, to write, to think, to interact positively with others, to investigate areas of personal interest, and to conduct interdisciplinary, individual, and classroom research. It would be redundant, and perhaps silly, of me to list all of the basic skills that are used in these tone setting activities. Let it suffice to say that in this kind of classroom environment it is natural for basic skill instruction to be contextualized—done in the course of real reading, real writing, and real thinking activities.

Another critically important area that Porterfield addresses is helping growing readers deal with the supports and challenges presented by a given text. Our goal is to assist growing readers in accomplishing the critical basic skills of monitoring their own handling of a text. We know that one of the characteristics that sets good readers apart from poor readers is this fundamental ability of metacomprehension—thinking about one's own comprehension. Kathy helps the reader understand the ways in which we can have students deal with the supports and challenges of a text.

Challenges or supports may be things such as level of interest in the book topic, background knowledge (both recognizing it and using it), personal experience with the topic, the genre itself, the relative difficulty of the vocabulary, and the physical set-up of the text. Helping readers recognize and deal with supports and challenges provides nearly countless opportunities to teach and reinforce basic skills in the context of real reading experiences.

Porterfield also talked about the power of the reading conference as a time for one-on-one instruction. Here is where some of the most significant reading instruction happens. She recognized that the conference itself became a stage for exploration of individual reading processes and the strategies children develop to become more efficient readers. The reading strategies she recommended focusing on during this time were: what to do when a reader comes to an unknown word, skipping unfamiliar words, and self correction. Mary Giard, in sharing the running records and miscue analysis done by her first graders amplifies these ideas.

Assuming that depth of understanding and the ability to communicate one's thoughts are basic skills Kathy showed us how, by the third literature study conference, readers had moved beyond the superficial details of the book. The discussions were much deeper. Students were able to focus on literary elements. Such growth would not be possible in a fill-in-the-blank classroom.

The number and kind of basic skills that may be taught in a given literacy event depend greatly on the nature of the event. Manning and Fennacy, in discussing shared reading with us, offered tremendously rich ground for skills instruction.

Deborah Manning and Jean Fennacy—Second Grade

With the exception of guided reading, none of the strategies we use to bring children to literacy affords us more opportunities to teach basic skills than do shared reading experiences. Consider the list of basic skills that are visited virtually every time we do shared reading with children.

✓ Knowledge of text features such as cover, title page, illustrations, paragraphing, dialogue;
✓ the concepts of author and illustrator;
✓ the concepts of publisher and copyright;
✓ book handling concepts such as text versus illustration, where to begin reading, when to turn the page;
✓ focus on sound/symbol relationships in frequently repeated words;
✓ making predictions, confirming and rejecting predictions;
✓ supports and challenges in the text that make it easy to understand and difficult to understand;
✓ selecting reasonable responses to the text.

Like Debbie Shelor, Deborah and Jean recognize the value of buddy reading. In this case, older children who are invited to be reading buddies with younger ones help the novice reader over some of the hurdles along the path toward independent reading. The major benefit they found in children reading with older buddies is that the younger child comes into contact with reading materials they find especially compelling. Here the basic skill of enjoying reading is highlighted and modeled.

Manning and Fennacy underscore the importance of novice readers engaging in reading-like behavior when sharing reading with a more experienced member of the literacy club. Basic skills that are taught or reinforced in this situation include:

✓ turning pages at appropriate times;
✓ relying on previous knowledge and illustrations;
✓ behaving like real readers;
✓ using the context as well as a story's syntax and semantic cues to support meaning making;
✓ increased attention paid to print;
✓ identifying specific words and phrases in context;
✓ using picture cues;
✓ matching oral production to the text;
✓ finally coming to control the whole of reading, the complex interplay between strategies and cueing systems.

Another basic skill issue which they address is supporting and nurturing the fragile reader.

For the fragile reader, finding ways to behave as a real reader rather than being singled out as "slow" is of paramount importance. Shared reading supports the least proficient readers. Reading a book within a group with a parent volunteer, a grandparent or the teacher affords these readers the opportunity to be successful as readers.

Mary Giard—First Grade

Mary described in her introduction how she and her students brainstormed a list of work they do. They listed as typical morning work: writing in draft books, conferencing with a peer or an adult, publishing work, doing research on a self-selected topic, writing mini-lessons, shared reading groups, guided reading groups, partner or buddy reading, reading to self, responding to text, listening to a read aloud or a tape, or taking a running record. Let's look at just two of these activities to discover the basic skill instruction embedded within each of them.

Research on self-selected topic. Consider the basic skill instruction and reinforcement that is possible through doing research on a self-selected topic:

✓ narrowing topic choices;
✓ considering what I know about a topic;

✓   identifying the questions I want to answer;
✓   identifying strategies to get my questions answered;
✓   computer and card catalogue skills;
✓   note taking;
✓   outlining;
✓   skimming and scanning;
✓   selecting relevant information;
✓   summarizing and organizing;
✓   presenting what I have learned.

Countless reading and writing skills are, of course, embedded within each of the areas identified.

Taking a running record.   When I first read Mary's chapter I was astonished at the idea that her first graders were taking running records on each other. I visited with her about this, and she assured me that she had not exaggerated the situation in her paper. Consider the basic skills that are integrated into this activity:

✓   the conventions of omission, insertion, rerun (reread), accurate reading;
✓   self correction, repetition, appeal for help;
✓   the ability to identify the nature of a miscue—semantic acceptability, syntactic acceptability, graphophonic similarity;
✓   using your experiences, making predictions;
✓   determining whether a rendering of a text makes sense;
✓   does my reading sound right?;
✓   does my decoding look right (beginning sounds, vowel sounds, ending sounds, and so on)?

Perhaps the best example anywhere of what children can do when the expectations are high is in Mary's classroom. Not only have her children learned the language of running records and miscue analysis, but they have learned to apply these concepts to their own and to each other's reading.

Mary told me the delightful story of how the fall after her children had devised the reading strategy list she shared in her chapter, a former student came to her one morning and said, "Mrs. G., do you have a copy of that strategy checklist we made last year? I would like to have a copy. Mary replied that she thought there was a copy in the file cabinet. As she handed the checklist to the little girl, the girl responded, "Thanks Mrs. G. I can really use this. I don't think my teacher understands strategies."

Not only does whole language instruction include basic skills instruction, it can take children to far greater understandings than traditional skill instruction ever could. Mary Kitagawa holds the same high expectations for her children that Giard holds for hers.

Mary Kitagawa—Fifth Grade

Mary's "small moment" lessons integrate a great deal of basic skill instruction. Recall that she models writing in which a small moment is enough for a topic. She and her students tell small moment stories. They shrink topics to portions that can be explored in small texts. Mary used the example that students cannot easily write in depth about "My trip to Disneyland," but can write a focused text about a small aspect of the trip: getting lost there. Consider the basic skills embedded with the small moment activity:

✓ brainstorming possible topics;
✓ identifying a topic;
✓ rough drafting;
✓ revision and response;
✓ polishing.

Kitagawa's description of the January and June examination and evaluation of writing portfolios is another prime example of basic skills instruction integrated within real reading and writing experiences. What does it take for a student to be able to identify five writing pieces to be evaluated—and to explain why those particular pieces were chosen? It requires that the student be able to think like a writer—to fully understand the writing process and to select pieces that exemplify his or her ability to use the process. It requires a degree of self-confidence—a sense of self as writer. While such characteristics may not appear on many basic skills lists, I suggest that they are, in fact, basic to becoming a life-long writer.

Donna Byrum and Virginia Pierce—Fifth Grade

None of the classrooms we visited had more opportunity to integrate basic skill instruction in authentic literacy events than with Donna and Virginia's theme cycles. In this classroom children use math, reading, writing, science, and social studies as tools for finding out more about the world around them. In this setting the basic skills are extended far beyond the traditional basics. The characteristics of responsible citizens, such as life-long learner, problem-solver, effective communicator, collaborative worker, quality producer, and involved citizen were the basic skills infused in the theme cycle work.

Kittye Copeland—Grades Five–Twelve

Copeland offers her students a real boost in becoming writers through the writing demonstrations she does for her children. Kittye explained that when she writes in the classroom, she becomes a member of the class that needs help, support and suggestions just as any writer in the group. Consider the basic skills that came into play as Kittye and the other writers in her class participated in response groups. Through the responses of other writers, Kittye further considered:

✓ improved use of vocabulary;

✓ improved sentence structure;

✓ improvements for greater clarity. In this exchange she was able to highlight:

✓ unity of ideas;

✓ sequencing;

✓ attention to detail;

✓ voice in writing.

Kittye's students were able to see that her first drafts were not complete works. They saw how she penciled in, crossed out, wrote marginal notes, and used other pieces of paper. As Copeland shared her piece in writer's circle, she was able to focus on basic editing skills such as spelling, subject/verb agreement, singular/plural agreement, and punctuation. These are wonderful examples of integrating basic skill instruction in real, authentic, living literacy events.

Teachers are sometimes reluctant to integrate basic skill instruction because they are afraid something will be overlooked—some critical skill will be left out and children will be harmed. Mary Jungdahl, a primary teacher, told me the story of how—though she wanted to think of herself as a whole language teacher—she worried about getting all of the basic skills covered. One day she had about ten minutes to fill before going to lunch. She decided the seize the moment and do a lesson on *plurals.*

She gathered the children around her and wrote the word, "box" on the board. She then asked, "How do I make this plural?" The children quickly responded with " b-o-x-e-s." After successfully pluralizing some more words, Mary wrote "cow" on the board, and again asked how to make it plural. A little girl put up her hand, Mary called on her, and she said, "To make that plural you would have to have a bull."

Mary decided at that moment to trust in the power of reading and writing and forego anymore isolated skill lessons.

How can a teacher be more comfortable with integrated skills instruction? There are three things the teacher who is worried about "covering the skills" can do. One, create a column on the lesson plan book or the anecdotal record page where the skills addressed in a given lesson may be listed. This running list can then be checked against the district or state curriculum guide. Two, keep a list of basic reading and writing skills in a desk drawer. Periodically pull it out and check which skills have been taught, reinforced, revisited, and mastered. Look for opportunities during reading and writing activities to highlight the skills that have not been addressed. Three, periodically collect writing samples and running records. List in the margin or on the back all of the skills for which mastery is evidenced in the work. These strategies have provided reassurance to teachers like Mary who just aren't comfortable *assuming* that the basics are being covered in daily reading and writing experiences. Are basic skills integrated with dramatic activities in the classroom? Let's revisit McGruder's class.

Sheryl McGruder—Second Grade

Sheryl said, "You might be thinking, 'But this has no academic value.'" Emphasis in dramatic activities is placed on the development of self-esteem, a sense of uniqueness and ability to create, and to problem-solve. These are basic skills. Furthermore, there is transfer from the dramatic activities to other areas of the curriculum. McGruder pointed out that once, for example, the concept of story is understood through dramatics, a clearer understanding of that concept is demonstrated in children's writing of story.

The ability to extrapolate beyond the text was listed as a basic comprehension skill by Carl Wallen (1972). Sheryl described how she uses drama to help children go beyond the text or the story and deal with the "what if" question. If children can change one element in a tale to see how the story will be affected, they must have a solid grasp on the concepts of story, sequence of events, and character interaction. Another way Sheryl used drama to look at the completeness of a story is by linking it to children's writing.

When some of the children in her class had written first drafts, she encouraged them to invite their classmates to dramatize the stories. After the drama the whole class talked about the experience—what they liked, what they wondered about, gaps in logic. This then gave the author of the story information to use in editing the final draft. Nowhere are the opportunities greater for integrating the basic skills of writing into real literacy events than in Denise DeFranco's class with its technology.

Denise DeFranco—Ungraded Five and Six-year-olds

Denise accurately points out that many children enter school with a vast knowledge of environmental print. We have many opportunities to teach or reinforce sight vocabulary and sound/symbol relationships as we engage children in discussion of environmental print. Remember Denise describing how one of her students helped Songkane find the right cubby that was labeled with the name. "See, it starts with an 'S.'" The richness of teachable moments with environmental print is extended with DeFranco's morning message.

Some teachers see the computer as a source of "skill and drill" activities. DeFranco dispels this myth with her examples of children interacting with reading with such software as *Discus Books*.

In Denise's classroom where the pupil/computer ratio is 4:1, the computer easily becomes a tool for word processing which children can easily access. Recall the story of Dean who upon completing work at a center decided to go to the computer and write a message about playing with Kyle—a rich opportunity for Denise to infuse basic skill instruction within or as an outgrowth of this real reason to write.

How Do You Plan Integrated Basic Skill Instruction?

The integration of basic skill instruction in authentic literacy events requires three things: a very knowledgeable teacher, careful planning, and a willingness to be spontaneous in one's teaching. Consider each of these conditions in depth.

A Very Knowledgeable Teacher

When whole language teachers integrate basic skill instruction in real literacy events they have no teacher's guide to follow. Gone are the workbook pages that seemed to carry us mindlessly through the skill maze. Instruction is pupil-driven; not text- or test-driven. The whole language teacher is a professional observer of children and very knowledgeable about reading and writing processes. These factors combined with attention to state and district curriculum requirements form the basis of curriculum design and execution.

Understands reading process. The whole language teacher understands the reading process. Reading is seen as an interaction between the thoughts of the author and the background knowledge and experiences of the reader which combine to create (or recreate) meaning. This teacher understands that when this interaction occurs the reader makes predictions about what will be in the text, samples from the myriad of available cues sufficiently to confirm or reject the predictions. The reader knows how to rethink predictions or reread the text if the predictions are rejected. If the predictions are confirmed, the reader knows how to integrate what has been read with his or her world view. This prediction, sampling, confirming, and integration are at the heart of the reading process. Knowledgeable teachers know how to help readers become increasingly adept at using this process.

Understanding cueing systems. Knowledgeable teachers also understand the cueing systems that operate when one reads. The semantic cueing system is comprised of the meanings of words, the syntactic cueing system is comprised of the principles that describe the relationships between words and the structure of sentences in our language. The graphophonic cueing system is all of the information available because our language is alphabetic and symbols represent sounds. The schematic cueing system is the knowledge, attitudes, and perceptions the reader brings to the reading act. All four of these cueing systems work in harmony to aid the reader in creating meaning.

Teachers must have a sufficiently refined understanding of all four of the cueing systems that they can assist readers in using the cues spontaneously as well as through carefully planned instruction.

Parallels between oral language and literacy. Whole language teachers appreciate the parallels that exist between becoming fluent as oral language speakers and become fluent in literacy. They see that the conditions that existed to facilitate fluency in oral language use must exist to bring children to fluency in reading and writing. Just as children formulated and tested hypotheses about language, so they need opportunities to generate and test hypotheses about print. They need support and encouragement as they interact with environmental print, as they engage with print in shared and guided reading, and as they learn the language with which they can talk about print. Children need many rich and varied interactions with print on a daily basis.

Children become fluent in oral language by connecting language to their experiences. So children coming to literacy need opportunities to come to reading experiences able to use what they know—to draw on that critical background knowledge. Children must see that print "talks" about things they know about.

As children are becoming fluent in oral language they clearly understand the purposes and functions of language—to meet needs, to attract attention, to get things done, and so on. So it is with children and literacy. They must have multiply opportunities to use print in ways that meet personal purposes—to function in a print rich world. The knowledgeable teacher creates ways for children to use print to meet needs, to attract attention, to get things done, to communicate with others. Children use print daily in a variety of ways for a variety of purposes.

Just as children understood that oral language was all about communicating meaning, so they must understand that literacy is all about meaning. Children need printed material that is meaningful and predictable and a teacher and parent who stress meaning over mechanics.

Understand process writing. Whole language teachers understand that writing is a process—a multi-faceted process. They understand that the way in which writers grow is through the use of the writing process across a wide range of genre, written for a variety of important purposes. They are able to help children with pre-writing activities, rough drafting, revision and response activities, revising and editing and publishing. They are also able to infuse basic skill instruction into these activities.

Fundamental to integrated basic skill instruction is a keen ability to observe children, identify their strengths, and to plan ways to guide them to their next learning steps.

Careful Planning is Key

I have heard uninformed teachers say, "Whole language is just a free-for-all, no holds barred classroom set up." Nothing could be further from the truth. Whole language teachers understand that creating a child-centered environment takes a great deal of work and a great deal of planning! Integrating basic skill instruction in real literacy experiences takes very careful planning as well.

There are several important planning steps to be taken.

Step One: Know the basic skills that are to be taught and reinforced at your grade level(s). This information may be found in both state and district curriculum guides. The teacher who is very insecure about what skills should be addressed at a given grade level may wish to consult a scope and sequence chart from a basal. Figure 10-1 illustrates typical phonic, structural and vocabulary skills listed for Grade Two and Grade Five. Figure 10-2 illustrates typical comprehension, literary and language mechanics skills

Figure 10-1   Typical Second and Fifth Grade Basic Phonic, Structural and Vocabulary Skills in Reading

Second Grade	*Fifth Grade*
Consonants initial final medial cluster digraphs	**Consonants** clusters digraphs
Vowels short long r-controlled schwa digraphs vowel patterns	**Vowels** short long r-controlled schwa digraphs
Syllabication Structural Skills base words suffixes inflectional endings compound words contractions syllabication	**Structural Skills** base words prefixes suffixes compound words contractions
Vocabulary Skills antonyms context clues homographs homphones pronoun referents synonyms	**Vocabulary Skills** analogies antonyms context clues homographs homophones idioms pronoun referents synonyms word histories

Figure 10-2   Typical Comprehension, Literary and Language
Mechanics Skills for Grades Two and Five

Grade Two	*Grade Fife*
Comprehension cause and effect characterization inferences and conclusions main idea prediction realism vs. fantasy sequence **Literary Skills** figurative language literature: form & characteristics rhyme **Language Mechanics** punctuation sentences typographic clues	**Comprehension** cause and effect characterization details fact vs fiction fact vs opinion inferences and conclusions main idea prediction realism vs fantasy sequence summary time relationships **Literary Skills** author's purpose, point of view comparison/contrast figurative language literature: form & characteristics story elements **Language Mechanics** punctuation typographic clues usage

for Grade Two and Grade Five. The critical point here is that the teacher must know the skills that are to be taught.

Step Two: Identify the learning needs of the children. Through careful "kid watching," conferencing, and work sample study decide the strengths and next learning steps for each child.

Step Three: Be constantly on the lookout for ways to infuse basic skill instruction in daily, authentic literacy experiences. Consider the following two examples.

Second grade shared reading. Imagine that you were using *The King Who Rained* by Fred Gwynne as a shared reading text with a group of second graders. Naturally, you could focus on any of the phonic or structural skills listed in Figure 10-1, but this text lends itself especially to talking about idiomatic expressions, a skill on the second grade list. The time you were using *The King Who Rained* as a shared reading text, for what ever good reason(s) you had, would be a perfect time to also introduce or reinforce the concept of idioms.

The introduction or reinforcement of idioms should not be done separately from real reading and writing experiences. Nor should a text be selected *solely* because it lends itself to focusing on a particular skill. The skill instruction should lead naturally and easily out of the experience with the text.

Literature as a springboard to writing—fifth grade.   Notice that in Figure 10-1 *analogies* is listed as a fifth grade skill. Traditionally the concept of analogy would have been taught through lecture and then students would have been asked to underline analogies in a text created by someone else for that purpose. How differently analogies would be handled contextualized in real literacy experiences.

Imagine that you are sharing *Summer Is . . .* (1967) by Charlotte Zolotow with a group of fifth graders. Perhaps you have multiple copies and a group of children are reading it together. Knowing that analogies are a part of your fifth grade curriculum you decide to use this text to present the idea as a springboard to writing.

After reading and enjoying *Summer Is . . .* several times, you would present the idea of analogies. Simply put, analogies use something familiar to explain something else, as in "Summer is whirring lawn mowers on still afternoons and ice-cream cones and watermelon." Following the discussion of the meaning of *analogy* you might invite one more reading of the text to appreciate it for its analogies. Children would then be encouraged, using the *Summer Is . . .* model, to use analogies in a future writing piece. They might choose to select other topics such as "Happiness Is . . . , School Is . . . , Winter Is . . . , or even Reading Is . . . . "

Step Four: Identify each day those individuals or small groups with whom you need a "mini-lesson" to review or reinforce skills taught in the past. Use a current writing piece or a current reading selection as the vehicle for this reinforcement. Often children's writing pieces are rich resources for integration of skill instruction.

Step Five: Use the planning of a thematic unit as an opportunity to integrate basic skill instruction.

Thematic unit.   As teachers are realizing more and more that everything in the universe is connected, that learning is always tied to other learning, they appreciate the value of organizing curriculum and instruction around themes. Thematic units usually last several weeks and integrate instruction across the curriculum and the theme. A schedule of activities for thematic

Figure 10-3   Curriculum Web for the Theme: Food

READING
Read *Greedy Cat* by Joy Cowley, *The Cake that Mack Ate* by Rose Robart; *Pancakes, Pancakes* by Eric Carle *Alligator Arrived with Apples: A Potluck Alphabet Feast* by Crescent Dragonwagon; *Gregory, the Terrible Eater* by Mitchell Sharmat

WRITING
Write recipes, write invitations to a literary luncheon for parents, write menus, write a food column for the newspaper, write a thank you note for a dinner party, create text for *Pancakes for Breakfast* by Tomie DePaola, create a class ABC Book of Favorite Foods

MATH
Cook recipes using both English and Metric measures, interview a local produce manager to determining the weight of fresh fruits and vegetables ordered weekly by the store, graph or illustrate this information, collect packaging from each family in the class, weigh the waste each week and graph, food costs - lunch for a family for a week, grocery ads, cost of restaurant meals

FOOD

SCIENCE
Explore the chemistry of baking, experiment with changing ingredients in recipes, examine nutrition issues in today's world and economy, investigate ingredient statements and critique, chart or graph the varying amounts of daily vitamin requirements met in certain cereals favored by classmates. Read *Growing Vegetable Soup* by Lois Ehlert

SOCIAL STUDIES
Examine issues of world hunger and population growth, study ways to get relief supplies to starving populations and the related problems, explore the economic issues of food in our town (harvest, transportation, storage, jobs, etc.) Read *Bread, Bread, Bread* by Ann Morris, *Alphabet Soup* by Abbie Zabar

teaching occupies most of the school day. Only those subject-matter areas that are not treated thoroughly in the theme (ones that do not fit a particular theme or that are not under the teacher's control) are scheduled separately. The large blocks of time devoted to the theme allow time for developing many different activities and for in-depth exploration of the topics.

A curriculum web is a useful planning device for a thematic unit. Consider each of the cells in the curriculum web for the theme of *Food* in Figure 10-3.

The next planning consideration is how to infuse basic skill instruction into each of the cells (where appropriate) of the curriculum web for *Food*. Let's consider some of the cells separately to identify the basic literacy skills that might be integrated into each cell.

READING
Read *Greedy Cat* by Joy Cowley, *The Cake that Mack Ate* by Rose Robart; *Pancakes, Pancakes* by Eric Carle *Alligator Arrived with Apples: A Potluck Alphabet Feast* by Crescent Dragonwagon; *Gregory, the Terrible Eater* by Mitchell Sharmat

What are the basic skills that might be integrated into the reading cell. Consider these possibilities:

✓ the phonics, structural and vocabulary skills listed in Figure 10-1;
✓ the comprehension and literary skills listed in Figure 10-2;
✓ the language mechanics skills listed in Figure 10-3.

Specific examples (*assuming that children need this instruction*) include: examining the /gr/ sound that is repeated so frequently in *Greedy Cat*. Talk about other words that have this sound and list them on the board, note other texts in which we find the /gr/ sound, play with "Baaaaaa" in *Gregory, the Terrible Eater*. Talk about how animal sounds are written. Think of others and write them on the board.

> **WRITING**
> Write recipes, write invitations to a literary luncheon for parents, write menus, write a food column for the newspaper, write a thank you note for a dinner party, create text for *Pancakes for Breakfast* by Tomie DePaola, create a class ABC Book of Favorite Foods

What are the basic skills that might be integrated into the writing cell? Consider these possibilities:

- ✓ reinforcement of all phonic skills;
- ✓ encoding the elements listed under structural skills;
- ✓ writing details;
- ✓ writing inferences and conclusions;
- ✓ writing main idea and sequence;
- ✓ writing summaries;
- ✓ examining and using certain literary forms and characteristics;
- ✓ employing punctuation and other writing conventions.

> **SCIENCE**
> Explore the chemistry of baking, experiment with changing ingredients in recipes, examine nutrition issues in today's world and economy, investigate ingredient statements and critique, chart or graph the varying amounts of daily vitamin requirements met in certain cereals favored by classmates. Read *Growing Vegetable Soup* by Lois Ehlert

Consider the opportunities to integrate basic literacy skill instruction and reinforcement in the science activities of the theme. Among them might be:

✓ understanding cause and effect;
✓ reading and recalling details;
✓ examining fact vs. fiction;
✓ drawing inferences and conclusions;
✓ understanding main idea;
✓ making predictions;
✓ sequencing and summary.

Further, we could extend to reading and writing numerals, charting and graphing data, interpreting charts and graphs, observing and reporting findings in a variety of ways, and writing scientific reports.

Willingness to be Spontaneous

The final "ingredient" in integrating basic skill instruction in real literacy events is the willingness of the teacher to be spontaneous. Whole language teachers have fully realized that not all of the learning outcomes or instructional objectives for an activity can be specified in advance. Let's be clear. The teacher must always know the foundational objectives—the direction in which the children are headed—the next learning steps.

However, when you give children freedom to direct some of their own learning, all of the outcomes cannot be specified in advance. For example, in starting the food theme described above, I would first ask the children what they know about food and issues related to food, what they want to know—what their questions are, and how they plan to get their questions answered. Immediately, their responses to these questions would change the content of some of the cells despite the care I had taken in my initial planning.

Likewise, as I am roving the room, watching children work, I will notice instructional needs that I will decide to meet *on the spot*. These objectives could never be specified in advance, because I won't have a way of knowing the children's needs until I observe the need.

The integration of basic skill instruction in literacy events requires a double kind of planning really. In addition to the careful plans the teacher makes before starting a lesson, unit or theme, there are the instantaneous plans that are made and carried out hour by hour if not minute by minute. Being a good whole language teacher is a great deal of work!

The integration of basic skills in real literacy events is certainly not as easy as handing out a workbook or a worksheet. But it makes so much more sense to teach the basic skills *in the context in which the children are using them*. This becomes possible when a very knowledgeable teacher engages in careful planning, and is willing to be spontaneous with some aspects of instruction.

References

Harp, B. & Brewer, J. A. (1991). *Reading and writing: Teaching for the connections.* Orlando, FL: Harcourt Brace Jovanovich.

Wallen, C. (1972). Competency *in teaching reading.* Chicago: Science Research Associates.

Children's Books Cited in the Chapter

Carle, E. (1990). *Pancakes, pancakes!* Saxonville, MA: Picture Book Studio.

Carle, E. (1986). *Papa, please get the moon for me.* Natick, MA: Picture Book Studio.

DePaola, T. (1978). *Pancakes for breakfast.* Orlando, FL: Harcourt Brace Jovanovich.

Dragonwagon, C. (1987). *Alligator arrived with apples: A potluck alphabet feast.* New York: Macmillan.

Ehlert, L. (1989). *Eating the alphabet: Fruits & vegetables from A to Z.* Orlando, FL: Harcourt Brace Jovanovich.

Ehlert, L. 1987). *Growing vegetable soup.* Orlando, FL: Harcourt Brace Jovanovich.

Gwynne, F. (1970). *The king who rained.* New York: Windmill Books, Simon and Schuster.

Morris, A. (1989). *Bread bread bread.* New York: Lothrop, Lee & Shepard.

Robart, R. & Kovalski, M. (1986). *The cake that Mack ate.* Boston: Joy Street Books, Little, Brown and Company.

Sharmat, M. (1980). *Gregory, the terrible eater.* New York: Four Winds Press.

Zabar, A. (1990). *Alphabet soup.* New York: Stewart, Tabori and Chang.

Zolotow, C. (1967). *Summer Is . . .* New York: Thomas Y. Crowell.

Epilogue

BILL HARP

Our journey through nine wonderful classrooms has ended. Remember my concern before we started, that by focusing on specific strategies in each chapter we might create the myth that whole language instruction is just that—a collection of strategies? I'm sure that I don't have to tell anyone that isn't true—not after reading these teachers' descriptions of their work. Here, as Dorothy Watson pointed out, we have seen "learning fields alive with the essence of whole language and they are filled with important and growing things like kids, stories, songs, plants, play, and language, language, language." There are some critical themes that emerge from these classrooms which help us to be better informed whole language teachers.

Whole language teachers are set directors rather than educational technocrats. In each of these classrooms we saw teachers setting the stage—in carefully planned ways—for children to explore, experiment, poke and feel and learn. The learning became the children's agenda rather than the teacher's. We saw this in Shelor's room with something as simple as letting the children decide where to sit. "Kelly, wanna sit at the conference table this week so we can have some privacy?," asked Emily.

We saw another wonderful example of children empowered to learn—taking responsibility for their learning—in Debbie's room with the story of Chris. Recall that Chris had chosen to read *Little House on the Prairie* but decided **on his own** that it was too difficult. After trying three choices, Chris was still not settled on the book he was going to read next, but he finally found a happy fit. The true beauty of the story is that Chris was in charge of his learning, and he finally read *Little House* six months later.

We got further insight into how critical careful planning is on the part of the teacher when Kathy Porterfield explained that in order to build a

199

literate community in her classroom she must operate from a defined philosophy or the "classroom would become nothing more than a collection of
activities." Over and over again we saw that these whole language classrooms were places where teachers created an environment and designed
instruction from a solid knowledge base and a carefully honed philosophy.
Copeland described it by saying, "Instead of being in charge, I'm in collaboration with students helping them decide their needs and purposes to
learn about the uses of language." The teachers were truly set designers,
not shufflers of papers or barkers of commands.

**Whole language teachers are continuous learners—they are part-
ners in the learning enterprise.** We saw this in Kathy's room when she
explained that when she began having children write responses to their
readings she expected quality responses weekly. But she learned that overuse of this rich technique can lead to "workbook" kinds of responses and
even contempt on the part of the students.

Kittye Copeland revealed herself as a teacher/learner in her conversation about demonstrating reading and writing to her students. By letting her
students see her struggle with selecting just the right word or phrase in
writing, she was letting them see her learn as a writer. I was moved by her
statement, "The knowledge of the power we hold as thinkers when we use
reading and writing to better ourselves as learners must become all our
students' curriculums."

Mary Giard underscored the importance of herself as teacher/learner
when she said, "I love to learn and I have always hoped that our room
would not only be an atmosphere of learning but a place of great joy. I have
always wanted to create an environment in which we could all learn and
prosper."

**In whole language classrooms children are reading and reading
and reading—they are literally immersed in texts.**

This theme surfaced in virtually every classroom we visited. It was beautifully demonstrated in Shelor's room. Because she wants children to see
how literature can be connected to all aspects of her children's lives, there are
bags, baskets, and shelves filled with books of all kinds in every area of the
room. In whole language classrooms children are reading authentic texts—
texts that confirm what they know about how language works. They are
reading books of their choice from a wide variety of children's literature.

It is also clear in these classrooms that whole language instruction in
reading is not the "book flood model." I am afraid that some teachers think
they are creating whole language instruction by filling a room full of books
and kids and that somehow the two will magically mix and learning will
occur. In instance after instance we saw how these teachers engage children in instruction in reading and writing.

Porterfield spoke of "more formal reading instruction" beginning after
her children were accustomed to the mechanics of literature study groups.
Byrum and Pierce gave us insight into how much of the instruction is

spontaneous—capturing the "teachable moment" as children are exploring, experimenting, and creating meaning.

McGruder helped us to see that by carefully creating opportunities to use drama—from storytelling with finger puppets to more sophisticated plans—that the concept of story was developing. This more fully developed sense of story carried over into reading and writing activities.

Manning and Fennacy underscored the importance of providing really good literature for children. They said, "The most important aspect is that once the children have had a taste of the text they will want more. The text must draw on the children's interest and fascination."

In whole language classrooms children are writing and writing and writing. As we moved through these classrooms we saw children writing for a variety of purposes and audiences. We also saw children experimenting with writing a range of genres. We saw personal experience narratives, poetry writing and "small moment" writing in Kitagawa's room. We saw children writing responses to their reading in Porterfield's room. We saw children using word processors in DeFranco's class, and on and on it went.

However, one of the characteristics that sets these whole language classrooms apart from traditional classrooms is the nature and quality of teacher response to children's writing. Mary Kitagawa's description of how she responds to journal writing is a bold counterpoint to the traditional "good," "interesting," or "great job." Mary offered us specific techniques for formulating responses such as trying to use present or present progressive verbs ("I see that you are recalling just how the kitten sounded."), avoiding questions ("Hmmmm, my curiosity is raised about this."), using the child's name occasionally, and praising sparingly and always avoiding unspecific praise. This piece was a mini-lesson for all of us in creating authentic, timely, nonthreatening, and meaningful responses to children's writing.

Whole language teachers value the power of successive approximations. Time and again we saw examples of ways in which whole language teachers value successive approximations as legitimate forms of learning. Denise DeFranco talked about the power of successive approximations and how she celebrates early attempts at reading and writing rather then "correcting" them. I enjoyed the way she gave her students confidence to write by telling them they were writing "the kindergarten way."

Manning and Fennacy underscored the power of shared reading as a support to the emerging reader by explaining that "during whole class experiences with songs, big books, poetry, chapter books and the class newspaper, these students behave as readers and read along as best they can. Never are they singled out for the lack of proficiency." Their successive approximations at fluent reading are honored and supported.

Perhaps no where in our classroom visits did we see successive approximations honored more than in Giard's classroom where the children were doing their own miscue analyses. Recall her unforgettable story about the two children who had done running records on each other's reading, had noted the miscues, and had recorded the strategies they had employed in dealing with the miscues. They were truly honoring each other's attempts at fluency.

Whole language teachers fully expect their students to succeed. In these whole language classrooms we saw a rejection of the medical model applied to education. No where did we see teachers who begin by asking what is wrong with the child so that they might write a prescription for fixing the problem. Kitagawa said, "As much as possible I expect my students to read and write in the same ways that accomplished adult readers and writers do. As co-readers and co-writers, we also serve each other as co-spectators."

Consider the faith Byrum and Pierce have in their students that they would begin the school year by asking, "What do you want to learn this year?" Porterfield fully expects students to succeed in literature study groups without her there all of the time! Manning and Fennacy fully expect that with a proficient reader to lead the way and a non-threatening atmosphere, children will succeed in shared reading. Giard quietly reminds us that we often *underestimate* what our students are capable of doing. To think that first graders can actually understand the reading process well enough to independently engage in miscue analysis is astonishing. I doubt that Mary Kitagawa ever questions whether any of her children will be writers. And I could go on and on.

In retrospect I have decided that I didn't need to be concerned about structuring this book so that each chapter focused on a particular strategy that we are finding powerful. As a complete fabric this tour through classrooms has not resulted in the impression that whole language instruction is simply a set of discrete parts. Within each chapter we have had the sense of wholeness, the understanding that whole language teachers work hard to understand students, literature, learning, teaching, and themselves.

I trust that the reader shares with me the overwhelming sense as Kathy said, "The process and the teacher are always becoming."

KEEP SEARCHING FOR THE ANSWERS

Contributors

Bill Harp is Professor of Reading Education in the Center for Excellence in Education at Northern Arizona University. He received his Ed.D from the University of Oregon. Drawing on his experience as an elementary school teacher, a principal, and university professor, he authored the popular "When the Principal Asks" column for *The Reading Teacher* (1988–1989). He is coauthor, with Dr. Jo Ann Brewer, of *Reading and Writing: Teaching for the Connections* (1991), published by Harcourt Brace Jovanovich, and editor of *Assessment and Evaluation in Whole Language Programs* (1991 and 1993).

Kittye Copeland is presently a teacher of a multi-aged (K–6) school and a reading instructor at Stephens College in Columbia, Missouri. She is one of the first members of the Mid-Missouri TAWL group that formed in 1980. She has shared whole language with other teachers through workshops, conferences, and publications. She is the past chair of the National Council of Teachers of English Whole Language Assembly.

Denise DeFranco teaches an ungraded primary class for students aged five and six at Hunters Woods Elementary School in Reston, Virginia. She is a frequent presenter at Fairfax County teacher inservices on issues relating to early childhood, integrated language arts, and technology. As a teacher researcher, Denise has observed the effects of technology in the developing literacy of "at risk" students. She is an enthusiastic advocate of using computers to meet the needs of her students.

Jean Fennacy is currently Director of Reading and Language Arts at Fresno Pacific College. She received her Ed.D from the University of Southern California with a specialization in early literacy. She is particularly interested in putting whole language theory into classroom practice at the college level.

Mary Giard received her M.E.D. from the University of Maine, Orono. A Literacy Specialist, she is a first grade teacher at Abraham Lincoln School in Bangor, Maine. Active in staff development and classroom research, she was the recipient of the International Reading Association's Outstanding Contributor to Literacy Award for Teacher as Research, 1992, and the National Outstanding Teacher Award, 1989, presented by the Center for the Expansion of Language and Thinking.

Mary M. Kitagawa is currently teaching fifth and sixth grades at the Mark's Meadow Demonstration School in Amherst, MA. She previously spent twelve years teaching Yaqui and Mexican American students at Richey Elementary School in Tucson, Arizona. Mary received her M.A. in English as a Second Language from the University of Arizona. She and her husband, Chisato Kitagawa, coauthored *Making Connections with Writing* (1987), published by Heinemann.

Virginia Lazenby Pierce is currently teaching first grade in Sherman, Texas, while on sabbatical leave from Austin College where she holds a position as Associate Professor of Education. She received her Ed.D from Texas Women's University. Her areas of special interest include literacy development in young children, authentic learning experiences, and literacy and social consciousness.

Donna Lewis Byrum is a classroom teacher on leave to serve as an instructional specialist for schools in North Carolina, Tennessee, and Texas. Through ongoing staff development she supports teachers as they move toward a more holistic philosophy of teaching. She also serves as a lead facilitator for the Richard C. Owen Whole Language in the Classroom Workshops.

Deborah Manning is a teacher in the Fresno Unified School District and on the adjunct faculty at Fresno Pacific College, where she received her M.A. in education. She is currently investigating family literacy portfolios and is very involved in encouraging parent participation in school.

Sheryl McGruder teaches second grade at Fairview Elementary School, in the Columbia Public Schools, Missouri. She received her A.B. from San Diego State College, California, and her M.A. in Curriculum and Instruction from the University of Missouri. She is active in her local TAWL group, serving as treasurer and as co-chair of the 11th and 12th annual TAWL renewal conferences in Columbia, Missouri.

Kathryn Elizabeth Porterfield received her M.S. in Special Education from Portland State University, and has taught in special education classrooms for the past ten years. She is currently teaching in an intermediate, multi-age classroom in the Centennial School District in Portland, Oregon. She is the recipient of the Centennial School District Special Education Teacher of the Year Aware and the Oregon Milken Foundation Award.

Debrah Lynne Shelor teaches primary grades in the Albemarle County School System in Charlottesville, Virginia, where she pursues her interests in children's literature, integrating all areas of the curriculum through thematic teaching. She focuses on the assessment and evaluation of student learning, and participates in the process of "teachers teaching teachers" by observing and consulting with colleagues across the school division and in other areas of the state. She received her B.S. in Early Childhood Education from James Madison University, Virginia, and has completed graduate courses at the University of Virginia, Longwood College, and the University of New Hampshire.

Index